The Other John Adams,
1705–1740

A South East View of ye Great Town of Boston in New England in America (detail). Engraving, 1725? John Harris, after William Burgis. Courtesy of the I. N. Phelps Stokes Collection, Miriam and Ira D. Wallach Division of Art, Prints and Photographs, The New York Public Library, Astor, Lenox and Tilden Foundations.

The Other John Adams, 1705–1740

Benjamin Franklin V

Madison • Teaneck
Fairleigh Dickinson University Press
London: Associated University Presses

Associated University Presses
2010 Eastpark Boulevard
Cranbury, NJ 08512

Associated University Presses
Unit 304, The Chandlery
50 Westminster Bridge Road
London SE1 7QY, England

Associated University Presses
P.O. Box 338, Port Credit
Mississauga, Ontario
Canada L5G 4L8

The paper used in this publication meets the requirements of the American National Standard for Permanence of Paper for Printed Library Materials Z39.48-1984.

Cataloging-in-Publication Data
is on file with the Library of Congress.

PRINTED IN THE UNITED STATES OF AMERICA

To Jo, Abigail, Rebecca, and Elizabeth
and to the students who have taught me

Contents

Acknowledgments

I AM GRATEFUL TO THE DEPARTMENT OF ENGLISH, UNIVERSITY OF South Carolina, for supporting my research on this book. Donald J. Greiner and Donald T. Siebert read early drafts of the manuscript and made helpful comments. Ward W. Briggs Jr. and Scott J. Gwara translated Latin passages. Patrick G. Scott located elusive sources. Leon E. Jackson provided useful books. Stanley W. Dubinsky helped with computer problems. Donald L. Jones and Kevin Lewis clarified religious issues. Numerous reference librarians at the Thomas Cooper Library, University of South Carolina, helped me immeasurably, always with good humor.

I appreciate the assistance of the following individuals who are not associated with my university: Florence Archambault, Sidney E. Berger, Robert Binswanger, J. B. Cahill, Frank J. Carroll, Richard L. Champlin, Laura W. Cutler, Brenda Dunn, Allie Fraser, Claudia Funke, H. Hobart Holly, Bertram Lippincott III, Jan Malcheski, Russell L. Martin III, David Miller, Robert M. Mitchell, Susan D. Moran, Clarice Muntz, Kim Olson, Hope W. Paterson, Ron M. Potvin, Jennie Rathbun, Boyd Reese, Edwin G. Sanford, Howard T. Senzel, Anthony W. Schipps, David S. Shields, Virginia H. Smith, Jennifer Tolpa, Christina T. Toulouse, Travis Westly, Alice C. White, and Harold F. Worthley.

The Other John Adams,
1705–1740

Introduction

JOHN ADAMS (1705–1740) IS LITTLE KNOWN EVEN AMONG SCHOLARS OF early American culture, for understandable reasons. Trained for the ministry at Harvard, he failed in his calling; of a literary bent, under his own name he published only an ordinary sermon. He died in his mid thirties. Why write a book about this man unknown to us?

Adams's importance derives from events that occurred during the decade of the 1720s. This was a time of great change in American life, especially in New England, and particularly in Boston. Secular realities were weakening the influence of the century-old Puritan establishment. The Congregational Church—the church of the Puritans—was in transition. Doctrinal issues sometimes created concern, even schism, within congregations. This was the case in Newport, where the young Adams was called to assist Nathaniel Clap, the father of Newport Congregationalism, who refused to administer the ordinance of Holy Communion to his parishioners. In time, Adams and the disaffected members of Clap's congregation established the Second Congregational Church, where Adams offered them Communion. An examination of the Clap-Adams dispute demonstrates how the decades-old question of who is eligible to receive the Lord's Supper continued causing difficulties in the 1720s. In this case, Clap hewed to the old way; Adams, to the new.

Adams was mostly progressive as an author, in both verse and prose. His poems—published anonymously in newspapers primarily in the 1720s and in a book published posthumously in 1745—indicate that he was one of the first Americans influenced by the neoclassical English poets, such as Pope, and by the religious sublime of Sir Richard Blackmore. The neoclassical mode would dominate American verse for most of the remainder of the century; Blackmore's influence was short-lived, but important. Adams was the first American to publish a translation of Horace and part of the Bible in an American or British periodical.

In 1727, Adams, his uncle Matthew Adams, and Mather Byles collaborated anonymously on Proteus Echo, the second essay series published in an American newspaper. In doing so, they showed the influence especially of Joseph Addison and helped introduce the urbane essay to American letters. Of the three authors, John Adams wrote the greatest number of essays for the series.

Adams, then, was in the literary vanguard of the day and participated in a religious conflict that was part of the evolving Congregational discussion over doctrine. He reflected and contributed to the changing cultural realities of the 1720s. A discussion of events of the time helps place him in cultural context.

Art often reveals societal concerns and realities. Tolstoy's *War and Peace*, Tchaikovsky's "1812" overture, and Picasso's *Guernica* depict war, for example, while Steinbeck's *The Grapes of Wrath*, Harburg and Gorney's "Brother, Can You Spare a Dime?," and Walker Evans's photographs reflect the Great Depression. So did early American writers and artists indicate the nature of their society. Michael Wigglesworth's *The Day of Doom* (1662) evidences theological crises of the day. John Foster's *Richard Mather* (ca. 1670), the first woodcut print known to have been published in America, shows the seriousness and religious dedication of Mather and, by extension, of his time and place. Early American artists and engravers also interpreted society. Howard Pinkham writes that *"the work of our early American engravers makes a useful guide to the past, showing us not only what cities and towns looked like, but also what New Englanders in the eighteenth and nineteenth centuries thought was important."* In his study of engravers' likenesses of Massachusetts through the mid nineteenth century, Pinkham goes on to say that the engravings "had to reflect the political, social and economic values of the community."[1] These comments are especially astute when applied to one of the earliest and most important views of Boston, William Burgis's *A South East View of ye Great Town of Boston in New England in America,* an engraving of the Boston waterfront dating from the mid 1720s.[2]

Although we cannot know the accuracy of all the details of Burgis's scene, it offers one person's impression of maritime and cultural realities, realities involving change. Burgis focuses on approximately fifty ships and boats in the harbor between his vantage point and the city. Those nearest the viewer, all of which fly the Union Jack, are the most pronounced; at least one less significant vessel displays the flag of another country, possibly Denmark. Despite artistic problems (for instance, scale), such a substantial number of vessels in a relatively limited expanse implies the nature of the harbor and waterfront: vibrant, boisterous, commercial, open, international. The scene suggests the variety, richness, and complexity of life.

Because Boston appears in the background, it is relatively insignificant in the context of the water and ships. So much is compressed into this panoramic view that the town appears as an array of indistinguishable buildings, with the exception of approximately a dozen churches and meeting houses, their spires rising over the city. Religion can be seen, then, as dominating Boston, the home of latter-day Puritans. Godliness presumably suffuses and defines the city's culture; the people have been and possibly are devout, serious, and good. But with the city and its churches appearing in the distance, on the horizon, as though fading from view, Burgis implies that the churches and therefore religion are less significant than the ships. He reinforces this point by depicting the Long Wharf jutting from land in the upper center of the scene. The wharf eased the transfer of goods to and from seafaring vessels by permitting ships to dock where workers could reach them. Indeed, this wharf was "more important than any building, public or private, and . . . of greater effect on the advancement of the town than any enterprise . . . undertaken" to its construction in 1710.[3] More succinctly, the ships that docked there "were the source of the town's prosperity."[4] In the engraving and in reality, the Long Wharf connects Boston to the world; it serves as an umbilical cord, as a provider of life to the community through trade and the people involved in commerce, many of whom, especially those from abroad, doubtless do not share the citizens' religious beliefs, and some of whom probably have no faith at all. Further, the ships' masts overwhelm in visual prominence and number the similarly vertical spires on shore. Spars on masts create images of crosses, thus suggesting that shipping, and what it represents, is supplanting the Congregational faith of the Puritans as the religion of the future, if maritime realities have not already become more important than Congregationalism. That is, Burgis depicts the opening of Boston to the newnesses of the times—goods, people, ideas, beliefs—at the expense of the old, relatively narrow way of perceiving life. Traditional religion, however, remains important, as the distant, spire-dominated city of Boston indicates.

Puritan life in America started becoming secular upon the arrival of the *Mayflower*. In 1620, William Bradford and the other passengers needed immediately to confront such a nonreligious concern as physical survival, which involved finding food, braving the elements, and enduring Indian hostilities. A century later, the religious fervor of the first Puritans in America had diminished considerably, while secular concerns had gained in importance. Change, though, is seldom easy, as it was not in the 1720s when religion became liberalized and continued giving way to worldly interests. Although saying that society was chaotic at the time of Burgis's rendering of Boston harbor would be inaccurate, events unsettled the status quo, as Charles E. Clark implies when he refers to it as "an especially rancorous decade."[5] Industry expanded. Trade blossomed, especially with the West Indies. The number of imported goods rose dramatically. Shipbuilding became an important industry. Less positively, prices rose, and the cost of living increased. The citizenry had to confront threats, uncertainties, religious conflict, and other difficulties.

One threat came at sea, where pirates so menaced Boston ships and therefore the city's tranquility that buccaneers "gave the clearest form to ruling-class fears about the casting aside of religion, strenuously denying religious teachings and wisdom."[6] This attitude, if not fear, may be observed in a 1723 sermon that Cotton Mather delivered in Newport at the execution of twenty-six pirates. The divine believes that their behavior stemmed not only from disregarding religion, but from active hostility toward it: "The wicked ones bid intolerable *Defiances to Heaven* in their Blasphemies. *Monstrous Undutifulness* to their Superiors is expressed by them. They *Mock* the Ministers and Messengers of God, with outragious Insolencies."[7] Such behavior should not be surprising from men who uttered "Horrid *Oathes*," spoke the "Language of Fiends," sang "Bawdy, & Filthy *Songs*," engaged in "*Dishonest Gaming*," frequented the "*House of the Harlot*," and abhorred "the *Churches of God*."[8] Puritans the pirates were not.

Whether or not Cotton Mather identifies the cause of the pirates' actions accurately, he could have been expected to demonize the buccaneers because they threatened his status in society. His grandfathers, Richard Mather and John Cotton, were among the most revered early Puritans, and his father, Increase Mather, was no less significant. Cotton Mather himself was the major Puritan of his day. Through hostilities, irreligion, and blasphemies, the pirates threatened the Mather dynasty and the faith that had inspired the family.

Pirates were not the only threat to Bostonians in the 1720s. At this time, political life was difficult as Governor Shute quarreled with legislators over his salary, paper money, timber rights, and their designation of Elisha Cooke Jr. (pro-paper money and voice of the "people") as their speaker. Relations between the governor and legislators were strained. Later in the century, Thomas Hutchinson wrote that during this period "the contests and dissentions in the government rose to a greater height than they had done since the religious feuds in the years 1636 and 37,"[9] by which he means the Antinomian crisis involving Anne Hutchinson, from whom he was descended. Furthermore, Shute and his government had to determine how best to defend Massachusetts's interests against the Indians. Abenaki Indians wanted to retain land they considered theirs. Encouraged by the French, they tormented English settlers in Maine to the degree that war "had come to be considered a necessity by Massachusetts."[10] The resulting Three Years' War, or Dummer's War, or Rale's War (but better known as Lovewell's War, or Lovell's Fight, which was but one battle in the war) began in 1722, placing Massachusetts soldiers at risk. This conflict lasted until 1725, when troops from Massachusetts and New Hampshire finally defeated the Indians.[11]

Hostilities on the frontier doubtless discomforted many people, although they would not have affected others. For much of 1721 and into 1722, though, every Bostonian would have been concerned about the threat of serious illness and possible death. This was the time of a smallpox epidemic that had been "imported" from Barbados in April 1721 and did not subside until the following spring. Outbreaks of the disease occurred in Boston throughout the latter half of the seventeenth century and well into the eighteenth century. But the worst of these was the outbreak of 1721–1722.[12] It caused a panic: seven hundred of the approximately 10,500 residents fled Boston. Although commentators on this plague use different figures, William Douglass, who was there, records that of the nearly six thousand people who contracted the disease, 844 died, or one in seven.[13]

Inoculation was an option. What now seems a common sense procedure did not appear so then, either to most of the ten Boston doctors (including Douglass, the only one university trained) or to the population generally.[14] Cotton Mather argued in favor of inoculation; Zabdiel Boylston administered it. Yet who could fault doctors—men of little training—for not wishing to inoculate when no empirical evidence indicated that it would work? Who could blame people for not wanting to receive a small dose of the disease that was ravaging their city? While the vast majority of Bostonians did not catch smallpox, some of them avoided it because they had been inoculated. Of the almost three hundred people inoculated, six died, or one in forty-eight.[15]

In generating debate over the effectiveness and therefore the advisability of inoculation, the epidemic contributed to an important change in the dynamics of American culture. Partly because of Mather's intrusion into the medical world, the clergy suffered a substantial defeat. Ola Elizabeth Winslow states boldly that because of the controversy over inoculation, "the authority of ministerial leadership in secular affairs had been dealt a blow from which complete recovery could hardly be expected. The importance of ministers in the community would henceforth be in their own hands as individual citizens. It would not be pulpit power they would wield, such as previously had been recognized as authoritative."[16] That is, the early 1720s could be seen within this context as the time when what might be called the Puritan way relinquished its hold on Boston society, a judgment Burgis suggests in his depiction of the Boston waterfront and Cotton Mather implies in his Newport sermon.

The Congregational clergy also suffered a defeat within the church itself over the seemingly innocuous issue of singing. Because the beauty of instrumental music could distract parishioners from the serious business of worshiping God, and because its performance in church might seem too Catholic, it was not used during services. The congregation therefore sang psalms and other holy songs a capella, frequently by a technique called lining-out. This method required worshipers to sing a memorized tune after a church official read a line from a psalm and after a "precentor" (Samuel Sewall was one) established the pitch.[17] The resulting slow and discordant music ultimately became so unbearable that a number of men, including John Tufts (1721) and Cotton Mather's nephew Thomas Walter (1722), attempted to solve the problem by composing and publishing books containing melodies. The availability of such books, augmented by the introduction of singing schools to Boston, contributed to the displacement of lining-out by what became known as regular singing, which resembles the singing of congregations today without instrumental accompaniment.[18]

The issue was not only musical; the debate over singing also concerned power. Who, finally, controls the church, the ministers, who generally favored regular singing, or the congregations, who usually preferred lining-out? Linda R. Ruggles notes that "the opponents of reform regarded Regular Singing as a move away from the congregational practice of local autonomy toward the more regularized form of Presbyterianism with its governing synods."[19] This belief coincided with a growing anticlerical feeling among Congregationalists.[20] When many congregations resisted regular singing because it was new, a challenge, and a threat, ministers reassured them by demonstrating that regular singing was not an innovation, but that it had biblical sanction. Although lining-out gave way to regular singing, congregations, not ministers, ultimately decided the issue, thereby affirming that they, not the clergy, controlled matters of church governance.[21] After all, such was—and is—the Congregational way.

From the apparent publication of an almanac compiled by William Peirce in 1639 (no copy is known to exist), secular publications came off the Cambridge and Boston presses. The trend continued through the decades and into the 1720s. For example, a majority of the books published in these towns from 1720 through 1725 are religious in nature, with sermons by such men as Benjamin Colman, Thomas Foxcroft, Cotton Mather, Increase Mather, and Benjamin Wadsworth published and presumably read frequently. Many of the books published during this period were secular, however, even though ministers wrote some of them. The early 1720s saw the publication of Latin textbooks, tracts about smallpox inoculation, a catalogue of the Harvard library, music books, a history or two, political and governmental documents, and almanacs, including the important, long-lived one (1725–64) compiled by Nathaniel Ames that influenced Benjamin Franklin's better known but possibly less engaging *Poor*

Richard's Almanac. These and other publications reflect the nature of the times: while people remained interested in religion, they also wished to read about other issues including health, culture, and politics. Writers and printers satisfied these needs with books on such topics.

The 1720s also saw change effected through the new medium of newspapers. *Publick Occurrences Both Forreign and Domestick* had appeared in 1690, but it was suppressed after the first issue. Upon beginning *The Boston News-Letter* in 1704, postmaster John Campbell and his printer, Bartholomew Green, had no competition until James Franklin began printing the *Boston Gazette* in 1719 under William Brooker, another postmaster. Charles E. Clark notes that "the *Gazette* was somewhat livelier and better looking than the more systematic but less varied *News-Letter*, but there was little to distinguish the two publishers politically."[22] The existence of an additional newspaper benefited Bostonians because Franklin and Brooker offered them an alternative to the "dulness" of the established paper and were dedicated to publishing European news in a more timely manner than Green and Campbell.[23] After Samuel Kneeland replaced Franklin as printer of the *Gazette* in 1721, Franklin started *The New-England Courant*, the most spirited of the three Boston newspapers active in the early 1720s.

Unlike the *News-Letter* and *Gazette*, which addressed "the power elite," the *Courant* identified with and appealed to "the lower orders of town and country."[24] It also "introduced the voice of contention into the local world of printed discourse" by becoming embroiled in controversies.[25] These included smallpox inoculation (which it opposed) and attempts to control the press. (When the General Court forbade James Franklin to continue as publisher and imprisoned him, his brother, Benjamin, succeeded him.) The *Courant* also encouraged ministers to speak publicly only about what they know and not about medicine and other secular topics outside their area of expertise. Additionally, it criticized divines for their apparent sense of infallibility. Because of such censuring of the clergy, Samuel Mather branded Franklin and his contributors the Hell-Fire Club, a view Mather's father, Cotton, shared. That the men who wrote for Franklin's newspaper, the Couranteers, felt free to deride the religious establishment—and Cotton Mather in particular—constitutes another indication that ministers were losing power and respect, at least among some Bostonians, in the third decade of the eighteenth century.

The *Courant* also broke new ground by publishing the writing of sixteen-year-old Benjamin Franklin in 1722. His fourteen Dogood papers are witty, insightful, educational, and occasionally cutting as they comment on character types, institutions, and literature, among other topics, in an engaging, even irrepressible manner. For example, in the seventh and most famous of these papers (18–25 June 1722), Mrs. Dogood quotes from an amateurish elegy (it is Franklin's creation) in order to praise American verse generally, thereby implying that it is weak, as it then was. In the second paper (9–16 April 1722), Franklin presents a minister, later named Clericus, who teaches Silence Dogood about language, not religion, and who in the fourth selection (7–14 May 1722) recommends that she enroll her son in college. Upon telling Clericus that she has dreamed that the college is a center for dullness, he identifies it as Harvard. This is the autodidact Franklin's criticism of the privileged, learned men of his time. In the Dogood papers published in the *Courant*, the youthful printer's devil introduces what might be called urbane letters to Bostonians.

Whether Harvard was dull is irrelevant because of its obvious importance on many levels. One event there from the same year as the Dogood papers, but now largely forgotten, is of practical and symbolic significance: the college replaced its eight-foot telescope with one of twenty-four feet, a gift of Thomas Hollis.[26] This new instrument enhanced significantly the ability of interested parties to expand their field of vision, to probe the skies, to seek, through one medium, the meaning of the universe. The opening of the heavens to examination helps substantiate the message of Burgis's view of Boston harbor: Boston (including Cambridge) of the early 1720s is not the provincial area it once was; it embraces the new, attempts to fathom the unknown, and accepts the other.

Harvard enrollments were increasing to the degree that the school could not comfortably house the students. As a result, the college overseers spent most of their money on the construction of Massachusetts Hall, which was completed in 1720.[27] Furthermore, from 1708 until 1724 Harvard president John Leverett, despite strong resistance, liberalized the college, helping it evolve from primarily a training ground for ministers to a school that prepared students for various occupations. Leverett went so far as to have Anglicans teach divinity.[28] The appointment of such "outsiders" parallels the general liberalizing of the Congregational church (salvation is now believed to be available to people who repent, and not only to the elect, as had been thought), which was a reaction against "the emptiness of the Puritan tradition."[29] In the years around 1720, then, the belief "that saints and worldly men were at war with each other, a war that would end with the coming of the kingdom and the triumph of the saints"—a view propounded by the Mathers and others who, "in imagination, still liv[ed] in the puritan century"—was under attack in Cambridge as well as Boston.[30] This was a time not of hard-line Puritanism but rather of theological reconciliation, understanding, and, in a sense, ecumenism.

The growing interest in things secular occurred for a variety of reasons, including the temper of the times, the lessening of religious intensity, the influence of English letters, the opening of the world through shipping and trade, the growing prosperity of citizens, the authority of science, and the availability of a variety of books and newspapers. The movement from religion toward secularization may be illustrated most vividly, perhaps, by observing that during the decade of the 1720s Increase Mather (1723) and Cotton Mather (1728) died, and Benjamin Franklin was published for the first time. The religious skeptic replaced the great Puritans. Yet Franklin had connections with the Mathers. He had heard Increase Mather preach, and he knew Cotton Mather. The latter influenced him directly. In a letter to Samuel Mather (12 May 1784), Franklin acknowledges an indebtedness to the ideas Cotton Mather expressed in *Bonifacius* (1710) (usually known as *Essays to Do Good*).[31] Not only does Franklin use the last two words of the popular title for his first fictional persona and ask himself in *The Autobiography* what good he has done each day, but he would go so far as to devote his life to bettering society. The old influenced the new; and that newness, Franklin and his ideas, would span the century and help establish the United States.

1

Background and Ministry

EZRA STILES TERMS THE HARVARD CLASS OF 1721 "THE LEARNED class." Among its members were Charles Chauncy, adversary of Jonathan Edwards and ardent foe of the Church of England; Isaac Greenwood, the initial Hollis Professor of Mathematics at Harvard and founder of a school of experimental philosophy; Ebenezer Parkman, frontier minister and one of the best-read men of the time; and Ebenezer Turell, Congregational divine who opposed the itinerant preachers of the Great Awakening, compiled the documents that serve as the memoir of his wife (Jane Colman Turell), and wrote a biography of his father-in-law, Benjamin Colman, under whom he had studied. Unlike Chauncy, Parkman, and Turell, some classmates who trained to become clergymen failed to excel or even succeed in their calling. They included Joseph Champney, Nathaniel Hancock, Noyes Parris, Barnabas Taylor, and Jabez Wight.[1] Another of the ordinary clergymen was John Adams, who died young.

Little is known about the family of John Adams. His maternal great-grandfather was the minister John Wheelwright, brother-in-law of Anne Hutchinson. Adams's maternal grandfather, the merchant and lawyer Anthony Checkley, was a member of the Ancient and Honorable Artillery Company of Massachusetts, which he apparently served as captain. Following his participation in the overthrowing of Governor Sir Edmund Andros, Checkley was appointed the first attorney general of Massachusetts in 1689, a position he retained until at least 1703. Adams's father, a Boston merchant known as Captain John Adams, moved, presumably with his family, to Nova Scotia no earlier than 1710, the year he participated under the leadership of Sir Charles Hobbey in an expedition against Annapolis Royal, where he settled. There he became a trader, real estate agent, and contractor. Among his official positions was membership on the Nova Scotia governing council, which he served for twenty years beginning in 1720; elected president of the council in late 1739, he was removed from this position the next year. When his son died in 1740, Captain John Adams returned to Boston, where he apparently remained until his death sometime after 1745.[2] His brother Matthew Adams, who wrote for James Franklin's *New-England Courant* and whom Benjamin Franklin mentions in his *Autobiography* as having lent him books, was a major figure in the life of the younger John Adams.[3] Another brother, the minister Hugh Adams, served as a link between his nephew John Adams and Cotton Mather, a connection that assumes importance in the context of one of the nephew's poems.

Not all sources concur about where and when the subject of this study was born: some state Nova Scotia, while others offer Boston; they cannot agree on 1704 or 1705. Although his precise place and date of birth cannot be determined with certainty, the best evidence indicates that he was the last of four children and the only son born to John and Hannah Checkley Adams—his siblings were Avis, Hannah, and Anne—and that he was baptized in Boston, on 26 March 1704/05, or 1705 (new style), the city in which he was probably born.[4] In all likelihood, he lived in Canada with his family from approximately age four until returning to Massachusetts for matriculation at Harvard in 1717. Little information exists about his college life or, until 1727, activities following his graduation. In the summer of 1722, while traveling to see his family in Nova Scotia, Abenaki Indians engaged in the early stages of the Three Years' War attacked his boat.[5] Some scholars state that Adams received the M.A. degree from his alma mater, and Clifford K. Shipton notes that for this degree Adams "denied that remittitur Peccatum, ubi non restituitur Ablatum" [sin is forgiven where, when the sin is once removed, it is not reestablished].[6] No document of which I am aware indicates that the college awarded him this degree, however.[7] If it did, then he probably received the M.A. around the year 1724, because most men who became Congregational clergymen pursued the master's degree during the three years following receipt of the bachelor's.[8] Adams could have been awarded the master's *ad eundem gradum* [to the same degree], without the college keeping a permanent record of it.[9]

Adams became a published author in 1726 when his translation of an Horatian ode appeared anonymously in the 23–30 April issue of *The New-England Courant*. Then, throughout most of 1727 and into 1728 he participated in Proteus Echo, a series of literary essays (including some poems) published in Samuel Kneeland's *New-England Weekly Journal* and modeled on *The Spectator* and *The Tatler*. Also in 1727, he moved to Newport, Rhode Island, to assist Nathaniel Clap at the Congregational church.[10] Ordained there in April 1728, Adams assumed what would become a troubled pastorate until his dismissal in early 1730 for reasons that cannot fully be determined.[11] He was an occasional member of the Newport Society for Promoting Virtue and Knowledge by a Free Conversation.[12] Following his tenure in Rhode Island, he spent four years at Harvard, possibly as tutor, but also possibly pursuing his master's degree. In 1735 he interviewed for the position of assistant to Jedidiah Andrews at the Philadelphia Presbyterian Church. In the same city in March of the following year he delivered the first sermon of Presbytery (on Isaiah 35:2); also in 1736 he preached at a Boston almshouse and was one of numerous subscribers to Thomas Prince's *Chronological History of New England in the Form of Annals*. Adams was in Boston in March 1737, suffering from delirium; he died in Cambridge on 23 January 1740, at age thirty-four. Paul Dudley, member of the Superior Court of Judicature, notes that "for some considerable time before he died [Adams was] much distempered in his brain so that his candle went out in a snuff." Hibbert Newton, husband of Adams's sister Hannah, administered Adams's estate, while Matthew Adams served as literary executor. In late May, Adams's books—which included Melchior Adamus's *Vitae Germanorum Theologorum*, works by Aristotle in both Greek and Latin, and John Owen's *Theologoumena Pantodapa*—were sold.[13] Such are the known facts of John Adams's life.

Adams's death was noteworthy. His obituary appears on the second page of John Draper's *Boston Weekly News-Letter* of 24–31 January 1740. Written by Matthew Adams, it provides one person's sense of John Adams's character ("it deserves to be engraven in Letters of Gold on a Monument of Marble") and quality of mind ("Genius"), as well as the regard in which the late cleric and writer was held.[14] Although Paul Dudley, who was also writing in 1740, tempers some of this praise by stating that "the

Character given of [John Adams] in the newspapers [is] extravagant,"[15] there is no reason to doubt Matthew Adams's accuracy in noting the people of importance—he identifies them by position, not by name—who attended Adams's funeral: the pall bearers were John Winthrop, professor of mathematics at Harvard; Nathaniel Appleton, Henry Flynt, Nathan Prince, and Joseph Sewall, all fellows of the college; and an unidentifiable master of arts. Among the mourners were Edward Wigglesworth, professor of divinity; Edward Holyoke, president of Harvard; and Spencer Phips, lieutenant governor of Massachusetts. In short, some of the chief academic and political figures of the day in Boston and Cambridge paid their respects to John Adams. His body was displayed in College Hall before being buried near Harvard.

Matthew Adams's obituary of John Adams concludes with this sentence: "But sufficient to perpetuate his Memory to the latest Posterity, are the immortal Labours and Composures of this departed Gentleman; who, for his Genius, his Learning, and his Piety, ought to be enroll'd in the upper Part of the highest Class, in the Catalogue of *Fame*." A grieving uncle can be forgiven this outpouring; yet he identifies the reasons why John Adams should be remembered. Although few of his services to humanity (if this is what Matthew Adams means by "immortal Labours") can now be substantiated, the details of one are accessible;[16] and his literary productions ("composures") constitute the major reason for remembering him. They consist of a sermon, poems (including translations, an imitation, and paraphrases), and essays, a significant body of work largely and undeservedly neglected by scholars of early American letters.

MINISTRY

While the decade of the 1720s was one of increasing secularization, religion remained important. As might be expected, changing cultural attitudes were reflected in religion: as society became more open, so did the Congregational church, though not without struggle, tension, and debate. For decades, Congregational ministers had discussed and written about the qualities people needed to possess in order to receive Holy Communion, for example, and the church had not resolved the issue by the time John Adams became a minister. Events relating to the Lord's Supper inspired him to move from Boston to Newport, caused dissension between him and the established minister there, and led to the establishment of a new church.

Because the notion of religious toleration informed the establishment of Rhode Island does not mean that its religious leaders were more immune to contention or less jealous of their authority than divines elsewhere, then or now, as Adams discovered from the reception he received from Nathaniel Clap in Newport. Clap (born 1668; Harvard 1690) arrived in this town in January 1696, though he did not establish the First Congregational Church (of which he was ordained the initial pastor) until 3 November 1720. The delay was due to his perception that too few people could demonstrate evidence of saving faith and therefore did not qualify for church membership. Once organized, the church apparently flourished until 1723, when Clap's unwillingness to offer Communion to the small congregation led to understandable animosity between the minister and his flock. Upon determining again that they did not exhibit adequate proof of conversion, he denied them the Lord's Supper for a number of years; he also refused to baptize an infant because the child's parents could not demonstrate their spiritual rebirth.[17] Although these denials might seem harsh, Clap was honoring values held by the seventeenth-century Congregationalists, which were waning in his own time. He was, though, neither the first nor the last eighteenth-century Congregational clergyman to deny Holy Communion to a congregation. Early in the second decade of the century, Edward Taylor refused it to the members of his church in Westfield, Massachusetts, in order to control malcontents; for four years in the 1740s Jonathan Edwards in Northampton, Massachusetts, denied it to all the members of his congregation because they could not confirm their regeneracy. Angry, they dismissed Edwards, primarily over this issue.[18]

The biblical authority for withholding Communion presumably comes from 1 Corinthians 11:27–34, especially verses 28–29: "But let a man examine himself and so let him eat of that bread, and drink of that cup. For he that eateth and drinketh unworthily, eateth and drinketh damnation to himself, not discerning the Lord's body." While John Calvin observes that limiting the Lord's Supper only to sinless people excludes everyone who ever lived, or will live, a document that many eighteenth-century Congregational ministers swore to uphold specifies the types of people who should be prohibited from receiving it.[19] The eighth item in the fourteenth chapter of *A Platform of Church Discipline* (1649), better known as the Cambridge Platform, addresses this issue: "The suffring of prophane or scandalous livers to continue in fellowship, & partake in the sacraments, is doubtless a great sinn in those that have power in their hands to redress it; & doe it not."[20] The Half-Way Covenant of 1662 also focuses on the requirements for receiving Communion. In words derived from the verses of 1 Corinthians quoted here, it states in the fourth proposition that church membership is not enough to qualify individuals to receive this ordinance, that people must "be able *to examine themselves, and to discern the Lords body*; else they will *eat and drink unworthily, and eat and drink damnation* or judgement, *to themselves*, when they partake of this Ordinance." It specifies that "the Lords Supper is the Sacrament *of growth in Christ*, and of *special-communion* with him I *Cor.* 10. 16. which supposeth *a special renewal and exercise* of Faith and Repentance in those that partake of that Ordinance."[21] Further, in addressing the same issue the members of the Reforming Synod of 1679 state, "It is requisite that persons be not admitted unto Communion in the Lord's Supper without making a personal and publick profession of their Faith and Repentance, either, orally, or in some other way, so as shall be to the just satisfaction of the Church; and that therefore both Elders and Churches be duely watchfull and circumspect in this matter."[22] Consequently, if people were "prophane or scandalous livers" (according to the Cambridge Platform) or if they did not know that Christ resides within them and that they possess "Faith and Repentance" (as required by the Half-Way Covenant) or if they could not profess their conviction and contrition publicly (as specified by the Reforming Synod), they—even the church members—were to be excluded from the Lord's Supper.

The issue that divided the Newport church was part of a doctrinal dispute that began late in the seventeenth century when Solomon Stoddard, Jonathan Edwards's grandfather, liberalized the requirements for receiving Holy Communion in his Northampton church. Finding the provisions of the Half-Way Covenant inadequate for promoting a sense of saving faith among his flock, he offered Communion to parishioners who could not demonstrate evidence of their salvation in the hope, ultimately, that the

Lord's Supper itself would serve as a converting ordinance. To him, ordinances "were not ends in themselves . . . [but rather] means to the one central experience, that of conversion and continued growth in God's grace."[23] In making this dramatic change from the accepted practice of limiting the Lord's Supper to people who could show evidence of saving faith, Stoddard met resistance from such divines as Increase Mather, Cotton Mather, and Edward Taylor, who argued that Stoddard was violating "the principles of New England's founders, and . . . the sanctity of the Supper."[24] The Mathers and Taylor disagreed with him strenuously, with the Mathers—especially Increase—publishing tracts against this new practice and Taylor protesting to Stoddard privately.[25]

Clap would have sided with these men, Stoddard's opponents. We do not know how Clap interpreted words such as "prophane" and "scandalous"—assuming that he based his decision to withhold Holy Communion on the Cambridge Platform; we also have no way of determining if the members of Clap's church acted impiously, however defined. We can conclude, however, that on the basis of his understanding of documents like the Cambridge Platform and the Half-Way Covenant, and the recommendations of the Reforming Synod, Clap could have justified his refusal to offer Holy Communion to the parishioners he deemed unworthy. But in the decade of the 1720s, people increasingly viewed seventeenth-century Puritan values as effete and were therefore generally accepting of the liberalized attitude toward the Lord's Supper expressed by Stoddard, who died in 1729. They expected to receive Communion. Clap, therefore, honored the old way while his congregation required the new. Any minister brought to Newport to satisfy these people would come into conflict with Clap.

On 20 July 1724, the Newport congregation asked their pastor's permission to receive the Lord's Supper elsewhere. Clap refused. As a way out of this dilemma, a year later a group of church members entreated him to accept an assistant, who would presumably satisfy their need. Again he refused. Taking matters into their own hands, which the Cambridge Platform authorizes, they engaged Benjamin Bass (born 1694; Harvard 1715) to assist Clap. Following Bass's tenure, they obtained the services of twenty-two-year-old John Adams, who arrived in Newport on 5 August 1727.[26]

After permitting Adams to help him officiate at services for several months, Clap decided against accepting him as a colleague. With the patience of the congregation exhausted, a number of Clap's parishioners broke from their minister in order to engage someone, Adams, who would offer them Communion. Because a church could not be established until it had a pastor, Clap's dissenters needed Adams; and he needed them because an aspiring minister could be ordained only after a congregation selected him as its pastor.[27]

Clap presumably disapproved of Adams because he thought the newcomer unqualified to be a minister; in all probability, he also disliked Adams and did not wish to share with him the religious power that had been Clap's for decades in Newport. Because of the inability of the principal parties to settle their differences, nine of the thirteen men in Clap's parish requested the assistance of a council in settling the dispute:

> wee whose names are hearunto anexed desiers in behalf of our selves and the rest of the church to call a councell of churches in order to the healing of what may be amis among us and we desier our Reverend paster mr Clap to joyne with us in chuseing and sending for those churches that may be thought proper if his consent may be had otherwise to proceed forthwith and wee Desier it may be on wendsday the first of november next. october the 11 day. 1727.

> Richard Clark
> John Raynolds
> Job Bissell
> James Cary
> Edward Rossam
> Kendall Nichols
> Joshua Statson
> Elisha Gibbs
> Ebenezar Davenport[28]

Samuel Sewall records in his diary that Thomas Prince, John Webb, and Thomas Foxcroft left Boston for Newport on 25 December 1727, presumably to talk with Clap about resolving the problems in his church.[29] If this was their reason, they failed in their mission. John Comer, minister of the First Baptist Church in Newport at the time, notes that on 2 April 1728, other "Presbyterian Ministers came to town to regulate ye affairs of Mr. Clap's congregation."[30] They were Joseph Baxter of the First Congregational Parish in Medfield, Massachusetts; Richard Billings of the First Congregational Church in Little Compton, Rhode Island; Richard Brown of the First Congregational Church in Wakefield, Massachusetts; Nathaniel Eells of the First Congregational Parish in Norwell, Massachusetts; Thomas Foxcroft of the First Church in Boston, where he was a colleague of Adams's Harvard classmate Charles Chauncy; and John Webb of the New North Church in Boston. These men were assisted by delegates George Barber, Samuel Basset, Thomas Church, John Cushing, Daniel Henchman, Thomas Nicholls, and Jonathan Williams. Baxter served as moderator.

Clap made the task of the councilors difficult by refusing to respond to their questions about the parishioners' written complaints. Ultimately, the men found against Clap, concluding that for four years he had withheld Communion improperly and in defiance of the advice of neighboring clergy. Baxter and his associates determined that Clap's recent administering of the ordinance to a few members of his flock (presumably the non-dissenters) did not constitute adequate reason for ruling in his favor, found that the Newport minister had admitted people inappropriately to membership in his church, noted irregularities in his conducting of the baptismal rite, believed that he should have accepted Adams as a colleague, judged that his behavior toward Adams demonstrated "reproachable self will'dness,"[31] and averred that there was no legitimate reason to delay Adams's ordination as minister of a church composed of former members of Clap's congregation. The dissension within Clap's church was so severe that the mediators believed matters would not improve even if Adams eliminated the tensions between the two men by leaving Newport. Yet the protesters were willing to remain with Clap if he would accept Adams as an assistant. He refused. The adjudicators therefore concluded in the following manner:

We now in the name of our Lord Jesus Christ Earnestly Intreat and exhort Mr. Clap and the Brethren who oppose Mr. Adams' Settlemt to consider these things in the fear of God, and Endeavor respectively a better regulation of their Temper and Conduct for the restoring lost peace and repairing the injured honour of Gospell order and religion. In particular, as uprightly Judging it the best and most propr Expedient for the end; We advise and beseech Mr. Clap and the Brethren to give their consent to the ordination of Mr.

Adams, as a colleague with him in the ministry, or give us forthwith some satisfactory reason (if any such they have in reserve) why they refuse it; or if they continue to refuse their consent, without rend'ring any sufficient reason for their conduct, and because we apprehend the ordaining Mr. Adams a colleague with Mr. Clap in the Pastoral Charge of one and the same flock, under the present circumstances against Mr. Clap's comfort, and the inclination of so great a part of the people, is not desirable: Therefore we advise the aggrieved members to appeal to the Church for a release from their special bonds and relation to them, and We desire the Pastor and brethren with him to give them a speedy and loving dismission in order to their Embodying into a Distinct Church by themselves: Which being done, we advise, that the New-formed Church, together with their associates renew their call to Mr. Adams and invite him to take the pastoral care of them and if they desire a speedy ordination, we cannot but Advise Mr. Adams to consent unto it.[32]

Following these recommendations, Adams and his people organized the Second Congregational Church of Newport, with Adams ordained as its pastor on 11 April 1728.[33]

A sense of the seriousness of and tensions surrounding this issue may be gleaned not only from the number and quality of divines involved in it, but also from sermons delivered in the week leading up to Adams's ordination, as well as from correspondence between Clap and Adams of a month earlier. According to John Comer, Clap delivered two of the sermons; Nathaniel Eells, Thomas Foxcroft, Joseph Baxter, and Adams gave one each. Although only Adams's sermon was published, we can infer the nature of the other sermons because we know from Comer's diary the Bible verses on which the men based their texts.[34] Council members Eells, Foxcroft, and Baxter hoped for peace among the Newport Congregationalists; Clap attempted to justify his position regarding Communion, the disenchanted parishioners, and Adams; and Adams strove to gain the confidence—if he did not already have it—of his congregation.

On 4 April, Eells preached from Clap's pulpit on Genesis 32:26, 29 ("And he said, Let me go, for the day breaketh. And he said, I will not let thee go, except thou bless me. . . . And Jacob asked him, and said, Tell me, I pray thee, thy name. And he said, Wherefore is it that thou dost ask after my name? And he blessed him there"). These verses concern Jacob's desire for blessing from the mysterious foe with whom he wrestles, an angel who injures his thigh. If Eells used this story of Jacob to comment on the issue of the day in Newport, as seems likely, he probably noted that following the encounter between Jacob and his adversary, Jacob became a better man than he had been before this confrontation. In order to soothe Clap—especially if Clap attended the sermon, as he probably did—Eells would have likened Jacob to Clap, a man who the day before Eells delivered his sermon had suffered a defeat when the councilors, including Eells, had ruled against him and in favor of Adams, although they had not yet announced their findings.[35]

Congregational ministers traditionally presented two sermons on Sunday, as Clap did on 7 April, the last day he would preach in the meeting house, where Adams and his congregation would assemble subsequently. The council members were among the people listening to Clap, as was John Comer, who found the sermons "wonderfully adapted to ye circumstances."[36] In the morning, Clap preached on Jeremiah 15:19 ("Therefore thus saith the Lord, If thou return, then will I bring thee again, and thou shalt stand before me: and if thou take forth the precious from the vile, thou shalt be as my mouth: let them return unto thee; but return not thou unto them"). In this verse, Jeremiah laments that God has failed him. God responds by saying that if Jeremiah wishes to remain a true prophet, he must rid himself of self-pity and repent of his accusation against God. Jeremiah "must **utter what is precious, and not what is worthless** if he is to be God's mouth."[37] In applying this verse to his conflict with the congregation and Adams, Clap presumably contended that his withholding of the ordinance was "precious" to God and stated that Adams, in promising to administer Holy Communion, might please certain people, but his gesture would be worthless because the recipients were unworthy of receiving the Lord's Supper. Thus, on the issue of Communion, Clap probably argued that he—not Adams—was God's spokesman.

In the afternoon, Clap preached on Isaiah 14:32 ("What shall one then answer the messengers of the nation? That the Lord hath founded Zion, and the poor of his people shall trust in it"). This verse concludes the oracle that presents Judah as secure because he relies on God, unlike the Philistines who are doomed because of their premature rejoicing at having defeated the Assyrians. It states that God will break men who challenge His authority. God favors people who do His bidding; when faced with adversity, human beings must place their faith in God, not themselves.[38] Clap probably likened his disenchanted flock and Adams to the Philistines and compared himself to Judah, a man respectful of, dutiful toward, and dependent on God.

We can deduce, therefore, that Clap was not conciliatory in his last sermons in the meeting house. He also probably depicted Adams as something of a false prophet, a man who, in attempting to please the members of his church, was setting them up for ultimate disappointment.

According to John Comer, approximately thirty minutes after Clap concluded his afternoon sermon, Thomas Foxcroft preached in the same meeting house on John 17:11 ("And now I am no more in the world, but these are in the world, and I come to thee. Holy Father, keep through thine own name those whom thou hast given me, that they may be one, as we are").[39] This verse indicates that Foxcroft called for understanding, if not unity, between the factions. As a member of the council of ministers, he would have had reason for seeking peace. Thus, in his sermon he probably pleaded for each party to show tolerance toward the other, while acknowledging that the sides might not soon resolve the basic issue that separates them.

The next day, 8 April, the council moderator, Joseph Baxter, delivered a sermon. He spoke on Genesis 13:8, a pacifying text appropriate, in its call for brotherhood, for the occasion ("And Abram said unto Lot, Let there be no strife, I pray thee, between me and thee, and between my herdmen and thy herdmen; for we be brethren"). Following this sermon, the members of the council announced the results of their deliberations of five days earlier.[40]

We do not have to make an educated guess about the nature of Adams's sermon, as we do about the sermons by Eells, Clap, Foxcroft, and Baxter. We can consult its complete text because James Franklin, who began his Newport printing career in 1727, printed and sold it in 1728 as one of the first publications in that city; Thomas Fleet sold it in Boston.[41] *Jesus Christ an Example to His Ministers* is Adams's only published sermon and his sole composition to appear as a separate publication during his lifetime.[42] Precisely why it was published we do not know, although Franklin might have thought the controversy would generate interest and therefore sales. Furthermore, because he had known Adams in Boston, where he published one of Adams's translations of an Horatian ode—Adams's first publication—in *The New-England Courant*, Franklin might have published the sermon partly out of a sense of friendship. As was the custom, the writers of the preface to this sermon note that it was "printed at the Desire of many," a claim that could in this case be accurate.[43] If Adams's parishioners encouraged Franklin to publish it, then they followed the pattern of laymen who often were responsible for the publication of "routinely prepared sermons," which, with qualification, is a fitting characterization of Adams's text.[44] Its publication, however, sets Adams apart from two-thirds of all American Puritan ministers from the first five generations (born through the early years of the eighteenth century), who published no book. He was one of the 11 percent who published only a single tract.[45]

That Adams delivered his own ordination sermon assumes significance in the context of other such sermons published in the early eighteenth century. J. William T. Youngs Jr. has found that until then, the men being ordained generally gave their own sermons. In doing so, they implicitly acknowledged that the clerical power they were receiving emanated from the congregation that was hearing their words. But as time passed and the clergy replaced congregations as the dispensers of clerical authority, a minister other than the one being installed presented the ordination sermon. Youngs notes that of the ordination sermons published in America between 1728 and 1740, Adams's is the only one to have been delivered by the person being ordained.[46] Adams's sermon is therefore an important document in the context of a changing religious attitude in the 1720s.

Councilors Joseph Baxter, Richard Brown, Nathaniel Eells, Thomas Foxcroft, and John Webb wrote the preface to *Jesus Christ an Example to His Ministers*. In it they note that Adams was surprised when they asked him to deliver the sermon for his own installation. Why did they make the request, when having a minister give his own installation sermon was already considered passé?[47] It was probably instigated by Thomas Foxcroft, who, in his sermon of January 1725/26 at the ordination of John Lowell in Newbury, Massachusetts, laments the passing of the tradition of having the clergyman being installed preach at such an important event.[48]

The writers of the preface explain that Adams consented to the publication of his sermon reluctantly, but that he agreed to it after receiving assurance that it would be accompanied by a preface explaining that time constraints had prohibited him from writing a new sermon for his ordination. These men also accept responsibility for any deficiencies in the text. According to them, in other words, Adams may or may not have felt comfortable delivering a mostly recycled sermon on a day important to him and his congregation, but he apparently did not want readers to think it typical or that he had sought its publication. Rather than charming, his apparent modesty seems defensive, as it should have been. His ordination was the climax to the long, acrimonious struggle between Clap and his congregation, an event of signal importance for all Newport Congregationalists, including Adams. And for this event he revised an old sermon. If he exhibited a similar lackadaisical attitude toward his pastoral duties, his parishioners would have had reason to tire of him, as they did fairly quickly.

Although I have not located the manuscript of this sermon (it probably has not survived), internal evidence indicates that for this occasion Adams wrote most of the application, beginning on page 39. Without question, new material appears on pages 39 ("my self in particular, who this Day, by the strange and unexpected Providence of God, am to be set apart and consecrated to the Evangelical Ministry"), 43 ("BUT I shall now turn the *Application* of the Discourse upon my self, and the particular and important Solemnity of the Day"), and 52–56 ("What Need have I, the most unfit and unworthy of the Servants of Christ, to intreat the Prayers of my reverend Fathers and Brethren, who have been instrumental to bring me into so near Approach to so awful a Charge?").[49]

Baxter, Brown, Eells, Foxcroft, and Webb relate something more than Adams's defensive attitude about the sermon, however. Their comments imply that Adams is a worthy minister because he embodies the virtues of the seventeenth-century Puritan fathers, thus linking him with spiritual forebears who were important to all Congregationalists but especially to such conservative ministers as the Mathers, Edward Taylor, and Clap. Connecting Adams with a presumably more religious if not purer era is significant in the context of the early eighteenth century, when some ministers, probably including Clap, were attempting to halt the secularizing of society and trying to remind their people that a life is fulfilled from above, not from earthly accomplishments.[50] In allying Adams with the likes of Richard Mather and John Cotton, then, Baxter and the others probably wished to convince Clap and the parishioners who remained with him that Adams was a true Congregationalist, one in the tradition of the American church fathers. Furthermore, in stating that recent college graduates should be placed at the head of both old and new congregations, the writers of the preface imply not only that the present belongs to the young, but also that Adams should establish a new church with the individuals who had separated from Clap, as the councilors had determined in their deliberations about the dispute in Newport. Implicitly criticizing Clap for refusing to bring people to Christ, they hope that Adams will perform this basic ministerial task. After wishing Clap long life, they offer their central statement about Adams:

> And we esteem it a happy Circumstance, that when a Number of'em [i.e., people disenchanted with Clap], thinking they were call'd of Divine Providence thereto (by reason of some special Incidents in their Affairs) were lately, by the Advice and Assistance of a Council of Churches, embody'd into a Church State by themselves, God has graciously provided for them in Mr. *Adams*, a Pastor who we trust will build on the Foundation already laid, and make it his study to preserve Gospel-Purity and Gospel-Order in the House of God, to promote the Salvation of Souls.[51]

Every reader in Newport and many readers in Boston must have understood what the "special Incidents" were. In concluding with the following statement to faithful people generally, the councilors imply one more criticism of Clap: "Let us walk in *Love*, as *Christ also hath loved us. . . .* Above all things put on *Charity*, which is *the bond of Perfectness*, and most illustrious Part of the Image of Christ."[52] They believe that Clap, in withholding the Lord's Supper, exhibited neither love nor charity, qualities that Adams presumably possessed and was willing to demonstrate to his congregation.

In *Jesus Christ an Example to His Ministers*, Adams follows the traditional form of explicating a Bible verse (John 12:26: "If any Man serve me, let him follow me; and where I am, there shall also my Servant be. If any Man serve me, him shall my Father honour"), discussing it, and then applying it, in this case to Adams himself. While it is well written and logical, the explication is unexceptional. The importance of this sermon resides in the application, where Adams shows admirable restraint in refusing directly to assail Clap, the man whose obstinacy led to Adams's presence in Newport. Yet despite Adams's reluctance to rebuke him by name, the application is a veiled criticism of—if not an oblique attack on—Clap.

From among his previously written sermons, Adams might have elected to use this one because John 12:26 requires people generally and ministers particularly to serve Christ; when they do, they honor God. Given the nature of the tensions of the day, this was an appropriate text. Adams focuses on clergymen not only because the Bible verse instructed him to do so, but also because this topic was by then customary in ordination sermons. J. William T. Youngs Jr. has found that in order to emphasize "the professional significance of ordination, . . . most of the ordination sermons published before 1740 not only [deal] primarily with the ministry, but [stress] the peculiar importance of ministers."[53] Adams also discusses clergy because he wishes to identify himself as someone who will satisfy all pastoral duties, as, he implies, Clap does not. Adams notes that while clerics cannot match the purity and perfection of Christ, they can and should strive to emulate Him as much as possible. In the explication, he specifies an area in which Christ serves as an important model: "No Duty was there, either of the ceremonial, civil or moral Law, or of Christianity, of which [Christ] was the Author and Example, so far as it related to him, that he neglected, or did not joyfully perform, even tho' it was most difficult and cross to Flesh and Blood."[54] We do not know if Adams composed this sentence specifically for his ordination. Among the listeners approving of his emphasis of this point would have been Adams's new congregation, the parishioners Clap had frustrated and alienated; certainly they understood Adams as implying that Clap, in having denied them the Lord's Supper, neither emulated nor served Christ.

In the application of this sermon, Adams describes the ideal minister. Among other things, he believes that a clergyman should demonstrate charity and love. He must think himself inadequate and his flock, good. Instead of criticizing his congregation that is necessarily imperfect, he must "condescend to their Weakness, and make the best Interpretation possible, not only of their lesser Slips, but greater Failings: Doing all the Good he can to all, and as little Hurt to any as he is capable; *willing to spend and be spent* for his People, and the whole World; and even to die, were he sure it was God's Will he should thus contribute to the Salvation of the meanest and most despised Person in it."[55] This implied promise to serve the needs of his parishioners differs from Clap's treatment of them. Clap wished to punish them until they rose to his expected level of behavior or belief; Adams desires merely to help them as best he can. Furthermore, Adams states that a minister's

> Zeal for God, should burn with a prevailing Heat, [and] it ought also to be tempered with the cooling Considerations of Prudence. In whatever he undertakes, he should be careful not to act with a doubting Conscience, but always preserve a clear Understanding, a warm & vigorous Heart. He must be wise & cautious not to give Offence, but become all things to all so far as is consistent with his Duty; doing nothing rashly and precipitantly, but upon mature and calm Deliberation, keeping not only his Tongue from speaking, but hls [*sic*] Ears from hearing Evil. And it may be sometimes Prudence as well as Modesty, for a Minister, not to exercise something of the Power Christ has given him, rather than stretch himself beyond his own Sphere and Line.[56]

That is, Adams highlights ministerial qualities that he possesses or aspires to have but that are alien to Clap. He implies that Clap has emphasized his parishioners' inadequacies, not their positive attributes, and that lack of prudence has caused him to act carelessly and hastily. To Adams, Clap obviously went "beyond his own Sphere and Line" by being too exacting with people who relied on him for spiritual guidance and support.

Most tellingly, Adams believes that

> The Ordinances of God [a minister] should dispense to all proper Subjects; and so far as the Keys and Censures of the Kingdom are committed to his Charge, must resolve to manage and administer them, tho' for doing his Duty in this, and other Respects, he is despised, vilified, and his righteous Soul is forced out of his Body, leaving it stained with his own Blood. In fine, He should be thoroughly furnished to every good Work: And as in every Action of his Office, act under the Influence of the Presence, and depend upon the Strength of Christ, so also consider what he would do, were He in the same Place in the Flesh.[57]

Here, Adams criticizes Clap for refusing to act as Christ would and as he, Adams, intends to conduct himself with his congregation, although he does not define what he means by "proper Subjects." Clap probably would have responded to Adams's statement by saying that he, Clap, would like to administer the Lord's Supper but cannot because of the parishioners' deficiencies.

Adams concludes the sermon predictably by noting his own unworthiness and his need for the congregation's assistance in leading them well. At the time of his ordination, he had no way of knowing that these people who wished for his success—and whom he wanted to help—would soon find him unworthy of their confidence. His wish for an effective ministry did not come true.

While Adams might have written and delivered more substantial sermons, in terms of theology, than *Jesus Christ an Example to His Ministers*, its substance is nevertheless appropriate for the occasion of his ordination and demonstrates something of his subtlety as a writer; indirectly but successfully, he addresses the issue that had led to his presence in Newport and to the establishment of and his involvement with the Second Congregational Church of Newport. Read without knowledge of the conflict between Clap and Adams and at a distance of almost three centuries, the sermon seems routine; in the context of the controversy of the time, it assumes a different, more valuable character.

The commentary on the conflict between the two divines ends in *Jesus Christ an Example to His Ministers* with Joseph Baxter's "Charge" to Adams and Richard Brown's "The Right Hand of Fellowship," which follow the sermon. Baxter addresses the central issue directly by exhorting Adams to "FEED the Whole Flock, over which you are now made an Overseer. Feed not only the Sheep, but also the Lambs of the Flock, with that Food which is suitable for them."[58] Furthermore, "WE charge you duely and carefully to administer the Seals of the Covenant, *viz*. Baptism and the Lord's Supper, to all proper Subjects."[59] Not only did Adams's parishioners want their new pastor to satisfy them as Clap would not, but Baxter insists that he do so as long as they are "proper Subjects." Although he, like Adams, does not explain what he means by this phrase, he does not suggest that they must meet requirements similar to those that Clap has established. He probably intends to imply that people qualify for receiving Holy Communion if they are ordinary, clean-living, religious human beings who accept the tenets of their faith, a definition so general and inclusive that many Congregational ministers—but not all of them, and certainly not Clap—then and in the recent past would have agreed with it. Even more clergymen would endorse such a definition after 1728 until the advent of the Great Awakening around the year 1740, when in many churches a public declaration of faith became a requirement for a person to receive Communion.[60]

Richard Brown alludes to the dissension between Clap and Adams in his final words to Adams, words that might seem conventional in another context: "live and walk in Love, and see that you keep the Unity of the Spirit in the Bond of Peace, and so the God of Love and Peace shall be with you."[61] Unfortunately, "the God of Love and Peace" did not long reside in the Second Congregational Church of Newport.

Clap's two sermons and Adams's *Jesus Christ an Example to His Ministers* are not the only statements by the disputants about the issues here under discussion. The controversy led to an exchange of letters between Clap and Adams. As best as I can determine, each man wrote but one letter to the other. Clap's hostility toward—possibly even hatred of—Adams caused the elder man to write to the younger a month following Clap's final sermons in the meeting house. Unlike the civil tone that characterizes the correspondence between Solomon Stoddard and Edward Taylor over essentially this same issue,[62] Clap's tone is so extraordinary that the letter—and Adams's response to it—warrants quoting in full:

"May 6, 1728

"Sir

"I have understood that you have proposed to administer the Supper of the Lord to some of your Company, amongst whom I cannot hope that three Persons are qualified according to the Gospel to partake at the Table of the Lord, if you were qualified to administer that holy ordinance. But I never thought you fit to preach in this place, whither I had been advised by Ministers & Christians, in the name of the lord Jesus Christ long before you was born: Therefore should know how Things are better than you, or any other Persons now living in the World: And am yet here for the Defense of the Gospel, however unworthy; and am not sure that I am released from all obligations to preserve the Purity and prevent the prophaning of the holy Institution of Jesus Christ, who has hitherto preserved me, and I dare not betray his Interest, after he has done so many Things imediately by his almighty power for this Advancement of his Kingdom here; and I believe he will still do more and some terrible Things in Righteousness for the vindication of his Holiness, notwithstanding all the Endeavours of his implacable Adversaries—and I hope & dare still trust the King of Zion with my Soul & the souls of his dear Flock, that he has bought with his precious Blood, & brought & still kept under my pastoral Care, notwithstanding all Endeavours of [Seducery?]—and tho' I don't pretend to any authority, yet I think I may solemnly in the fear of God caution you against proceding <u>to encourage openly ungodly Sinners in their Heaven Daring Impiety, & their presumptuous profanity in striving to prostitute the tremendous Mysteries of Religion to gratify their wicked Lusts.— But if you are so ignorant or so hardened, or your Conscience be so stupified by your ungodly Company that you'll rashly venture to Seal their Damnation to their Souls, and to Sink your own Soul into deeper Damnation, so, as to be made visible & eternal Monuments of the terrible Vengeance</u> of the righteous & holy God, who will not be mocked, Remember you have been warned, & I have endeavoured thus far to deliver my Soul, and wish the Lord may have Mercy on you that you may find the Strait Gate and Keep the right Way to Life Eternal—and tho' you dont value my Favor and Friendship, yet I suppose you will not alway every where find a more cordial & faithful Friend to your Soul & name than your despised, reviled, & openly & causelessly and therefore unjustly condemned

> Neighbour
> You-know-Who."

P. S.   What is the Reason annexed to the Third Commandment?
        Leviticus 10.3.
"For Mr John Adams."[63]

This letter indicates how seriously Clap considered the administering and receiving of Holy Communion. He states that it must be given only to qualified people and that it should not be offered casually just because individuals desire it. Their worthiness, not their wish, is the important issue. However admirable his yearning for purity among worshipers, Clap undercuts his argument by allowing for the possibility that a few of his former parishioners, now tended to by Adams, might qualify to receive the Lord's Supper. If this is the case, then why had Clap not offered it to them all along? Had he administered it, they would not have left him for Adams. Why deprive them because their brethren fail to meet his definition of worthiness?

But the question of the flock receiving Communion is only half the issue, as Clap presents it. The other half concerns Adams's qualification for offering the Lord's Supper. Clap knew Adams well. Because Clap doubtless observed Adams carefully when the two men worked together, the older one might have noticed from the younger actions or attitudes that somehow disqualified Adams from preaching, in Newport or elsewhere, and made him ineligible to administer Holy Communion. Clap might also have thought that if Adams gave it to people Clap deemed unworthy of receiving it, the new cleric would damn their souls. The councilors disagreed with him on both points. Although Clap does not detail the nature of Adams's shortcomings, perhaps the established divine's assessment of the newcomer as unworthy is correct: Adams's tenure with his own church would be brief and unsatisfactory, a time apparently filled with tension.

No matter how accurately Clap evaluates Adams and his congregation, the tone of this letter diminishes the force of Clap's observations. Clap thinks himself *the* Newport Congregational minister; the presence of another one—Adams—seems to threaten him. Clap concludes the body of the missive by presenting himself, accurately, as an experienced minister offering advice to Adams. It is within the realm of possibility that Clap intended for Adams to benefit from the comments in the letter. However, no reader of it—including Adams—could think of Clap as Adams's friend, if only because of its hatefulness and Clap's petulant, adolescent signature, "You-know-Who."

Clap reinforces his points in a postscript. In referring to the third commandment ("Thou shalt not take the name of the Lord thy God in vain; for the Lord will not hold him guiltless that taketh his name in vain," Exodus 20:7), he suggests that Adams, in offering Communion to people unqualified to receive it, disrespects God's desire and that, therefore, God will hold Adams responsible for having violated this commandment.[64] Furthermore, in referring to Leviticus 10:3 ("Then Moses said unto Aaron, This is it that the Lord spake, saying, I will be sanctified in them that come nigh me, and before all the people I will be glorified. And Aaron held his peace"), Clap might mean that he thinks the younger clergyman risks invoking God's wrath because he lacks righteousness. One explicator of this verse explains it in the following manner:

> The point is that those who by virtue of their office are called to draw near to God constantly place themselves in a perilous, as well as a privileged, position. Whatever they do or fail to do, they must bear in mind that God is absolutely unique above all other creatures. Any act, or failure thereof, that may detract from the deity's absolute holiness, and thus tend to treat God in a light, trite, or unthinking manner, would immediately expose those who draw near to possible danger. If God is not sanctified by those who are supposed to know best, by virtue of their constant opportunity to draw near in acts of serving the people for God, God will be sanctified in the eyes of the people by swift judgment and wrath upon all trivalizers [sic] of the ministry.[65]

If this reading is correct, then in citing Leviticus 10:3 Clap suggests that in withholding Holy Communion from people he thinks unqualified to receive it, he honors God's word and, by implication, gains God's approbation; and he intimates that in offering it to some of these same people, Adams places them at risk of damnation through his violation of God's command.

Adams responded to Clap's attack. Despite, according to him, being busy and ill, he composed on 11 May a lengthy, considered letter to Clap in a tone admirably restrained given the viciousness of Clap's correspondence with him:

> Sir
> Tho I am very busy to Day, and besides not in a very good State of Health, I think it my Duty to answer the Letter you sent me the last Night by the Hands of messieurs <u>Malem</u> & <u>Rosum</u>[.]
> <u>You have understood</u>, you say, I have purposed to administer ye Sacrament to some of my Company. If by Company, you mean Church, we are both agreed; But if this Expression was used out of Contempt, and is too plain an Allusion to a certain person and his company we read of in the Beginning of ye Bible, as I have heard you had sometimes in common Conversation compared us to them I leave him both to defend, & answer for it who wist it, which if he cannot do I pray God the unjust Calumny may not be laid to his Charge. Next you express your want of Charity for so many as three persons in this Company, conceiving they are not prepared ["qualified" is lined out] for this holy Ordinance; & also seem to doubt, if not fully say, I am not qualified to administer it. The Reason you give for my

not being so, because you never thought me fit to preach in this place, I shall give this mild Answer to, that it is not conclusive unless your Thoughts of me are infallible which I presume you do not pretend to. But however I should have been very glad if you had let me known what real Faults you have to charge against either of us, to disqualifie the one to receive, & ye other to administer the sacred Supper and till you give me some better Reasons for your ill Opinion of both of us, than you have done in this Letter you must pardon me, Sir, If what you say appears the less forcible since I have learn't to call no man Master unless he gives me a sufficient Reason for his Assertions.

You tell me you was sent here by Ministers & Christians, & was not I so too? But you came here long before I was born and so have a much greater knowledge of things than I or any living now in ye World. But, Sir, suffer me to say, that tho' you have been here all this while upon the spot, yet you have been all along ["this while" crossed out] liable to Mistakes. Your Informations of many things may have been wrong. being perhaps received from persons ignorant, prejudiced, overbusy, not to say, malicious. And I must have a greater Opinion of you than any Man in the World which I will assure you sir I have not to take your bare Word without any Reasons for it for at least, not to say worse, your strange and unusual Conduct.

As for those many wonderfull things God has done for you, you seem to say, by your Ministry, immediately by his almighty power, I must say, that is no proof at all[.] My Church is not fit for the Sacrament; for God very often gives his immediate Assistance to good Men, without patronizing their Actions which are otherwise. And besides this seems to contradict what you have sometimes said to this effect that but few have converted under your Ministry. however, Sir, I heartily thank God for all the Success he has granted you which I hope has been greater than your Fears.

What terible things God is about to do to this place or ye World, I am ignorant of; But having acted according to my best Reason & Conscience and I hope out of a sincere Love to him; I trust he will give me Grace to acquiesce in all his Dealings with me and others.

As to your seeming Insinuation that I am a Seducer. I can bear it with the greater patience and Forgiveness, since my great Master has been called so before me; But in Return to it shall say, I believe, Sr, you are a most worthy Servant of Jesus Christ, & have a singular Love and Esteem for you as such.

For The Caution you give me in the Name of ye Lord [letters lined out] so far as you do it out of Love for God and Love to me I esteem and thank you; But as to my encouraging openly ungodly Sinners in their heaven-daring Impiety &c[.] It is a light thing for me to be judged of Mans Judgment & being innocent I can [face?] what you say with the Patience & Meekness of Jesus. But to be revenged on you shall say that I believe ["Sir, you are a most worthy Servant of J. C." lined out] Mr Clap endeavours to encourage all Goodness in all Mankind, and forever to discourage the Contrary.

If you call the Desires of my people after the Sacrament presumptuous profanity, I shall mildly reply I humbly conceive Sir you are Mistaken. And as for the Charge of my keeping ungodly Company you know who was charged with Being a [friend?] by publicans & Sinners.

The dreadfull Threatnings you use against me in case I am faithfull to my Ordination Oath, tho it strikes me with Horrour to see a good Man left to such Expressions; yet will have no Effect upon me to detain ye Ordinances from my people to ye great Dishonour of God, wounding my own soul, & Grief of all good Men, for [I can be only?] plain with you I never thought your refusing the Sacrament to your people for four Years together the best part of your Character. And God forbid I should follow your Example in this or any thing else any further than as it is comformable to that of Christ. I should then indeed be afraid of being made the publick & eternal Monument of the Vengeance of God;

In the Mean Time, Sr, let me beseech & caution you as you will answer it at ye dreadfull [Base?] of God, no ways to molest or hinder me in ye stedfast prosecution of my ["study" lined out] Duty but to encourage & treat me as a Father.

I heartily pity and pray for you, always make mention of you in ["every" lined out] my prayers publick, private, & secret. I wish you the same Blessings you do me, I highly value & Esteem you Favour & Friendship but that of God much more & am your very unjustly censured Friend as well as Dutifull son in ye Gospell

John Adams

Matthew 18.15. 16. 17.
Acts 25.16[66]

Adams defends himself against what he thinks are unfair criticisms that Clap does not present in adequate detail. Throughout Adams appears strong and confident in his position on administering Holy Communion, as he should have been given the decision of the councilors and the liberalized attitude toward the Lord's Supper in Congregational churches generally. Most importantly and convincingly, he states that he will follow not Clap's example of behavior, but Christ's. To illustrate the point: Clap criticizes Adams for consorting with the ungodly people who had left Clap's church; Adams responds by saying that even if Clap characterizes these people accurately, which he does not, he, Adams, is behaving as Christ did when keeping the company of "publicans & Sinners." What Christian, including Clap, could deny the force of Adams's argument?

In his quibble over Clap's use of the word "company" instead of "church," Adams apparently refers to "company" as it appears in Genesis 32:8, 21 ("And said, If Esau come to the one company, and smite it, then the other company which is left shall escape. . . . So went the present over before him: and himself lodged that night in the company"). Here, Jacob divides his possessions into two groups so that one of them might survive an expected attack by Esau, whom Jacob had once defrauded.[67] If Adams means to invoke this story of Jacob and Esau, then he possibly interprets Clap's use of "company" as insulting because it suggests unethical behavior on the part of Jacob, thus implying improper actions by the people who had left Clap's church.

Like Clap, Adams concludes his letter with references to Bible verses. In order to justify his letter to Clap, Adams cites Matthew 18:15–17, verses dealing with church discipline: "Moreover if thy brother shall trespass against thee, go and tell him his fault between thee and him alone: if he shall hear thee, thou hast gained thy brother. But if he will not hear thee, then take with thee one or two more, that in the mouth of two or three witnesses every word may be established. And if he shall neglect to hear them, tell it unto the church: but if he neglect to hear the church, let him be unto thee as an heathen man and a publican."

The verses reflect Adams's situation. In writing this letter to Clap, Adams honors the fifteenth verse by corresponding directly with him, thereby keeping their animosity private. Although no evidence indicates that Clap responded to this letter, the spiteful nature of his missive to Adams suggests that the older man would not have embraced his adversary as a brother. Yet people were aware of these men's dispute, and the council of ministers had examined it and ruled in Adams's favor. Luckily for all concerned, Clap accepted the ministers' recommendation that some members of his congregation form a new church with Adams as their minister, thereby keeping him, Clap, from becoming, from Adams's view as indicated by the seventeenth verse, "an heathen man and a publican."

Adams also cites Acts 25:16, which reads, "To whom I answered, It is not the manner of the Romans to deliver any man to die, before that he which is accused have the accusers face to face, and have licence to answer for himself concerning the crime laid against him." Here, Adams emphasizes one of the major points in the letter proper: that he cannot adequately defend himself because Clap's charges lack specificity, as they do.

The tenor of Clap's letter to Adams indicates that the older man is jealous of his authority and hateful toward his former parishioners and Adams, unbecoming qualities suggesting that his congregation probably had more than one reason for seeking relief from his despotic ministry. Richard M. Bayles seems restrained in terming Clap's "ideas of discipline and church government . . . severely rigid" and characterizing the clergyman as "an eccentric person."[68] In the exchange between the two Newport divines, the young, inexperienced Adams emerges as the more sympathetic man and the one with the more reasonable position on the issues being discussed, precisely as the councilors concluded.

Upon the resolution of the conflict between Clap and Adams, tensions apparently subsided quickly as the Newport Congregationalists seem to have accepted the presence of two of their churches and ministers in the community. Adams sent his letter to Clap on 11 May 1728; the next day Adams administered Holy Communion for the first time to the Second Congregational Church of Newport.[69] According to John Comer, two days after this event Clap preached on an unknown text to "a considerable auditory" in his parsonage.[70]

Unfortunately for everybody involved with the Second Congregational Church, its congregation did not long remain content with Adams. Although he presumably offered the Lord's Supper regularly, he did not mollify his parishioners to the degree that Baxter and the other councilors hoped he would. In an action that must have delighted Clap, on 25 February 1729/30 Adams requested dismissal from his pastorate:

Gentlemen of the Church & Congregation—
You Cannot I suppose be altogether insensible of the Occasion of our present meeting. It is not that I want a sincere desire to serve you (for I have as great a Desire to do it as a minister can well have for his people) that I now call you together upon so melancholly a Design as to ask a Dismission from you. But I have been sensible a long time

that I was incapable of sustaining so great & difficult a place as mine
was—and as the principle of my serving with you at first was to pro-
mote religion so when I find that I cannot longer be serviceable to
the Interest of it amongst you the very same principle inclines me to
ask a seperation—

I wish you all blessings and that God may make up in the successor those defects you have seen in me[.] I give you many thanks for
all your kindness to me and am sorry that the Event of things have
not answered to my Expectations & Endeavours[.] I Desire to look
into this dark scene of providence with humility & hope we shall all
of us submit to divine will and that God will hear my prayers by granting the most sincere wishes that are possible for your welfare. I Desire to part in love and hope you will be unanimous in Granting me a
dismission and I wish the God of peace may be with you all—[71]

While Adams alludes to difficulties he encountered as minister
of the church, he does not detail them other than to acknowledge
an inability to sustain the promotion of religion among his people
and the congregation's finding of flaws in him. What these defects were we do not know. J. William T. Youngs Jr. notes that a
minister's "day-to-day effectiveness depended upon his ability to
maintain a sympathetic and understanding relationship with his
people," a relationship that Adams was, perhaps, unable to establish or sustain. Youngs also observes that congregations expressed their disapproval of ministers by sleeping in church,
singing unenthusiastically, and so forth, which might have been
the case with Adams's people.[72] They could have intimidated him.
Maybe he just did not much like performing ministerial duties,
a possibility implied by his casual attitude toward his ordination
sermon. Other than Adams himself, Timothy Alden, writing in
1814, makes the most specific comment about Adams's problems; unfortunately, he, like Adams, does not provide details:
"Mr. Adams . . . soon became discouraged from the inimical disposition of mr. Clap and the divisions in the place."[73] Alden might
well imply, as David S. Shields concludes, that "Clap's agitations
forced [Adams's] dismissal,"[74] although Adams himself suggests
that his difficulty with the members of the Second Congregational Church concerned only him and them. In his letter, he
does not obviously allude to Clap.

The four church members who wrote to Adams in response to
his request for dismissal also do not mention Clap. On the same

day that Adams wrote his letter to them, they responded, granting his request:

> At a meeting of the Church & Congregation under the pastorall charge of the Revernd Mr. John Adams at his own request. The Reved. Mr. John Adams, the Church & Congregation aforesaid judging, it may tend most to the Glory of God & the interest of's holy religion in this place, that Mr. Adams be dismissed from his pastorall charge and care over us, & Pursuant to Mr. Adams's request, 'twas put to vote, whither a Dismission should be granted, & was carried in the affirmative— (Nemine Contradicente)
> We therefore do lovingly & peaceably Dismiss the Reved. Mr. John Adams from his pastorall care & Charge over us; wishing him all happiness—
> Signed in behalfe of the Church & Congregation—
>
> > Job Bissell Deacon
> > Nathan Townsend
> > Richard Clark
> > Benjamin Ellery[75]

As an indication of their lack of enthusiasm for Adams, these men do not offer him a letter of recommendation, as John Comer, writing that same day, notes in his diary when outlining Adams's career in Newport:

> This day Mr. Adams' church met to give him a dismission from his charge, which was accordingly done, but no letter of recommendation. He came to this Island August 5, 1727. Mr. Adams preached in the schoolhouse January ye 21, 1728; was ordained April ye 11, 1728; was dismisst, February ye 25, 1730; removed out of town March ye 2, 1730; his people had contended with him about a year. Though there be troubles yet God's foundation is sure.[76]

Like Adams, Alden, and the men who wrote the letter of dismissal, Comer does not specify the nature of the troubles that existed between Adams and his parishioners.

Following his tenure with this church, Adams had only brief pastoral experience in Philadelphia. He should not have been surprised at his inability to secure a ministerial position. At this time, few Congregational ministers were removed, and those who were had difficulty finding another church to serve. Adams was, therefore, both a rarity (he was discharged) and unexceptional (once dismissed, he was tainted).[77]

Adams might not have lasted long as the initial minister of the Second Congregational Church of Newport, but it survived. Until the Revolution, James Searing, Samuel Fayerweather, and Ezra Stiles succeeded Adams as minister of the church he and Clap's disgruntled parishioners established in 1728. The last of these men, coincidentally, was born in 1727, the year Adams arrived in Newport. It is Stiles who in 1770 transcribed notes about the Adams-Clap matter upon which most subsequent accounts are based.[78]

The Clap-Adams dispute might be said to have ended in 1740. Adams died then, with his Newport experiences far behind him. This same year, according to Ezra Stiles, Clap "of his own accord came & partook at the Lords Supper in this very 2d Cong Chh, with this 'ungodly Company'—all the Members of the first gathering being still living."[79] That is, either because Clap had become reconciled to the existence of the church Adams and Clap's disenchanted flock had founded or because he became milder as he aged or for some other reason, Clap signaled his acceptance of his former malcontents—if not of Adams—by gracing their church with his presence and by partaking there of the ordinance that had driven them apart because of Clap's refusal to offer it. Writing early in the nineteenth century, Timothy Alden concludes his comments about the tempestuous relationship between Clap and Adams with the hope that the antagonists are "in a world, where all is harmony and love," implying, because of their contentiousness, that there is some chance that they are not in heaven.[80]

In an age when the typical minister served a church for twenty-five years or more, the cantankerous Clap cared for his people for that long before establishing the First Congregational Church of Newport, which he then served for a quarter century; Adams tended to his church for fewer than two years. Adams's brief ministry is significant only in relation to Clap, and Adams and his congregation are central to the most notable problem of Clap's long tenure in Newport.[81] Yet their disagreement constitutes an example of bitter contention between Congregational divines over the question of who is eligible to receive Holy

Communion, an issue that had been debated for decades but that came to a head in Newport with Adams's arrival in 1727. Clap implied his agreement with the position of the Mathers and Edward Taylor that the Lord's Supper should be administered only to church members who could demonstrate evidence of saving faith; Adams demonstrated his sympathy with the position of Solomon Stoddard, who had challenged orthodox thinking by offering Communion to people who could not provide evidence of their salvation. It is unclear whether Adams, like Stoddard, considered Holy Communion a converting ordinance.

In addition to changing the Congregational dynamics in Newport, the conflict between Clap and Adams was also important because it led to the establishment of the Second Congregational Church. Furthermore, Adams delivered his own ordination sermon at a time when ministers generally did not. His actions regarding this sermon—making an old one topical—indicate a casualness toward it and, possibly, his ministry. Nevertheless, when he alludes in it to the controversy with Clap without mentioning him, Adams demonstrates some sophistication as a writer—conveying an important message obliquely—a skill that he would use elsewhere. That the sermon was published matters because most Congregational ministers published nothing. Someone, or some people, thought it worth reading and preserving. The Clap-Adams dispute proved the power of the congregation. The members of Clap's church were disenchanted with their minister, so they called Benjamin Bass and then Adams to assist Clap; when Adams's flock tired of their minister, they forced his resignation. The councilors acknowledged the congregation's power.

In providing temporary relief to long-suffering people who had worshiped with Clap, Adams satisfied the main reason for his presence in Newport. In so serving his congregation, he demonstrated a generosity of spirit in the face of adversity and provided a genuine service to humanity, although few people benefited from his actions, and no one did for long. Perhaps Matthew Adams was thinking of these things when mentioning John Adams's "immortal Labours" in the obituary of his lamented nephew.

2

Poetry

When writing sermons and involved in a local debate over a Congregational change in perspective about the Lord's Supper, Adams was composing poems and essays. A liberal on the issue of Holy Communion, at least within the context of Nathaniel Clap's attitude, he was also forward looking in some of his creative literary undertakings. His verse is among the first American poetry inspired by relatively recent English poets who had generally been ignored or who were writing during the 1720s. He modeled his essays primarily on those of Joseph Addison. (I address Adams's essays in the next chapter.)

Until approximately Adams's time, American poets usually sought inspiration from religious writers. Anne Bradstreet was influenced by the verse of Guillaume du Bartas; Michael Wigglesworth, by the theology of John Calvin; Edward Taylor, by the techniques of such poets as Richard Crashaw, John Donne, and George Herbert. In the 1720s, John Adams, Mather Byles, and Jane Colman Turell were among the first Americans inspired, in varying degrees, by the verse of the more recent Richard Blackmore, John Dryden, and Alexander Pope; they helped introduce neoclassical poetic values to American verse. Whether earlier American poets were aware of Dryden is unclear, and they were ignorant of Blackmore until Benjamin Colman brought copies of his books to America in 1699. A contemporary of Adams, Byles, and Turell, Pope was possibly unknown in America until 1715, when Englishman Francis Knapp, who had settled in Massachusetts, addressed a poem to him. Blackmore wrote religious poems; Dryden and Pope were secular, often satirical, and concerned with aesthetics. Pope quickly became the major influence on American poets and would remain so until the time of the American Revolution half a century later.

Dryden and Pope offered literary sophistication in poems written in heroic couplets. Through antithesis, balance, parallelism, and other techniques, they mastered this form that probably dates from Chaucer. Their intelligence and technical adroitness informs their verse, as does their wit, Pope's in particular. The example of such a poem as *An Essay on Criticism* helped liberate some writers partially from the religion-dominated poetry of their American forebears. Recognizing great poetry is one thing; creating it is another. While Adams and other poets acknowledged the genius of Dryden and Pope and were inspired by them, American poets of the 1720s failed to create verse similar in quality to that of the English masters. This was so for a number of reasons: they were not as talented or sophisticated as the British writers, and they—Adams and Byles specifically—often wrote religious verse because as Congregational divines they were naturally concerned about sacred topics. This is not to say that one cannot write compelling religious poetry, as Adams did in the Blackmorean style. Rather, these writers had one foot planted firmly in the past (a significant emphasis on religion) and another in the present (increasing interest in things secular and concern with new literary styles and techniques), thereby reflecting one aspect of the cultural dynamics in America, especially in Boston, in the 1720s.

Adams is also notable as the first American translator of an Horatian ode and of a Bible verse to be published in an American or English periodical. His brief discussion of poetic theory, written at approximately the same time that Cotton Mather was making the major statement on this topic in the 1720s, further suggests his importance and commands our attention.

Until the time of Adams, Americans wrote verse in considerable quantity, although the quality is not often impressive, at least in the context of English poetry. In British America, the first book published is a poetical treatment of the Psalms, a volume known as *The Bay Psalm Book*, which appeared in 1640, only twenty years after the landing of the *Mayflower*. The first collection of American verse to include a number of secular poems is Anne Bradstreet's *The Tenth Muse*, published in London in 1650, two decades after the arrival in Massachusetts of the *Arbella*, on which Bradstreet was a passenger and which was in the vanguard of the great migration to America. The first American best seller was neither a sermon nor a history, but rather Michael Wigglesworth's frighteningly memorable *The Day of*

Doom (1662), a 224-stanza poem that some Puritans, presumably including Edward Taylor's wife Elizabeth, committed to memory. As religious fervor lessened in the early years of the eighteenth century, some Americans—Sarah Kemble Knight, Nicholas Noyes, and Richard Steere, for example—composed verse of value, although it generally lacks the intensity and artistry of the poems of Bradstreet, Wigglesworth, and Taylor. During this period, though, Edward Taylor, who had begun his preparatory meditations in 1682, wrote many of the poems in his second series of meditations. Because his verses, with the exception of two stanzas of one poem, were not published until the twentieth century, in his own day Taylor was not known as a poet.[1]

For historical, quantitative, and qualitative reasons, Bradstreet, Wigglesworth, and Taylor are generally considered the foremost American poets of the Puritan era.[2] *The Tenth Muse* is the first published book of poems by someone living in British America; *The Day of Doom* responds to tensions in American religious life at a time when Puritan leaders were enacting the Half-Way Covenant as a means of bolstering church membership; Taylor's poems show the depth of religious feeling in a man with numerous worldly responsibilities, including preaching, farming, doctoring, and tending to a large family. Although Bradstreet patterned some of her early poems on the verse of du Bartas, in time she developed an individual voice that expresses love for her father, husband, and children; that laments the death of relatives, including grandchildren; that conveys gratefulness for her and her family members' recovery from illness; that expresses gratitude for the safe return of loved ones from long journeys; and so forth. Wigglesworth merged form and content so expertly that New Englanders devoured *The Day of Doom*. Of them, one in thirty-five owned a copy of the first edition of his book. These people found it so meaningful that they "read [it] to pieces," as Harrison T. Meserole has suggested. As a result, no copy of the 1,800-copy first edition is known to exist.[3] Like Bradstreet, Taylor possessed an individual, personal voice. In his poems, he is concerned primarily about his relationship with God and whether he is of the elect, with the resulting tension enhancing the effectiveness of his verses. While these and additional qualities help elevate Bradstreet, Wigglesworth, and Taylor above the other seventeenth-century American poets, such authors as Edward Johnson, who included poems in *The Wonder-Working Providence* (1653), and Benjamin Tompson, whose *New Englands Crisis* (1676) treats King Philip's War, also wrote verse of substance.

Early in the eighteenth century, poetry remained a popular mode of expression. Americans not only wrote a large number of poems, but they bought and read them. From 1700 through 1729 (the year Edward Taylor died), there were, according to my count, approximately fifty volumes (including broadsides) of verse published in America, almost half of them translations of psalms. Occasionally, poems appear in books written predominantly in prose, as is the case with those composed by Edward Johnson, Sarah Kemble Knight (her journal of 1704–5 that was not published until 1825), and John Williams (*The Redeemed Captive Returning to Zion* [1707]). Beginning with the 1704 publication of *The Boston News-Letter*, the new medium of newspapers provided versifiers with access to a large audience, and the occasional presence of poems on a front page indicates that they helped sell papers. To indicate how times have changed, any contemporary arts editor pressing to include verse prominently on the front page of a newspaper would soon be walking the streets. As a culture, we value poetry less, not more, than did the seventeenth-century Puritans and their immediate progeny.

The two major surveyors of American verse essentially ignore eighteenth-century poetry published after Edward Taylor's death and before Philip Freneau's first creations in the early 1770s. In *The Continuity of American Poetry*, Roy Harvey Pearce mentions Mather Byles, William Livingston, Thomas Godfrey, and Benjamin Church in one sentence in order to deride American poetry written at mid century.[4] Hyatt Waggoner discusses only Anne Bradstreet, Edward Taylor, and Joel Barlow before devoting two pages to Freneau in *American Poets*.[5] One can understand why critics considering the grand design of American poetry dismiss the creations of Byles and others. Pearce is only slightly too cynical in saying that they are remembered "not because of the poems they wrote, but just because they wrote poems."[6] Indeed, who but a specialist could name one of these poets, let alone identify one of their poems? Within the context of romantic and post-romantic aesthetics, their verse seems uninspired. Within the context of their own time and aesthetics, it is significant, sometimes even accomplished. Yet almost half a century separates the last of Taylor's preparatory meditations, written in 1725, and Freneau's earliest poems, or about one-seventh of the time between Bradstreet's *The Tenth Muse* and the present day. Of all the periods of American poetic creation, this one is the least known.

John Adams's poems serve as a good introduction to the poetry written at the beginning of this era. They, and the verse of other Americans such as Mather Byles and Jane Colman Turell, indicate that some intelligent men and women then courted the muse according to the English poetic standards of the day.[7] These well-read colonists emulated Alexander Pope, most obviously by composing poems in heroic couplets, which he and other neoclassical poets favored. Adams, Byles, and Turell also embraced, knowingly or not, the spirit of Pope's admonition to write "what oft was *Thought*, but ne'er so well *Exprest*."[8] Favoring such familiar topics as natural occurrences, politics and government, religion, and the death of friends and public figures, they probably did not make many truly exceptional poetic expressions. Because of their skills and inclinations, they attempted to refine, in a manner of speaking, but not particularly to invent. If great writers define the literary fashion or break from it, however, then the American poets of Adams's era were important to their time and place because they established the American literary mode while attempting to break from the poetic tradition of Bradstreet, Wigglesworth, and Taylor, and these poets' European influences, though Adams and the others probably did not know of Taylor's verse.

Adams's poetry has elicited little serious analysis. In "The Publisher to the Reader," which introduces Adams's posthumously published *Poems on Several Occasions*, Matthew Adams praises his nephew's creations:

> As the Volume consists, mostly, of divine Subjects, it will doubtless be grateful to the Vertuous, and as it is interspers'd with a vast Variety of Beauties, it cannot but be pleasing to the Ingenious. Here, will be a sufficient Play for the most extensive Genius, and here we shall find an Improvement for the brightest Imagination. While Fancy is mounted, and upon the Wing in her gayest Attire, the Judgment sits with the Reins, directing in a calm and compos'd Gravity, whilst a glowing Piety is urging her rapid and aspiring Progress, even to the very Heavens. Nature and Art seem to go Hand in Hand, and both

are subservient to Vertue thro' the Whole of his Composures. Here is Musick for the Ear, Landskip for the Eye, and a rich Repast for the highest Understanding. Devotion it self, might improve by the Fervours of his Piety, and even Angels (I had almost said) might admire at his Sublimity.[9]

Perhaps mercifully, no subsequent writer comments so unrestrainedly about these poems.

Half a century after Adams's death, a writer signing himself A. published "Remarks on the Poetical Character of the Rev. John Adams, A. M." in the April 1789 issue of *The Massachusetts Magazine*. While commenting astutely about American poets of Adams's time ("Sense was never sacrificed to sound, and as they very judiciously did not build their hope of immortality on this foundation, external elegance and harmony of numbers are the last things to be expected"), he does not argue for Adams's quality as a poet other than to say, amid quotations from "On Society," that Adams "describes the emotions by which we are involuntarily moved... [;] such descriptions characterize the true poet, and distinguish him from the mere tagger of rhymes."[10] In other words, A. finds Adams capable of evoking the sublime, an ability Matthew Adams identifies at the conclusion of his introduction to *Poems on Several Occasions* and that David S. Shields, the most thoughtful critic of John Adams, also praises.

Writing in 1809, John Eliot avers that Adams's creations are similar in quality to other American poems of the early eighteenth century. In 1821, Samuel Knapp judges Adams's poems "certainly above mediocrity[, although] many of them [are] not in a very good taste." He does not detail the tasteless aspects of the verse. Although Knapp considers Adams's version of Revelation a failure because of inappropriate rhyme, he notes that the imagery (unspecified) in Adams's elegy of Cotton Mather "is alone sufficient to give him a high rank among our early poets." In 1829, Samuel Kettell recognizes that Adams's poems "give as good evidence of a cultivated mind, as any other written at that period," although he searches "in vain for those flights of the imagination and characteristics of sublimity spoken of in the introductory remarks [to *Poems on Several Occasions*] of a too partial friend." The Duyckinck brothers in 1855 find Adams successful in translating Horace and comment without elaboration that *Poems on Several Occasions* "does not deserve the neglect into which it has fallen." Francis S. Drake (1872) thinks that Adams's poems "evince a lively fancy, and a harmony of versification remarkable for that period." Moses Coit Tyler in 1878 states that Adams in his verse "sounded no note that was not conventional and imitative."[11]

Among twentieth-century commentators, Oscar Fay Adams declares in 1904 that John Adams's verse "shows . . . no very especial marks of poetic talent." In a book published thirteen years later, Samuel Marion Tucker refers to the diction in Adams's elegies as "more natural than Pope's" and believes that some of Adams's poems "reveal a more purely æsthetic purpose and a more careful style than can generally be found before the later years of the century." Writing in 1938, Stanley J. Kunitz and Howard Haycraft conclude that Adams's verse is "patently imitative. Had he 'descended' more often to that stark simplicity which he but rarely achieved, he might have escaped the charge of drowsy conventionalism which is posterity's verdict on his work"; Kunitz and Haycraft do not offer examples of simplicity in Adams's poems. In solving authorial problems in 1940, C. Lennart Carlson states, without documentation, that Adams was a "poet of perhaps even more importance than Mather Byles." Clifford K. Shipton in 1942 implies that Adams as versifier is notable only because America of his time had few poets. More charitably, Theodore Hornberger suggests in 1946 that "we may safely leave the works of Mather Byles, John Adams, . . . and other would-be 'wits' to the specialist, remembering, however, that they were the literati of their day and, whatever their deficiencies, cherished the tradition of belles-lettres in a world frequently too busy for art." In the most comprehensive (if incomplete) article about Adams, John C. Shields in 1983 notes Adams's classicism and Platonism and judges, without evidence, that Adams's translations in some cases are "equal if not superior to their originals in imagination and power." He also praises Adams for being one of the first American belletrists. Of the commentators on Adams, only David S. Shields argues convincingly for his importance. In so doing in 1984/85, he offers compelling reasons for reading Adams—his verse in particular—as we shall see. Recent histories of and guides to American literature that mention Adams usually limit discussion of him to a derivative sentence or two; such books as *American Colonial Writers, 1606–1734* (1984) and *The Columbia Literary History of the United States* (1988), both edited by Emory Elliott, ignore Adams. In an essay in *The Cambridge History of American Literature* (1994), David S. Shields mentions Adams briefly. He also comments on Adams in passing in "Eighteenth-Century Literary Culture" (2000).[12]

POEMS ON SEVERAL OCCASIONS (1745)

Poems on Several Occasions contains almost all of John Adams's known verse. In structuring the contents of this volume, someone arranged the poems in six unmarked sections. In all probability this person was not John Adams and was almost certainly Matthew Adams. The first section contains five religious poems, beginning with "An Address to the Supreme Being," concluding with "Dedicated to the Honour of Christ," and also including translations of a psalm and verses from Canticles. The second contains verses about melancholy, contentment, joy, and society. Seven biblical translations comprise the third group, with translations of six Horatian odes constituting the fourth. Before concluding the collection with the long translation of Revelation, Matthew Adams grouped, as the fifth part, six personal poems. The poems in this collection present problems that make assessing John Adams's artistic accomplishment problematic. The difficulties relate to issues of text and authorship.

Textual and Authorial Issues

Because the title page of *Poems on Several Occasions* ascribes the contents to John Adams, one naturally assumes that he was responsible for them. But was he? More specifically, did he compose the poems as they appear in this posthumous collection? Questions of text and authorship arise not only because Adams could not have seen the book through the press, but also because four of these poems were published in newspapers and revised before their inclusion in *Poems on Several Occasions*, as another poem also appeared in a newspaper before publication in a collection of poems edited by Mather Byles. Who made these textual emendations? Furthermore, what do these changes imply about the texts of the other poems in this book?

Surely John Adams wrote the manuscripts (which apparently do not exist) on which the poems are based and was responsible for the newspaper texts, although typesetters possibly altered, innocently, a few letters or marks of punctuation as they set the poems. We can, however, document the changes made to these newspaper poems before their publication in *Poems on Several Occasions* and Byles's *A Collection of Poems* (1744) and can infer the identity of the men who edited them. We cannot know, though, whether the texts of the previously unpublished poems in *Poems on Several Occasions* differ from the manuscript originals or if the versions of any of the selections in the book reflect Adams's final wishes.

The alterations to the four newspaper poems later published in *Poems on Several Occasions* vary in quantity. Adams's translations of Psalm 104 and 1 Corinthians 13 both contain approximately a dozen revisions, while the translations of Horace's ode 2.16 and Psalm 148 underwent considerable rewriting. The emendations, which range from the inconsequential to the significant, generally benefit the poems.

In *The New-England Weekly Journal* of 20 November 1727 appears Adams's 132-line translation of Psalm 104, the first translation of a biblical text by an American to be published in an American or English periodical.[13] The poem details God's creation of the world. Whoever prepared this poem for book publication omitted an introductory prose paragraph that accompanies the poem in the newspaper. Signed O., but written by Mather Byles, it praises the translator (Byles does not use Adams's name) and observes his stylistic indebtedness to *The Creation* (1712) by Sir Richard Blackmore.[14] Someone also changed the title of the poem from "The Hundred and Fourth Psalm, Paraphrased" to "Psalm 104th Translated." (Below, I discuss paraphrase and translation, as well as imitation.) The editor made some significant changes to the text.[15]

In the newspaper version of the second verse of this psalm, Adams describes aspects of "Heav'ns Eternal KING" (l. 2) in the following quatrain:

> Whose outward Skirt, ting'd with cælestial Blew,
> O'er His fierce Brightness like a Curtain drew;
> Least, from his dazling Glory, rushing rays
> Of streaming Lustre should our Sight amaze.

(ll. 7–10)

The emender of this poem noticed in line 9 the inappropriateness of the word "Least"—possibly a mistake by the newspaper type-setter—and changed it to the more suitable "Lest" sometime before the publication of the translation in *Poems on Several Occasions*. Elsewhere, in rendering the twenty-third verse of the psalm, which affirms man's labor as part of God's structuring of the world, the editor rewrote

> With constant Course of vigour, bless Mankind,
> At Morn their toil begin, at Evening end
>
> (ll. 81–82)

as

> With constant Vigour all Mankind is blest,
> At Morn their Toil begins, at Evening Rest.
>
> (50.20–21)[16]

The rhyme in the later version ("blest"/"Rest") is superior to that in the earlier one ("Mankind"/"end"). The first lines of these couplets mean different things. The newspaper text asks God to bless human beings, while the later one states that God has already blessed them.[17] The editor also changed the final two lines of the poem. The quatrain that this couplet concludes treats verse 35, which reads, "Let the sinners be consumed out of the earth, and let the wicked be no more. Bless thou the LORD, O my soul. Praise ye the LORD." Here is the newspaper version of the couplet:

> My Soul thy Name with in-most ardour bless,
> You num'rous Worlds your grateful Songs express.
>
> (ll. 131–32)

The editor changed these lines to

> My Soul, the LORD with in-most Ardour bless,
> And let all Worlds their grateful Songs express!
>
> (52.11–12)

possibly to make the provider of the action unambiguous and to avoid the "you . . . your" construction.

 "A Paraphrase on the XIII. Chap. of the I. Corinthians" (the chapter deals with the importance of charity, or love) appears in *The New-England Weekly Journal* of 17 March 1729. Like the poem based on Psalm 104, this one received relatively few substantive alterations before its appearance in *Poems on Several Occasions*. Some of the changes matter little (for instance, retitling the poem "Charity. Being a Paraphrase on the 13th Chapter of the 1st of Corinthians" and replacing the word "big" with "swell'd" in line 6).[18] Others are more significant.

In the King James Version of the Bible, verse 8 reads, "Charity never faileth: but whether there be prophecies, they shall fail; whether there be tongues, they shall cease; whether there be knowledge, it shall vanish away." The newspaper text of Adams's poem treats the first three words of this verse as "Immortal Charity shall lift its Head" (l. 45); in *Poems on Several Occasions*, the words become "Love shall, immortal, lift its beauteous Head" (59.13). Although the earlier version is succinct and straightforward, the revision is less so because of the word "beauteous," which the editor added to enhance the appeal of love. In a line of iambic pentameter he accommodates this two-syllable adjective by changing the three-syllable "charity" to the monosyllabic "love."[19] The editor also placed "immortal" within commas in order to emphasize an—the?—important aspect of charity, a point that is muted in the original text.

The most significant changes to this poem occur in the concluding quatrain, where the first couplet treats the twelfth verse of 1 Corinthians 13, which reads, "For now we see through a glass, darkly; but then face to face: now I know in part; but then shall I know even as also I am known." The second couplet addresses the thirteenth verse: "And now abideth faith, hope, charity, these three; but the greatest of these is charity." The newspaper version of these verses is as follows:

> Now through a Glass we see but trembling Rays,
> . Of that, whose blazing Light will strike the Face.
> When Faith and Hope, with Knowledge all expir'd,
> Leave endless Charity to be admir'd.

> (ll. 29–32)

Revised, the lines read:

> Now thro' a Glass we see but glimmering Rays,
> Of that, whose Light will strike with op'ning Blaze:

When Faith and Hope, with Science, all expir'd,
Shall leave triumphant Love to be admir'd.

(59.21–24)

Both "trembling" and "glimmering" (in the first of the lines quoted here) convey a sense of mankind's inability to understand God fully, which is the meaning of one part of the twelfth verse. The other part indicates a time when mankind will be able, through faith, fully to commune with God. Because of a sense of hopefulness, the word "glimmering"—with its suggestion of life—is more appropriate in rendering this thought than "trembling," which Adams presumably wrote and which implies fright rather than promise. The editor revised the next line in order to indicate that the "glimmering Rays" will ignite into an "op'ning Blaze."

The later version of the concluding couplet eliminates problems from the 1729 text. As originally published, the couplet constitutes a sentence fragment, and in the final line the word "Leave" violates the future tense Adams established in line 54 ("will strike"). The revised text removes the fragment by concluding the antepenultimate line with a colon, not a period, and uses "Shall leave" to solve the problem of tense. While the later text replaces "Charity" with a synonym, "Love,"[20] it emphasizes the power and importance of love by substituting "triumphant" for "endless."

Although the editor altered relatively little in Adams's translations of Psalm 104 and 1 Corinthians, someone—presumably this same person—substantially revised two of the newspaper poems before their publication in *Poems on Several Occasions*. This person changed numerous words and rewrote lines in Adams's translation of the sixteenth ode of Horace's second book (the ode to Grasphus, who is named Graspus in the 1745 text), which appears in *The New-England Courant* of 30 April 1726.[21] The editor reworked the original lines 19–20,

Whose Sleep no fears disturb, his Life no Care,
But at his Table dines on homely Fare

as

Who at his Table dines on homely Fare,
No Fear disturbs his Sleep, his Life no Care.

(68.5–6)

In the first of these lines, the subject-verb-object construction of the revision not only flows more naturally than the syntax in the original, but the 1745 text reverses the sequence of lines 19–20 in order to indicate a cause and effect relationship that is missing from the 1726 version. In the earlier rendering, the second of these lines does not follow logically from the first; in the later, the man sleeps well and leads a carefree life because of his simple diet.

The newspaper text has at lines 23–24,

> Condemn'd to breathe on Earth a narrow Space,
> We many Things, and mighty Projects chase.

Revised, they read,

> Condemn'd to breathe within the little Space
> Of fleeting Time, we mighty Prospects chase.

(68.9–10)

The absurdity of the original line 23 is obvious. How can one breathe a narrow space? In addition to eliminating this problem, the text in *Poems on Several Occasions* clarifies, with the words "Of fleeting Time," the point that Adams almost certainly intended to make. The editor revised the newspaper version in order to avoid the empty word "Things." The idea of chasing "prospects" indicates that mortals seek great goals in the time available to them on earth, a meaning different from and superior to chasing "Projects," although Adams might have written "Prospects" and the typesetter somehow changed it to the less effective word.

Further, in revising lines 27–28 from

> In vain our Haste, while in the conscious Soul
> The angry Gods their killing Horrors roll

to

> But vain th' Attempt to hide the conscious Soul,
> The angry Fates their killing Horrors roul,

(68.13–14)

the editor makes the religious subject ("Gods") secular ("Fates") and removes any hint of polytheism, a concept that could have offended some readers. The editor also rewrote "And mad with Fury, knaws his endless Chains" (original line 47, with "his" referring to Tithon) as "And, mad with Rage, knaws his eternal Chains" (69.3, where "his" refers to Tithenus). Although "Fury" and "Rage" are synonymous, the assonance of "Rage" and "Chains" makes the revision more euphonic than the corresponding line in the 1726 text. The easily comprehended "eternal Chains" is more effective than "endless Chains," an image difficult to imagine.

The most extensive changes to this poem occur at lines 29–36. In *The New-England Courant*, they appear as

> A guilty Gloom hangs hovering o'er the Ships,
> And in the Minds of running Squadrons leaps.
> Pursuing Cares bound swifter than the Deer,
> Chas'd by the bloody Hounds and trembling Fear,
> Or the fleet Pinions of the Eastern Wind,
> Which vail the Sun, and leave the Hours behind;
> While swift as Light the Clouds impetuous fly,
> And spread with Sackloth all the Azure Sky.

The editor, finding these lines inadequate, rewrote them in the following manner:

> A guilty Darkness hovers o'er the Ships,
> And running Troops with following Haste outstrips:
> Pursuing Cares bound swifter than the Deer
> Chas'd by the bloody Hound, and trembling Fear;
> Or than the rapid Pinions of the Wind
> Borne from the East; and seize upon the Mind.
>
> (68.15–20)

The 1745 version reduces the number of lines from eight to six and alters meaning significantly. Surely a difference exists between a guilty gloom (or darkness) oppressing sailors and somehow leaping in the minds of squadrons of men, as the 1726 text has it, and guilty darkness (or gloom) oppressing sailors and outstripping running troops from behind, as related in *Poems on Several Occasions*. Which version is more logical and visual I cannot say. The revision eliminates the redundancy of "hangs hovering" (29), however, and enhances the original lines 31–32 through enjambment and a more pleasing rhyme ("Ships"/"outstrips," as opposed to "Ships"/"leaps"). It also eliminates from the earlier version the superfluous couplet at lines 35–36, which includes the unbelievable image of clouds moving at the speed of light. In these lines and in most other alterations to Adams's translation of the sixteenth ode of Horace's second book, the revised text is superior to the original one.

John Adams's treatment of Psalm 148 first appeared in *The New-England Weekly Journal* of 12 May 1735; for book publication, it underwent the most substantial changes of Adams's newspaper poems.[22] The psalm requires all things to praise God. A typical revision, and one that strengthens the text, occurs at lines 20–21, which describe an aspect of God's power. The editor rewrote

> Gives down the finer Drops of silver Dews,
> Which o'er the glittering Lawns and Fields diffuse

as

> Gives down the finer Drops of sifted Dews,
> Whose varied Honours ev'ry Morn renews.

(4.4–5)

In the first of these lines, "silver" is predictable, while the unexpected "sifted" in the revised text delights because of its implied image of a sifter, God, dispensing the dew. The editor conveys the sense of the newspaper couplet in only one line—where the second line is largely redundant because dew necessarily covers lawns and fields when it settles on earth—thus permitting him to compose a new, non-redundant line to complete the couplet. Although "varied Honours" in the new line might be vague, the image of moisture renewing the morning suggests a freshness and hopefulness appropriate to God, the creator of everything, including dew. This revised second line also makes dew a daily blessing, thus implying that God's attention to the earth and its people will never end.

The most dramatic changes occur near the conclusion of the poem, where the editor skillfully reduced original lines 61–76 to six lines (5.59–64). The revision improves the newspaper text, although the two versions do not differ in meaning. The editor was most concerned about structure, unity, and momentum. The 1735 text has no stanza breaks; the revision has nine stanzas. Unlike John Adams, who twice uses the word "let" (as does the Psalmist, in verses 5 and 13) near the end of his poem (lines 79, 81), the editor employs it several times to link the last three of his stanzas and lend coherence and force to the concluding lines. He uses "let" as the initial word in the first two of the last three stanzas, and as the third word (following "But more,") in the last of them. Although Psalm 148 requires all living beings to praise God, these three stanzas implore selected animals to do so: in the first stanza, fish (5.9–16); in the second, lions and other animals (5.17–22); and in the third, people (5.23–6.4). The "let"s at the beginning of these stanzas do more than unify them, however. They lead to two more appearances of the word in the concluding stanza. This repeated imperative for living things to praise God therefore clarifies forcefully the meaning of Psalm 148. The earlier rendering of this psalm lacks the insistence and therefore the effectiveness of the revision.

I have detailed only some of the alterations—and they are representative ones—that an editor made to Adams's newspaper poems before including them in *Poems on Several Occasions*. This person took seriously his apparently self-imposed responsibility to the texts, if not to the poet, by changing words, phrases, and lines in order to rectify what he saw as their shortcomings.

The question of the identity of the editor remains unanswered. Although John Adams might have revised the poems, circumstantial evidence suggests that the person who gathered them and arranged for their publication (by Daniel Gookin) would have been more likely than the poet to have edited them. The text of a John Adams poem not included in *Poems on Several Occasions* helps resolve this issue.

Adams's "To a Gentleman on the Sight of Some of His Poems" first appeared in *The New-England Weekly Journal* of 9 October 1727 and was later published in *A Collection of Poems* by Mather Byles and other poets. This book contains mostly Byles's creations, but it opens with Adams's poem, although its author is not identified.[23] Byles gave it honor of place because he himself is its subject; he is the gentleman of the title. Beginning his book with this laudatory poem—Adams likens Byles to Apollo—permitted

Byles to prepare readers to admire his poems without appearing immodest.

Byles would have wanted this poem to be as artful as possible so it would reflect well on him in form as well as content. Readers noting textual problems might have thought the author of this poem ill qualified to judge Byles's poetic merit. In all probability, then, Byles read Adams's poem carefully before submitting it and other verses to the printer, Bartholomew Green Jr. So how does this 1744 text of Adams's poem differ from that of 1727? Hardly at all. In fact, of the five poems that Adams published in newspapers and that later appeared in either his *Poems on Several Occasions* or *A Collection of Poems*, it received the fewest alterations. Only five words are changed.[24] This fact assumes importance in the context of the length of "To a Gentleman on the Sight of Some of His Poems." At 141 lines, it is the longest of Adams's newspaper verses. Although it strikes me as reasonably well written, the person who revised some of Adams's newspaper poems so radically for publication in 1745 probably would have altered more than five words in a poem of such length. If this is the case, then the person who made so few changes to this poem about Mather Byles is probably not the one who altered the newspaper verses substantially before their publication in the collection of Adams's verse.

The last of Adams's poems to be published in a newspaper, the translation of Psalm 148, appeared in May 1735, although when Adams wrote it cannot be determined. From sometime in 1735 until 1737, Adams apparently led an unsettled life. The poet tried to establish himself in Philadelphia; unable to do so, he returned to Boston. If he pondered the book publication of his poems— there is no evidence that he did—personal uncertainty and its resulting frustration probably would not have permitted him the opportunity to think seriously about the nuances of verses he had written a decade earlier. In 1737, though, Adams, suffering from delirium, presumably would have been unable to revise his poems conscientiously and intelligently, even had he, when lucid, wished to do so. The one poem he would have had to revise during this period—assuming that he wanted to emend any of his verses—is, because of its date of original publication, his translation of Psalm 148, which underwent a considerable number of beneficial alterations. The realities of his life suggest, therefore, that Adams did not edit this poem, as he probably did not revise his other newspaper poems. If he did not revise his poems, then Matthew Adams, himself a writer, likely did. He was his nephew's literary executor, the person who wrote John Adams's obituary, and the man responsible for the introduction to and the publication of *Poems on Several Occasions*. If someone other than John Adams and the editor of the poems in this book revised Adams's poem about Byles in *A Collection of Poems*, then Byles probably did.

This circumstantial evidence is compelling. It suggests that while John Adams was responsible for the original manuscripts and for the texts of the newspaper poems, in the mid 1740s Matthew Adams revised four of the newspaper verses and Mather Byles edited one for book publication. Despite the likelihood that the revised texts do not represent the final wishes of John Adams, he probably would have approved of his uncle's efforts on his behalf and of Byles's minor retouching of one poem.

The poems that originally appeared in newspapers constitute a small number of the verses in *Poems on Several Occasions*. Even if I conclude correctly about the editorship of them, we cannot know how extensively, if at all, Matthew Adams revised the other poems in the collection, although the person who improved the four newspaper poems probably would have polished the manuscripts of the other verses he was preparing for inclusion in the same volume. Because no previous form of these other poems—either published or in manuscript—is known to exist, comparing the 1745 texts with earlier versions is impossible. How responsible John Adams was for the poems as they appear in this collection therefore cannot be determined. For the sake of convenience, I refer to them as his creations.

Theory

In *Manuductio ad Ministerium* (1726), Cotton Mather makes the principal American prose statement from the 1720s about poetry and style. In addition to defending his own "Massy" prose, he warns about seduction by the poetic muse. For him, poetry should be "*Sauce*" (a condiment), not "*Food*" (substance), an opinion all Puritan writers would have shared.[25] At approximately this same time, John Adams addressed even more specifically than Mather the nature of verse and the poet's relationship not with the muse but with God, the inspirer of his poetry.[26] "An Address to the Supreme Being, For His Assistance in My Poetical Compositions," which serves as a proem to *Poems on Several Occasions*, includes an early and valuable American poetic statement about verse, which makes its critical neglect surprising.

Adams and Mather agree that poetry is important, although both men predictably consider it less valuable than religion. Adams, for example, warns,

> Nor let me in the Poet loose the Priest,
> But know both what, and when to write is best.
>
> (2.17–18)

The most notable lines in "An Address to the Supreme Being" concern Adams's poetic ideal:

> Thro' all my Works, let Order clearly shine,
> And let me know the Reason of each Line.
> Give me to trace out Nature in each Thought,
> And let each Peice be to Perfection brought;
> A Subject for my Genius fit to chuse,
> Not vainly light, nor yet prophanely loose,
> But innocent, at least, if not sublime,
> And let my Numbers smoothly flow in Rhyme.
> May each Production, writ with Strength and Ease,
> The Ear, the Judgment, and the Fancy please.
>
> (2.3–12)

Such words as "Order," "Reason," "Perfection," "Rhyme," and "Judgment" characterize certain attitudes of the age, and they are derived, selectively, from Pope's *An Essay on Criticism* (1711). But because Pope in his poem also encourages individual expression—as Adams does not—and not just mimicry, Adams's and other American writers' reading of and narrow reliance on the great poet might place them among Pope's "*Vulgar*," who "through *Imitation* err."[27]

Most American poets of the time would have agreed with Adams's sentiments, although those of the previous century would have questioned Adams about the values implied in the last of these lines. Yet pleasing the ear, judgment, and fancy is not Adams's ultimate poetic goal. Rather, he hopes that he can write effectively in order to praise God, a sentiment his forebears would have embraced. To him, as with them, art is not an end unto itself, but rather a means to the end that Adams identifies.

"An Address to the Supreme Being" also offers evidence that, despite the foregoing, Adams did not fit easily into the neoclassical mold as established by Pope, that he was a sentient human being and not merely someone who blindly followed the conventions of the day. One of the chief poetic problems with Adams and his American contemporaries is that by writing to form and relying too heavily on models such as Pope, they often conceal their individuality, their voice. Therefore, anyone, including scholars specializing in the American poets of the early eighteenth century, would have difficulty distinguishing the verses of one of them from those of another. How, really, are Byles's poems different from Adams's? Adams's verses from Jane Colman Turell's? To them, following the best poetic models and writing to form are desirable; to us, generally speaking, they are not.[28]

Despite Adams's predictable words in "An Address to the Supreme Being," something is not quite right in this poem. The poet hints that in adhering to the poetic standards of the day, as he understands them, he restrains his true spirit, or at least an individual voice, that struggles for expression; and he fears that without divine assistance these inner feelings or forces will predominate, thus weakening his verse and possibly embarrassing him. He is so concerned about the inability of his superego to control his id, to use Freudian terms, that he addresses the crisis in the first sentence of the poem. He requests that God

> let Judgment hold the Reins,
> And curb my Fancy's fierce unruly Fire,
> Which else would, wild, to boundless Flights aspire.
>
> (1.2–4)[29]

While this sentiment is not unique to Adams among neoclassical poets, these lines reveal that Adams's truest self is passionate and yearns for freedom from restraint. Here, Adams deftly augments his meaning. Although the last of the quoted lines scans as iambic pentameter, the caesuras before and after "wild" emphasize this key word. These pauses, along with, in the preceding line, the repeated initial *f*s that approximate the sound of fire, constitute some of Adams's most accomplished writing. His sentiment suggests that an incomplete understanding of Pope forced Adams into wearing, uneasily, what he possibly perceived at some level as the shackles of the neoclassical mode. Or, to use the words of Matthew Adams in the introduction to *Poems on Several Occasions*, John Adams might mount fancy, but "Judgment sits with the Reins, directing in a calm and compos'd Gravity."[30] Reluctance to accept his emotions doubtless also stemmed from the Calvinist tradition of distrusting the profane and the passionate, qualities that Adams expresses in these lines from "An Address to the Supreme Being."

"Melancholly Discrib'd and Dispell'd" is one of Adams's most interesting poems because the poet essentially disavows his major accomplishment in it. The poet describes a man not to praise him but rather to undercut him, to deny him, to replace him with someone more appealing. Only the first twelve lines of Adams's seventy-line poem concern this man, a melancholiac:

> MUSE, sing the Man, whose overclouded Head,
> Is with a Mist of rising Shades o'er-spread;
> Whose Fancy, wild, a thousand Evils forms,
> And shakes and shudders at imagin'd Storms:
> Whose Mind in endless Whirls is toss'd around,
> Whose quivering Feet scarce touch the solid Ground.
> Look deep into the Caverns of his Mind,
> And, there, ten thousand monstrous Shapes you'l find;
> Gloomy as Night, and airy as the Wind.
> Deep drench'd in Melancholly's baleful Streams,
> Quick up his Brain ascend eternal Steams;
> And his dull Life flows heavily in Dreams.
>
> (17.1–18.6)

In the third line, Adams sets off with caesuras the adjective "wild"—just as he does at the beginning of "An Address to the Supreme Being"—this time to emphasize the nature of the melancholy man's fancy; and once again the technique serves him well, especially when augmented by the snake-like sibilance of the fourth line. Here, though, metrics matter less than description, which is vivid and memorable. One wants to know about this man.

So what exactly has caused this man's melancholy? The "rising Shades" enveloping him in the second line indicate his distress over death, either the actual death of family or friends, or thoughts of his own mortality. Regardless of the reason, it leads to what Adams identifies as melancholy but what the modern reader would likely term neurosis: the man conjures up "Evils" and imagines "Storms"; he is so distraught that his "quivering Feet scarce touch the solid Ground." Because of these problems, which to the unsympathetic Adams are as "airy as the Wind," the melancholiac barely functions in life; he floats through it as if in a dream. He has lost touch with reality because of an obsession with death.

When the focus of the poem shifts from the upset man to a content one at 18.7–12, Adams finally acknowledges that while obsession with death may appear to be the cause of the melancholiac's problems, it is only a symptom. Lack of faith in Christ really precipitates them. Adams makes this point by contrasting his straw man with a believer, who has an "easy cheerful Soul" even though life has not always treated him well. Adams doubtless believed what the poem says about the contented man, and most eighteenth-century readers of this poem probably would have agreed with him, as many today would also concur in his judgment. It is precisely this moralizing, though, that weakens the poem and diminishes what might have been a startlingly effective psychological poem. Had Adams chosen not to continue past his description of the troubled man, he would have created a dark poem that, because of its depiction of the melancholiac's psychic agitation, might have found its place in anthologies of American verse, thus rescuing him from obscurity. Yet he did not stop because he could not stop. To him, the troubled man is merely a distasteful convenience for dramatizing the balanced person, whom Adams wishes to embody Christian virtue.[31]

I do not wish to make too much of the opening verse-paragraph to this poem. Perhaps the best that finally can be said about Adams's unintentional accomplishment in it is that a century later—at a time of different literary aesthetics—this poet might have developed more convincingly than he does in "Melancholly Discrib'd and Dispell'd" his imperfect investigation of a man's psyche.

The Religious Sublime

Admired by Dr. Johnson, Locke, and Cotton Mather, but ridiculed by Dryden, Swift, and Pope, Sir Richard Blackmore was an important influence on Adams and American poets of his generation.[32] In the most persuasive and important essay treating John Adams, David S. Shields shows conclusively that Blackmore's *The Creation* inspired John Adams, Matthew Adams, Mather Byles, Jane Colman Turell, and Roger Wolcott to adopt an aesthetic, the religious sublime.[33] Blackmore's philosophical poem in seven books is, as Harry M. Solomon notes, "the best example of early eighteenth-century praise of God's handiwork."[34] Solomon states that in this book the English poet and doctor "uses science to increase religious awe, to destroy heathen arguments, and to verify that, as Locke and Newton assumed, God is as much an indispensable hypothesis for the astronomer and the physician as for the cleric."[35]

Although summarizing Shields's textured article necessarily perverts it, for the purposes of this study I epitomize his argument in the following manner. When a poet succeeds in limning objects vividly, the reader accepts the poet's fervor because the distinction between word and object has vanished. Such a situation is desirable in religious poetry where, through pictured supernatural objects and events, the poet, acting as God's device, can cause readers to comprehend God's "dynamics and design."[36] In perceiving creation poetically rendered, they would feel wonder, awe, terror, or elevation. As a means of showing God's presence in creation, John Adams and other poets writing in this style "translated" parts of the Bible and achieved sublime effects through descriptive passages (favoring adjectives over nouns), couplets, and the antitheses that couplets encourage. Shields mentions Adams's "On Society" as a particularly noteworthy example of the religious sublime, going so far as to term it "the greatest American poem in the Blackmorean mode."[37]

"On Society," the ninth selection in *Poems on Several Occasions*, contains three cantos of increasing length. In the first, Adams identifies "social Pleasure" as the agency that helps people through the difficulties of life.[38] By this term he does not suggest merely conviviality; rather, he means love and harmony, which originate in and reflect the nature of the Trinity. Adams states that because he is an earth-bound mortal, he cannot adequately depict heavenly reality.

Human beings, though, have access to divine love through angels, who, like the sun, send

> down perpetual Rays,
> Whence lower Spirits draw their common Blaze.
>
> (24.19–20)

People can see evidence of God's love: God does not permit the oceans to flood the land, and He keeps heavenly bodies moving in an orderly manner. That is, because He synchronizes nature,

> like a vigorous Soul, Society
> Runs thro' the World, and makes its Parts agree.
>
> (26.11–12)

Such harmony may also be observed in animals, even ones as seemingly insignificant as insects.

The second canto focuses not on nature and animals but on people who interact according to "social Laws, and social Joys" (27.6). Adams positions them "in the Centre of all *Being*" (27.2). He (apparently a bachelor) details the joys of marriage, noting that even the perfect Adam requested a wife in order to be fulfilled, as he was, for a time, in Eden, "the clear Current [of] Heav-'ns's fair Image" (28.8). Adams also addresses parent-child and sibling affection before stating that nature infuses people's hearts with love, which permits human beings to overcome hardships and which will last forever unless the beloved's "Contempt or Hatred quench the Fire" (31.16).[39]

The concluding canto deals with friendship, which, in its reasonableness, helps people subdue their "subject Appetites" (32.2). Friendship, however, has a more important function. In ideal form it directs one heavenward. Adams details what he would do if he were capable of examining the heavens:

> Oh, could I with a Seraph's Vigour move!
> Guided thro' Nature's trackless Paths to rove,
> I'd gaze, and ask the Laws of every Ball,
> Which rolls unseen within this mighty *All*.
> 'Till, reaching to the Verge of Nature's Height
> In GOD wou'd loose th' unwearied Length of Flight.
>
> (34.1–6)

Musing about nature with a friend could transport Adams ultimately to God.

While with his friend in nature, Adams would contemplate not only the heavens. He would also ponder sublunary existence where, despite virtues, people possess many faults. Their lack of rectitude leads them to hell, which Adams describes vividly:

The horrid Vault which flames with Seas of Fire.
And fiercely boils with Heav'n's eternal Ire;
Where pale Despair it's ghastly Triumphs spreads,
And Grief it's Tears in fruitless Rivers sheds:
Where endless Rage in fiery Transports reigns,
And strives to break it's adamantine Chains
In vain; forever fix'd, it roars, it raves,
And with loud Blasphemies th' *Eternal* braves.

(34.25–35.4)

Hell can be avoided, however. As a Congregational divine, Adams believed in the possibility of redemption, which Christ offers and which Adams allows for in this poem. He thinks that he and his friend could attain it by singing Christ's glory and becoming engulfed in His limitless love. After focusing on mankind, hell, and Jesus, Adams considers God. Because God is "Surrounded with a Robe of blazy Light" (35.12), Adams knows that he would not be able to see Him. The poet must approach Him through Christ. Adams perceives saints interacting in heaven and observes bright, jewel-encrusted crowns that outshine the sun.

This musing enhances the bond between Adams and his companion—as such thinking would intensify the relationship between any true friends—to the degree that he believes the friendship will continue in heaven following their liberation from "the puzzled Maze of Life" (36.16). In heaven,

> each will find his Friend a bubling Source,
> Forever fruitful in divine Discourse:
> No common Themes will grace their flowing Tongues,
> No common Subjects will inspire their Songs:
> United, ne'er to part, but still to spend
> A *Jubilee* of Rapture without End.—

(36.19–24)

The dash at the conclusion of this last line is significant, as is the one at the beginning of the next line. Together, these dashes indicate a change of focus, of mood, of tone. Until this point in the third canto, Adams has conjectured about the nature of things. The conclusion of the poem—the final six lines, which follow the dashes—focuses on earthly and human realities:

> —But oh! my Muse, from this amazing Height
> Descend, and downward trace thy dangerous Flight;

> Some Angel best becomes such lofty Things,
> With Skill to guide, and Strength to urge his Wings:
> To lower Strains, confine thy humble Lays,
> 'Till, by Experience taught, thou learn to praise.

(36.25–37.2)

Here Adams means that only angels, because of their proximity to God, can describe Him and heaven adequately. Adams, a mortal, cannot, although he hopes to learn to do so through the experience of his muse.

David S. Shields admires "On Society" for Adams's accomplishment in the Blackmorean mode. He explains:

> The poet asserts the connection between divine power and the sensible order; the poet surveys the order; once its design has been comprehended, a turn occurs—the order is shown to be a transparent vehicle of God's power; the poet encounters godhead in a climactic moment of feeling and insight.[40]

Adams does all these things in his poem, and more, although the depth and convincingness of his feeling and insight are open to question. As is the case with other writers inspired by Blackmore, Adams, as Shields notes, "represents nature only to dissolve it and discover the divine power animating it."[41] In this poem, Adams effectively depicts God enlivening nature.

Generally speaking, Adams succeeds in adopting various aspects of the Blackmorean technique; his accomplishment with details of the religious sublime is less obvious. "On Society" is highly descriptive, with numerous adjectives, as may be seen in the portrayal of hell (above) and in an effective quatrain about trees and wind from the first canto:

> THE tall and amorous Trees, with folded Boughs,
> Receive the Tempest, when its Fury blows;
> And when the Winds their sounding T[err]ors cease,
> The Zephyrs ask their Pardon with a Kiss.

(25.5–8)

Adams creates antitheses in his rhymed couplets, as in the following description of God from the third canto, where He is both invisible and visible:

Veil'd in his Essence, from our Weakness veil'd,
But all the GOD on all the *Son* reveal'd.

(35.13–14)

That is, in this poem Adams employs some of the methods, as David S. Shields identifies them, for creating a sublime religious experience in his readers. Yet while Adams succeeds in conveying God's plan to mankind, he seems less successsful in dissolving the distinction between word and object. I wonder how deeply this poem moved its readers, most of whom probably shared Adams's religious views. Although "On Society" deals with divine topics, to think that eighteenth-century readers believed the poem transported them to heaven strains credulity. In other words, the distance between the theory of the sublime and the actual response to the poem seems great. Perhaps the theory is, at least in the case of Adams, only a theory.

Personal Poems

Six personal poems are the most moving literary creations of John Adams because in treating the death of friends and the misfortune of Captain John Adams he comes close to a genuine expression of emotion, an expression that is thwarted elsewhere in his poetry. He is involved in his subject matter. In five elegies, he communicates his own remorse and either directly or indirectly attempts to console the survivors of people who have died recently. Additionally, in a poem about the blindness of his father, he regrets Captain John Adams's physical infirmity while anticipating the elder Adams's sighted existence in heaven. Matthew Adams arranged the elegies chronologically, according to when the subjects of the poems died and doubtless, therefore, according to when John Adams wrote them. Matthew Adams placed the verse about the poet's father between the first two elegies, possibly in order to indicate when in the sequence of personal poems John Adams composed it. The date of its composition is unknown.

The first of these poems paraphrases 2 Samuel 1, in which David laments the recent death in battle of Saul and Jonathan, father and son. In this poem titled "David's Elegy Paraphras'd," Adams applies the first chapter of 2 Samuel to the 1724 death of Josiah Winslow, his Harvard classmate whom Indians killed in

Maine in 1724 during the Three Years' War. Adams likens himself to David and Winslow to Jonathan, David's best friend. With genuine, if conventionally expressed, emotion, Adams states, perhaps predictably, that Winslow was no less heroic and worthy of lasting fame than the fallen biblical heroes:[42]

> BUT shall the Muse in melting Strains deplore,
> An ancient Loss, and pass a Modern o'er?
> Shall *Saul* and *Jonathan* eternal live,
> And all the Waste of envious Time survive,
> While WINSLOW's Fate employs a silent Woe,
> And Death shall seize his Fame and Body too?
>
> (75.15–20)

One accepts such a statement from a devastated friend of an apparently noble warrior killed in battle. One also accepts it because even then using David's lament in elegies was something of a convention; Urian Oakes's 1667 elegy of Thomas Shepard is one example of an earlier poem that uses this episode from the Bible.[43]

This poem benefits less from Adams's comparison of Winslow with Saul and Jonathan than it does from the poet's likening of a friend being killed by arrows to a lion being speared to death:

> So, a fierce Lion, when in darted Show'rs
> A Storm of Jav'lins round his Body pours,
> Foaming, he roars, and Lashes quick his Main,
> Then furious flys, and fills the Field with Slain;
> 'Till overcome by a Superiour Strength,
> He, falling on the Ground, projects his dreadful Length.
>
> (76.19–24)

Although the word "round" in the second of these lines is vague because it could mean either that the javelins land near or in the animal, the image is vivid and appropriate. Threatened with death, the lion strikes out, killing some of his attackers before they can destroy him. One can imagine Winslow reacting to the threat of imminent death in a similar manner. Unfortunately, because this poem does not sustain the comparison, it is all but lost in this 142-line panegyric. Another of its intriguing aspects concerns Adams's wondering if Winslow has been buried. His interest suggests Antigone's anxiety about the remains of her brother

Polynices in Sophocles's great play, with which Adams was probably familiar.[44]

"On the Sudden Death of Messieurs George and Nathan Howell," the second of Adams's personal poems, concerns the Howell brothers, ages fifteen (George) and thirteen (Nathan), who drowned in Boston in January 1728. While skating, they broke through the ice. They were the children of Nathan Howell, who died in 1716, and Katherine George Howell; they were also the step-grandchildren of Cotton Mather, who married their maternal grandmother, Lydia Lee George, in 1715. Adams wrote this poem to express his own remorse, certainly, but primarily to console the boys' mother, as may be inferred from these lines:

> Her matchless Grief no Bounds can know,
> But gushes in an endless Flow.[45]

> (81.11–12)

I cannot determine the precise nature of Adams's connection with the family, although "charming Youth" (79.9) indicates his possible familiarity with the victims.

After imploring Melpomene, the muse of tragedy, to open her "Springs of Sorrow" and "Let every Eyeball pour its Tide" (79.3–4), Adams captures convincingly the Howells' youthful excitement at skating on the ice and then their inability to save themselves when imperiled. As in the Winslow poem, here Adams augments an important event, the drownings, with a suitable image, in this case an earthquake:

> So when an Earthquake shakes a Town,
> And Nature's Works seem shudd'ring down,
> Th' Inhabitants with wild Affright,
> Out from their Houses pour their Flight:
> The Streets amaz'd no less than they,
> Haste from their quivering Feet to flee,
> Their rolling Eyes with Horror stare,
> Their Knees to Heav'n are bent in Prayer,
> In vain they cry, wide gape their Graves,
> A springing Lake the City laves.

> (80.19–28)

An earthquake struck Boston in late October 1727, with aftershocks continuing for the remainder of the year.[46] Likening the boys' drownings to an earthquake-jolted city is therefore appropriate within the context of the time. The youths were "Nature's Works"; their mother and other people almost certainly fled houses "with wild Affright" upon learning of the skaters' predicament. People caught in this earthquake might have bent their knees in prayer. Best of all, poetically, Mrs. Howell, friends, neighbors, and rescuers must have been so shocked upon learning of the disaster that their frenzied, desperate racing to assist the children could have caused them or an observer to think of the streets as fleeing their pounding feet. Personifying the streets in this manner creates a fitting image for the panic that naturally accompanies both an earthquake and actions resulting from news that a loved one is in danger.

The remainder of the poem is pedestrian; Adams knows that Jesus has taken the children to heaven, where they are liberated from life's cares. He uses these drownings predictably to encourage other people to prepare for unexpected death and to turn to Christ while capable of so doing.

Although effective imagery most recommends these poems on Winslow and the Howells, a general uniformity of mourning, passion, grief, and sense of loss weakens them and other of Adams's personal poems, although he seems sincere in all of them. The poet appears to be as devastated by the accidental deaths of children as at the apparently noble death of a college classmate. Perhaps the events affected him similarly. In "On the Death of the Late Reverend and Learned Dr. Cotton Mather, February 13. 1727,8," he expresses somewhat greater remorse, however, although Mather, unlike Winslow and the Howells, did not die young. To Adams, Mather was the great man of the time, the learned cleric, voluminous author, and eloquent speaker against whose magnitude all other contemporaries, when compared, would be found wanting. (Mather himself would have agreed with this assessment.) Such praise might seem excessive; but Adams, while perhaps lauding Mather immoderately by objective standards (although he is writing in a genre where excess is understandable), is correct; Mather was, by almost any positive measure, including the measures Adams cites, the most formidable American upon his death in 1728.

Adams's deep feeling for Mather indicates a probable personal relationship between the two men. Although I have discovered no irrefutable evidence to establish such a connection, strong circumstantial evidence exists. Given the size of the Harvard enrollments around 1720 (thirty-seven students comprised the class of 1721, for example), all of the students certainly knew each other, as, therefore, did Samuel Mather, Cotton Mather's son, and Adams. Because the former was a member of the class of 1723, Samuel Mather's first two Harvard years (1719–21) coincided with Adams's last two. It is not outside the realm of possibility that Adams, whose family then presumably still lived in Nova Scotia, became acquainted with young Mather and visited his home in Boston, thereby becoming friendly with the father of his fellow student.

In addition to Adams's concern about the drownings of Mather's step-grandsons and the poet's acquaintance and possible friendship with Samuel Mather, four indirect connections between Cotton Mather and John Adams suggest at least their familiarity with one another. First, Mather knew Hugh Adams, the brother of Matthew Adams and Captain John Adams, the poet's father. At the Braintree, Massachusetts, second parish, in September 1707, Mather delivered a sermon, *The Temple Opening*, at the ordination of Hugh Adams. Second, Mather was involved in the Nathaniel Clap affair. In a letter to Thomas Prince dated 13 January 1727—thirteen months before Mather's death at age sixty-five—Mather acknowledges having written to Clap at Prince's request to encourage Clap to cease the "great and public scandal that he had long persisted in," namely withholding Holy Communion from his Newport parishioners.[47] Surely Mather was informed when, seven months later, Adams was called to Newport to help with a problem that Mather wanted solved. He might even have recommended Adams for the position. Third, Mather was the uncle of Mather Byles, with whom Adams was active in literary affairs during the last ten months of Cotton Mather's life. Byles and Mather were neighbors. Fourth, John Adams was criticized for emulating Mather's "florid pulpit style,"[48] a charge that indicates his probable attendance at Mather's sermons, which Adams also implies in his Mather elegy:

> When *Mather* spoke, he hung each silent Ear,
> Or gain'd the Smile, or spread a serious Air;
> With deep Instruction ting'd the virtuous Mind,
> Scatter'd our Sorrows, and our Joys refin'd.

> Kindl'd our Thirst for Learning's sacred Springs,
> Rais'd up new Fields, and clear'd sublimer Things.
> His Speech was like the Rain which plenteous pours,
> Our Ears the Field to drink the dewy Show'rs.
>
> (86.19–26)

Whatever the nature of the relationship between the two men, Adams's poem conveys both respect and reverence for Mather.

Adams begins this elegy by stating that he will avoid writing about military men and wars, not because he cannot address them but rather because they are inadequate subjects. He is concerned with higher, more important matters:

> LET others sing the Hero or the Field,
> The glitt'ring Helmet, or the blazing Shield;
> The streaming Blood which dies the crimson Plain,
> When strow'd in wild Disorder lay the Slain;
> My Muse to higher Glories winds her Strings,
> Her Theme a Subject of the *King* of Kings.
> 'Tis Thee, O boundless JESUS, whom I praise,
> And from thy Servant strike Thee back Thy Rays;
> No mean Attempt will suit my tuneful Lyre,
> While *Mather* trembles o'er the speaking Wire.
>
> (83.1–10)

He wants to praise Jesus, which he can do only with His assistance. Adams asks elsewhere for Christ's encouragement, but in doing so here he conveys a clear sense of his own inadequacy vis-à-vis Mather. Adams wishes to celebrate and lament the great man, but he deems the task formidable. The dead Mather intimidates him.

In eulogizing Mather, Adams attempts a substantial poem but succeeds only modestly. He uses imagery effectively, as Samuel Knapp observed in 1821.[49] In particular, Adams juxtaposes light and dark images. In the second stanza, such words as "lighten'd" (83.12), "flaming" (83.13), "Light" (83.17), and "dawns" (83.18) describe Mather's "Bliss immortal" (84.4). In the third stanza, "Night" (84.12), "dark Eclipse" (84.13), and "Storms" (84.16) characterize the earth that has lost "the Saint, the bright Example" (84.20). Granted, Adams does not sustain this contrasting imagery throughout the poem, but his use of it in two stanzas reflects his sense of the state of Mather's spirit and of the people who mourn the great man. It also creates a context for the remainder of the poem, which primarily limns Mather as thinker, author, and preacher, although in a predictable manner.

In summarizing Mather's range of reading and knowledge, Adams creates a serviceable image:

> So spread the Fishing-Tribe th' expanded Net,
> In which the scaly Swarms promiscuous meet.
>
> (85.11–12)

The off-rhyme may or may not be artful, but the image of myriad netted fish illustrates well Adams's sense of Mather's enormous intellect, which housed not only numerous facts but deep learning.

Despite Adams's expression of sorrow and his effort to capture Mather's greatness, this poem contains at least one significant ambiguity. In the line "Ah Father! Why so sudden was thy Flight?" (84.11), does Adams intend the second word to mean the divine Father or Mather? Either way, the question implies that Mather died young, unexpectedly, or both. Neither is the case.

Of Adams's personal poems, this one about Mather is the most ambitious. Eager to mourn and praise, Adams doubtless spoke for many Americans—especially those in the Boston area—who, like Adams, considered Mather a religious, literary, and cultural icon.

If the Mather elegy is the most ambitious of Adams's personal poems, "A Consolatory Letter to a Near Relative on the Death of His Consort, July 2. 1733" is the most heartfelt. Here, Adams attempts to console the husband of Katherine, who died of an unnamed disease.[50] The title and the author's occasional use of the first-person plural pronoun indicate a close relationship between Adams and the widower—and thus Katherine—which explains Adams's heightened emotion in this poem.[51] Although Adams knows that this male relative is the person best qualified to write about Katherine, he realizes that grief inhibits Katherine's mate from so doing. The responsibility for memorializing her therefore falls to Adams.

Who is Katherine? Adams begins the poem by addressing her husband, implying that he is an author. Since the widower is the poet's relative, this man could be Matthew Adams, a writer who was married to Katherine (or Katharine) Brigdon. They wed in

1715, and she died sometime between the 1726 birth of their last child and her husband's 1734 marriage to Meriel Cotton.[52] Therefore, she could have died in 1733, the date of death indicated in the title of John Adams's poem. If she did—as seems likely, especially given Matthew Adams's remarriage the following year—she is the Katherine of the poem, and Matthew Adams is the relative John Adams attempts to console.

In this poem, Adams enumerates Katherine's qualities. To him, she was good, intelligent, loving, meek, virtuous, modest, truthful, and so forth. While such characterization might be predictable and while Adams is reluctant to provide examples of his aunt's attributes, Adams's depth of feeling for Katherine makes believable his depiction of her. He provides details about one of her qualities, however, and that is her intelligence:

> NOR were these Virtues doom'd to be confin'd
> To low Ideas, and a grov'lling Mind;
> But Art and Elegance, to Nature true,
> Touch'd into Life the Lines which Nature drew.
> Her ready Pen, to what she once essay'd,
> In soften'd Lights the justest Thoughts display'd;
> On the smooth Current of each gentle Line,
> Shone the fair Image of the Soul within.
>
> (91.7–14)

One would like to know the nature of "her ready pen." Did Katherine write letters? Poetry? Essays? Whatever her mode of composition, her writing ability indicates that she was an educated woman.

Unfortunately, the imagery in this poem is not particularly noteworthy. In fact, one image is less adequate than it might seem at first reading. In attempting to demonstrate how in life Katherine had united with her husband, Adams introduces the image of ivy, symbolizing the woman, climbing and covering an oak tree, the man:

> So, round the spreading Oak the Ivy bends,
> And graces with its Green, while that defends,
> But Death, too sudden, stepping in between,
> Has drawn a sable Curtain o'er the Scene.
>
> (91.17–20)

Adams did not consider the ramifications of this image. Had the ivy not died, in time it probably would have choked life from the tree. Surely he does not mean to say that had Katherine lived, she would have killed her husband. In editing John Adams's newspaper poems and possibly other verses for publication in *Poems on Several Occasions*, Matthew Adams would have been well advised to change or delete this image. He is, after all, the tree that Katherine's ivy might have killed.

Another part of this poem warrants comment. Adams's description of Katherine's present physical state attracts attention, although the following macabre, Poe-like image probably seems more shocking to sensibilities of the twenty-first century than it did to eighteenth-century readers familiar with "graveyard" meditations, of which these four lines constitute an early poetic example:

> Once gay with Life, within the Tomb embrac'd,
> The busy Worms devour the crumbling Guest;
> Wrapt in the Curtains of a solid Night,
> No more a Joy but Horror to the Sight.

(89.15–18)

It is an accurate description, no doubt, but hardly consolation to the person most grieved by her death, Matthew Adams.

This poem had an effect unlike any other of Adams's verses. Eleven years after the poet's death and six years following the appearance of the poem in *Poems on Several Occasions*, someone adapted "A Consolatory Letter to a Near Relative" to commemorate the death of another woman. "A Consolatory Letter to a Near Relative, on the Death of His Agreeable Consort, July 22. 1751" was published in *The Boston Evening Post* of 26 August 1751. The author of this poem, a resident of Annapolis Royal, Nova Scotia, used many of Adams's lines and composed some original ones to console an unnamed man over the death of Martha, his wife.[53]

The existence of this later poem raises the question of how someone knew of Adams's poem that was published only in *Poems on Several Occasions*, a volume that probably had a limited print run and could not have had much celebrity. Because relatives of John Adams living in Annapolis Royal would have had copies of his collection of verse, one of them might have modified his poem about Katherine. If not, the person who did probably knew of it from one them. One such relative was Adams's sister, Anne, the wife of William Skene, surgeon at the local military garrison until at least 1750.[54] Other Adamses might also have lived there then.

Who was Martha? Although neither death records nor protestant church documents exist for Annapolis Royal from that time, her identity can be inferred. She was probably Martha Shirreff Hamilton, daughter of William Shirreff, commissary of musters and judge advocate at the fort, which later became Fort Anne (named, as was Annapolis Royal itself, for Queen Anne). In June 1741, she married John Hamilton, captain-lieutenant with the 40th regiment of foot. Because in April 1752 the British agent for the regiment paid Hamilton's bills for black cloth, black sealing wax, and a mourning sword, someone in Hamilton's family had died relatively recently, but—given the shipping time to England and the nature of bureaucracy—almost certainly before late 1751. Furthermore, few Englishmen or Englishwomen lived in Annapolis Royal at the middle of the eighteenth century, so not many Marthas would have resided there. The only other Martha known then to have inhabited Annapolis Royal was Martha Bradstreet, who was still living in the 1760s.[55]

Evidence indicates, therefore, that following the death of Martha Shirreff Hamilton in mid 1751, someone of or intimate with the Annapolis Royal family of John Adams adapted the poem to comfort John Hamilton. This person might have been Anne Adams Skene, or her husband, William. It is unclear, though, why this person submitted the poem to *The Boston Evening Post*. If relatives of the Shirreffs or Hamiltons lived in Boston, the person who modified Adams's poem might have wished to console them in a public manner.

In "To the Rev. Mr. Turell, on the Death of His Vertuous Consort, Daughter to the Rev. Dr. Colman," Adams eulogizes two of his Harvard classmates' wives, Jane Colman Turell (spouse of Ebenezer Turell) and Elizabeth Taylor (mate of John Taylor), who died within three weeks of each other. It is Adams's least artful, most disappointing personal poem primarily because its two parts are distinct. In referring to the husband and father of only one of these women, Turell, the title anticipates the major problem with the poem, lack of unity. One can only conjecture about Adams's handling of this work. He might have eulogized

Turell soon after her demise on 26 March 1735, and, a few weeks later, composed a poem about Taylor, who died on 16 April. Alternatively, he could have composed it all following Taylor's death. Without question, though, Adams was aware of the problem this poem presents. In an attempt to link the two parts, he composed a quatrain to serve as a transition from Turell to Taylor:

> FAIN would the *Muse* her plaintive Numbers cease,
> And lose her Sorrows in these Realms of Bliss.
> But TAYLOR calls me downward, and demands
> Tears from my Eyes, and Cypress from my Hands.
>
> (99.3–6)

Although the first couplet refers to Turell and the second to Taylor, these lines do not satisfactorily unite the two parts of the poem.[56] The problem is especially perplexing in the context of Adams's elegy for Josiah Winslow, in which Adams treats biblical heroes in the first part of the poem and Winslow in the second. These two parts cohere because the second follows naturally from the first.

The section of the poem dealing with Turell is superior to that treating Taylor. This is partly because Adams implies his intimacy with Ebenezer Turell, and thus with Jane. He does this in the opening couplet, where he positions himself to observe the anguish on Ebenezer's face:

> WHY hangs such Sorrow on your pensive Brow,
> Say *Turell*, why the Tears so freely flow?
>
> (94.1–2)

This affection of the speaker (Adams) for the addressee (Turell) implies concern genuinely felt, which is not the case in the lines about Taylor. In them, Adams, addressing no one, appears unmoved. The part of the poem treating Taylor seems merely an appendage to the section about Turell.

In eulogizing Turell, Adams fashioned some attractive lines. One of his loveliest couplets concerns an effect of "Th' impartial Tyrant" (95.3), death:

> The Charms of Beauty wither from his Hands,
> As fades a Flower, and to a Tempest bends.
>
> (95.5–6)

He also writes convincingly when attempting to bolster Ebenezer Turell, although Adams had to be careful not to focus too intently on Turell's sorrow because "to grieve was not only to admit excessive attachment to a mere creature but to reject the comfort that faith should bring."[57] Adams needed to focus ultimately on the spirit of the departed, not on the survivor's loss. Adams states that Jane now inhabits a place far superior to earth, heaven:

> None that had tasted of sublimer Springs,
> Could feel a Thirst for these inferiour Things.
> As who a Lawn, distinct with silver Rills,
> Wou'd change for burning Sands, or broken Hills?
> Or in the Covert of a lonely Cell
> From all the beauteous Realms of *Phœbus* Steal;
> When smiling Prospects and unfading Greens
> Courted his Sight with their enamell'd Scenes,
> And all the Arch of Heaven's expanded Sky
> Burnt with unnumber'd Glories to his Eye?
> Thro' Death's dark Valley, winding out her Way,
> The Saint has open'd to a Blaze of Day.

(96.3–14)

However genuine his remorse in this poem, Adams offers little to distinguish Turell from other people he laments, such as Josiah Winslow and the Howell brothers. But Turell was then an important woman, primarily because she was the daughter and wife of notable men, Benjamin Colman and Ebenezer Turell respectively. She is even more significant now because of her accomplishments as a poet.[58] While this is not the place to discuss her verse, one would, nonetheless, like to know, from someone who apparently knew her, more than Adams offers about this woman and her poetic creations. He notes that

> NATURE had shed upon her ample Mind
> It's various Gifts, which Art had well refin'd.

(96.25–26)

In attempting to detail Turell's intellectual accomplishments, Adams unwittingly allies himself with writers who, in the century following the landing of the *Mayflower*, promulgate what we would call the sexist attitudes that Anne Bradstreet criticizes when lashing out at "each carping tongue, / Who sayes, my hand a needle better fits" than a pen.[59] Adams comments on Turell in the following manner:

> Politely read, what various Books she knew?
> Which on her Mind unfading Traces drew.
> Nor was She vain, nor stain'd with those Neglects
> In which too learned Females lose their Sex.
>
> (98.17–20)

That is, Turell was an intellectual because she read books (and wrote verse). Fortunately, from Adams's point of view, she kept her intellect in check; while remembering what she read, she did not permit herself to become vain, shirk her womanly duties, or assume a masculine bearing, which Adams believed learned women tend to do. His carping tongue is only slightly less harsh than John Winthrop's when the great Puritan notes in 1645 that Ann Yale Hopkins, who "had written many bookes," became insane "by occasion of her givinge her selfe wholly to readinge & writinge," activities that only men are properly constituted to pursue seriously.[60]

Except for in his lines on Elizabeth Taylor, Adams seems genuinely saddened in all his elegies by the loss of people who were meaningful if not close to him. Writing about them possibly provided him catharsis. These poems probably also comforted these people's survivors when they read the verses in manuscript. Most impressive of them are the poems on Cotton Mather, in which Adams attempts to honor the greatest man of his time and place, and on Katherine, in which Adams is deeply moved by her death. Least satisfactory is the poem on Jane Colman Turell and Elizabeth Taylor, primarily because of structural problems and of Adams's seemingly greater feeling for the former woman than the latter.

"To My Honoured Father on the Loss of His Sight" is the only personal poem that is not an elegy. Here, Adams attempts religiously to console the senior John Adams for the sight that had begun to diminish in the 1720s and that would fail almost completely by 1730.[61] Although the poet's father is physically blind, through Jesus he will be able to see again, eternally, in heaven:

> But, first your Frame must moulder in the Ground,
> Before the Light will kindle Worlds around.
>
> (78.17–18)

Adams uses musical imagery effectively to depict his father's future trek heavenward:

> You, who can touch the Strings to melting Airs,
> And with melodious Trills enchant our Ears,
> May, wing'd by Faith, to heavenly vocal Plains,
> In Fancy's Organ, drink sublimer Strains:
> The Sounds, which Love and sacred Joys inspire,
> Which pour the Musick from the raptur'd Choir.
>
> (78.7–12)

These lines imply that the father was a musician, possibly a violinist or guitarist.

In this poem of consolation and genuine but predictable religious expression, John Adams writes most convincingly in the concluding eight lines. Here, he creates an effective image:

> So, when a Stream has warbled thro' the Wood,
> Its limpid Bosom smooths and clears its Flood;
> The rolling Mirrour deep imbibes the Stains
> Of heav'nly Saphyr, and impending Greens;
> 'Till thro' the Ground, in secret Channels led,
> It hides its Glories in the gloomy Bed:
> 'Till, op'ning thro' a wide and flow'ry Vale,
> Far fairer Scenes the purer Streams reveal.
>
> (78.24–79.2)

"Warbled," the key word here, links the musical imagery with nature, thereby unifying the poem, at least aurally and visually. Yet these lines also restate symbolically and pictorially what has occurred, and Adams's sense of what will happen, to his father. The first four of the concluding eight lines represent the elder Adams's sighted life; the next two, his blindness and physical death. When in the last two lines the stream escapes what appears to be its underground death and emerges into an unencumbering and fecund valley, it unites with a part of nature more beautiful than the woods; and the stream benefits from this new environment by becoming purer than it was previously. The stream in the ideal valley parallels the blind man's eventual residence in heaven, where he will see perfect loveliness, of which he is a part. These lines symbolize the resurrection.

Although this stream image helps the poet make his point, it becomes less effective when considered in the context of its appearance in other poems in *Poems on Several Occasions*. It is present in the third canto of "On Society":

> BUT oh! what Joys thro' various Bosoms rove,
> As Silver Riv'lets warble thro' a Grove,
> When fix'd on Zion's ever-wid'ning Plains,
> The Force of Friendship but increas'd remains
>
> (36.7–10)

and in the translation of Psalm 104:

> The living Springs, dispers'd in num'rous Rills,
> Thro' Vallies glide, and glad the neighbouring Hills;
> Where all the Brutes drink in the crystal Waves,
> And the wild Ass his fiery Palate laves:
> Near these the winged Chorus of the Sky,
> On blooming Boughs their warbling Accents try.
>
> (49.5–10)

Adams employs it in the poem about Cotton Mather:

> Say Muse, how great the Compass of his Mind,
> Like a vast Ocean deep, and unconfin'd;
> Or like a River Gliding o'er the Plain,
> Deep and serene, which heav'nly Colours stain
>
> (84.21–24)

and again at the conclusion of "A Consolatory Letter to a Near Relative":

> So, gentle Rills, which narrow Channels bind,
> Thro' lonely Glades their weeping Riv'lets wind,
> 'Till, meeting with a Stream's impetuous Course,
> They join their Currents, and improve their Force:
> Now op'ning thro' a large luxuriant Plain,
> They draw the liquid Mazes of their Train;
> While rising Flowers confine the shining Crowd,
> And stain the Bosom of the Silver Flood.
>
> (94.11–18)

The sequence in which Adams uses this image cannot be determined. His treatment of it, though, indicates a tendency to reuse images and techniques that he found effective, as he also does in setting off the word "wild" in commas in "An Address to the Supreme Being" and "Melancholy Discrib'd and Dispell'd."

These six personal poems—on Winslow, the Howells, Mather, Katherine, Turell and Taylor, and Adams's father—are all in *Poems on Several Occasions*. One other quasi-personal poem not included in the collection requires comment. It appeared in a newspaper before being included in a book published seventeen years later, four years following Adams's death.[62]

In *The New-England Weekly Journal* of 9 October 1727, Adams published, in heroic couplets, the 141-line "To a Gentleman on the Sight of Some of His Poems," which I have discussed in the context of Adams's newspaper verse. The title is misleading because Adams focuses on only one of his subject's poems; although he identifies neither the author nor the poem he praises, internal evidence indicates that the poem is "Verses Written in Milton's *Paradise Lost*," which appears in the 21 August 1727 issue of the same newspaper. Because of its presence in Mather Byles's *Poems on Several Occasions*, we know that Byles wrote it.[63]

Adams compares the twenty-year-old Byles with Horace and Waller, among other poets, and invokes Apollo and Phoebus. The poem contains some attractive lines, in particular the concluding ones that establish Byles as Phoebus in order to show his poetic superiority to Adams and their contemporaries:

> So *Phabus* shining with immortal gleams
> Shoots down the golden glory of his beams.
> Nor when behind the hills his light retires,
> Are in the ocean quenc'd his radiant fires,
> But rising to their sight, the inferiour world
> Behold his flames with fiery vigour hurl'd.

(8.136–41)

Most notable is Adams's suggestion that because of Byles's accomplishment, America can boast—or might soon boast—of verse comparable in quality to British poetry:

> No more shall foreign wits our clime despise,
> And bless the indulgence of their milder skies.
> *Britannia's* Bards, forever may ye feel
> The inspiring Pow'r; and with his raptures swell.

May *Milton's* force and *Dryden's* smoothness join
With mingled lustre on your isle to shine:
But still regard with fond propitious eyes,
Your distant sons by your examples rise.
On us *Apollo* sheds his kindly light,
While we ascend *Parnassus* steepy height:
My friend can riding rein the furious horses,
And thro' the aerial kingdoms drive his course:
Can we reach the glittering Regions of the sky,
Where the still tracts of purest ether ly;
Or thro' the flow'ry fields of nature rove,
And gather garlands to adorn his love.

(6.68–83)

To his credit, Adams resists the temptation to elevate American verse above that written by British authors; to do so would be patently foolish and probably would not have occurred to him in any event. In fact, he goes out of his way to acknowledge the greatness of Milton and Dryden, and by implication other writers, doubtless including Pope.[64] Yet in showing awareness of a separate American artistic expression and suggesting that in Byles the colonists have a poet who might compete in the world arena, he anticipates similar interests of such a writer as Noah Webster over half a century later; and Webster's concerns helped create an environment that permitted Charles Brockden Brown to write his intentionally American novels.[65] Although such eighteenth-century British authors as Samuel Johnson and Oliver Goldsmith derided things American, the most pointed and derisive comment about American culture is possibly Sydney Smith's famous question of 1820: "In the four quarters of the globe, who reads an American book?"[66] Adams suggests that Byles is worth reading, although Smith would probably say that considering Byles a major man of letters merely reinforces Smith's point.

Translations

With the exception of "To a Gentleman on the Sight of Some of His Poems," all of John Adams's poems originally published in newspapers are translations, as are many verses in *Poems on Several Occasions*. In them, Adams renders Horace and parts of the Bible into English verse. He was qualified to do this because he had been trained in the art of translation, although "translation" does not fully characterize the nature of his work with ancient texts. During his grammar school years, language study was part of the curriculum for boys such as Adams who needed to demonstrate proficiency in Greek and Latin before being admitted to Harvard. Once enrolled, at morning and evening prayers they translated "from one sacred tongue to another."[67] Adams's translations of Horace indicate his command of Latin; if Adams translated verses from the original languages of the Old and New Testaments—as opposed to reworking English translations of these books—then he was demonstrably proficient in Hebrew and Greek. Although his translations, if any, from other languages are lost, Matthew Adams's claim that John Adams "was Master of Nine Languages, and had read all the most famous Greek, Lattin, Italian[,] French[,] and Spanish Authors, and had translated some fine pieces from several of'em,"[68] seems plausible.

Among the seventeen translations in *Poems on Several Occasions*, eleven are of scripture. Eight of these are from books of the Old Testament (Canticles, Judges, Lamentations, Psalms [four of them], and 2 Samuel), while three are from the New Testament (1 Corinthians, Matthew, and Revelation).[69] Adams's versions of the Holy Writ are much longer than those of the Authorized Version. In every instance but one he uses heroic couplets. With four eight-line sections, each part comprised of two ballad stanzas, Psalm 1 is the exception. Predictably, Adams's treatments of Bible verses do not possess the majesty of the King James renditions of these same texts. Why are his translations so different from the ones that had been used and admired for a century before he turned portions of the Bible into verse? How might his translations be appreciated?

No evidence of which I am aware indicates that Adams translated the entire Bible or even wished to present it all in poetry. For him, rendering parts of it into English verse was a literary exercise, although the appearance of some of his translations in *The New-England Weekly Journal* indicates that he wished for them to be read and for them to move people. Adams was not the only American to translate scripture poetically and publish his creations in the press, although he was the first to do so. Americans published approximately twenty such treatments of the Bible in periodicals from the late 1720s until 1765.[70] However, Adams's versions of the Holy Writ present a problem of nomenclature, of definition. I have used the word "translation" to describe the activity of Adams and other poets who made the Bible, or parts of it, available in English verse. No matter how accurate—translation renders a text from one language to another—this word does not adequately describe Adams's method. The poet himself admits as much by identifying his treatments of the Bible in different ways. Of his eleven reworkings of scripture, he classifies four as translations (Psalm 1, Psalm 24, Lamentations, and Revelation), four as paraphrases (Judges, Matthew, 1 Corinthians, and 2 Samuel), and one as an imitation (Psalm 148). Another, the translation of Psalm 104, appears as a paraphrase in *The New-England Weekly Journal* and as a translation in *Poems on Several Occasions*. (Matthew Adams, and not John Adams, might have changed the description of this poem.) The collection of Adams's poems does not identify the method of translation used in Canticles. Why does John Adams use words other than "translation" to describe his versions of Bible verses?

John Dryden, writing in 1680, identifies three approaches to translation. He uses the term "metaphrase" to mean a literal translation, "imitation" to suggest a free translation, and "paraphrase" to indicate a translation freer than metaphrase but less free than an imitation.[71] Dryden himself favored paraphrase. To him, metaphrase misses the spirit of the original text—Dryden terms it "servile"—and imitation captures more the spirit of the translator than of the text.[72] Obviously aware of these distinctions, Adams uses the second and third of these terms with his renderings of the Bible, but not the first. He would not have used "metaphrase" if only because in translating into verse the prose of some of his source material he could not have offered a literal translation; and he did not desire to translate in such a manner. Adams employs "imitation" accurately, according to Dryden's definition, while using "translation" and "paraphrase" interchangeably. But are Adams's translations and paraphrases similar to what Dryden means by "paraphrase"? They seem to be because Adams takes fewer liberties with the poems he identifies as translations and paraphrases than with the one poem he calls an imitation, his version of Psalm 148. Comparing his renderings of Bible verses with those of the same verses in the King

James Version and by other translators illustrates Adams's translating technique.

Matthew 6:9–13 is widely known in the language of the Authorized Version:

9   Our Father which art in heaven, Hallowed be thy name.
10   Thy kingdom come. Thy will be done in earth, as it is in heaven.
11   Give us this day our daily bread.
12   And forgive us our debts, as we forgive our debtors.
13   And lead us not into temptation, but deliver us from evil: For thine is the kingdom, and the power, and the glory, for ever. Amen.

Adams translates these verses as follows:

CElestial PARENT, whose admir'd Name
All Nature owns; and Angels speak thy Fame.
Thy constant Kindness wou'd our Tongues display,
When Morn begins, and Evening ends the Day.
Rule in our Hearts, and bow each rebel Thought,
Let every Virtue in our Souls be wrought,
Subdue our Wills, and form them to thine own;
Thy Laws our Counsels, and our Minds thy Throne:
Such let our blest Obedience be perform'd,
As Angels pay, with nobler Passions warm'd.
Descend, O sacred *Dove!* into our Breast,
And bring the Joys of everlasting Rest:
Sink every Wave, and smooth our ruffled Mind,
And let the Reign of Earth and Heav'n be join'd.
Descend in Show'rs of Bounty, and relieve
Our constant Wants; the daily Nurture give.
Scatter our Sins, like an offensive Cloud,
Let to our Penitence Thine Ears be bow'd;
Soften our Anger, and let Malice fly,
And fierce Resentment in our Bosoms dye;
Unwearied Injuries our Prayers inspire,
And our Forgiveness all our Foes admire.
Let Satan from the awful Guard retreat
Which Virtue gives, and own his foul Defeat;
From every Evil sheild our happy Lives,
Strong in the Tower which thy Protection gives.
Thy Kingdom widens o'er the starry Frames,
And grasps the rolling Worlds, and guides their Flames:
Thy Power sustains the Basis of the Whole,
And goes thro' Nature, like a mighty Soul.

Eternal Praises circle thro' the Skies,
And to Thy NAME the Hymns of Angels rise.

(56.1–57.18)

These treatments of the Lord's Prayer differ dramatically. Written in memorable prose, the first is compact and sonorous; the second, in verse, is lengthy and metrically undistinguished. Adams's text includes a number of elements absent from the Authorized Version. The translators had different goals. The earlier ones wished to present the Bible—and thus these verses—in a manner both easily understood and accurate, with their work based on other versions of the Bible as well as on the original languages.[73] Because Adams was not providing a translation of the entire Bible and thus was not intending to create a version of scripture that would replace another text, as the translators of the King James Version were doing, he did not have to worry whether his work would be endorsed by a religious or governmental group or how it would be received by a large religious audience. Adams also was not interested in translating the Bible precisely, although his translations of it generally retain the basic structure and main points of the King James Version. In his treatment of Matthew 6:9–13, for example, the first ten lines (56.1–10) correspond to verse 9 in the earlier text; 56.11–14, to verse 10; 57.1–2, to verse 11; 57.3–8, to verse 12; and 57.9–18, to verse 13. If he wished to render scripture more fully than other versions of the same material, he could; and he did. He took liberties with the text, as any poet would. His was a creative endeavor.

Adams's handling of the ninth verse of the Lord's Prayer typifies his approach to Bible translation. The Authorized Version presents the verse in ten words; Adams requires ten lines. He begins by stating the essential meaning of the verse: "Our Father which art in heaven, Hallowed be thy name" becomes

CElestial PARENT, whose admir'd Name
All Nature owns; and Angels speak thy Fame.

(56.1–2)

Does this translation appeal to readers familiar with the King James Version? Possibly—probably?—not. Yet the meaning is clear, and the lines are poetic, although eliding the "e" in "admir'd" violates the iambic meter of this line. Because he presents the sense of verse 9 in this couplet, he could, at this point, have moved on to translating verse 10. Why did he not do so?

Adams chose to compose eight more lines about this verse in order to augment the meaning of the first two lines, to demonstrate the degree to which mankind admires God. He details the desire of human beings to praise God's kindness, and he expresses the hope that God will make mortals as much like Him as possible. They must obey God. While legitimate enough logically, theologically, and poetically, these lines raise questions that Adams does not address, either because he did not see them as issues or because he could not resolve them. What, for example, does he mean by "each rebel Thought" (56.5)? If he believes that he himself occasionally desires to act profanely or possibly that he sometimes ponders whether God actually exists, he becomes more interesting to the modern reader than he might otherwise seem. Perhaps Adams intends to say only that he is as imperfect as any other person. Furthermore, referring to God's "constant Kindness" (56.3) begs the question of how unremittingly compassionate God is. To what, one wonders, does he attribute the tragedies of human existence? So although in lines 3–10 Adams elaborates on the initial couplet, he raises provocative questions that he fails to answer.

Adams also translates verse 13 expansively by treating in ten lines the material the King James Version presents in twenty-five words, including "amen." His couplets are serviceable, although again his lines have implications that he does not investigate. He calls mortal lives "happy" (57.11). What does he mean? Surely he could observe that not every human life is contented. Perhaps he suggests that we are happy because we are children of God. And in referring to God's power at 57.15–16 ("Thy Power sustains the Basis of the Whole, / And goes thro' Nature, like a mighty Soul"), he possibly implies pantheistic ideas that could have offended some readers, had they pursued the religious and philosophical ramifications of these lines.

The translation of Psalm 148, already discussed in the context of textual issues, offers better insight into Adams's technique than does that of the Lord's Prayer because we can compare Adams's poem with another more or less contemporaneous poetic rendering of this psalm, thus observing different approaches to the same material. Both of these translations appear in American newspapers, Adams's in 1735 and the other in 1739. The King James text reads as follows:

PRAISE ye the LORD. Praise ye the LORD from the heavens: praise him in the heights.
2   Praise ye him, all his angels: praise ye him, all his hosts.
3   Praise ye him, sun and moon: praise him, all ye stars of light.
4   Praise him, ye heavens of heavens, and ye waters that be above the heavens.
5   Let them praise the name of the LORD: for he commanded, and they were created.
6   He hath also stablished them for ever and ever: he hath made a decree which shall not pass.
7   Praise the LORD from the earth, ye dragons, and all deeps:
8   Fire, and hail; snow, and vapours; stormy wind fulfilling his word:
9   Mountains, and all hills; fruitful trees, and all cedars:
10 Beasts, and all cattle; creeping things, and flying fowl:
11 Kings of the earth, and all people; princes, and all judges of the earth:
12 Both young men, and maidens; old men, and children:
13 Let them praise the name of the LORD: for his name alone is excellent; his glory is above the earth and heaven.
14 He also exalteth the horn of his people, the praise of all his saints; even of the children of Israel, a people near unto him. Praise ye the LORD.

A translation of this psalm, submitted and possibly composed by S. W., appears on the front page of John Peter Zenger's *The New-York Weekly Journal* in the issue of 19 November 1739. It bears the title, "Part of the 148th Psalm Paraphras'd." I indicate the verses in the Authorized Version to which the stanzas correspond.

I [verses 1–2]

BEGIN *the high celestial Strain,*
Bright Seraphims, and sing
Triumphant Songs of grateful Praise
To Heav'ns eternal KING.

II [verse 3]

Thou Lamp of unexhausted Light
That rules the genial Day,
Shine, with the Silver Queen of Night;
His Praises to display.

III [verse 3]
Ye glimmering Orbs that gild the Skies,
     When Darkness veils the Light   10
Proclaim the Glories of your Lord,
     In Watches of the Night.
          IV [verse 4]
Ye murmuring Streams his Praise repeat,
     When thro' the Vales ye flow;
Bend down your Heads ye lofty Pines,
     And Praise him as ye blow.
          V [verse 8]
*Young **Zephyrs** bear on all your Wings,*
     His Glorious Name away
To distant Shores, and foreign Climes,
     The lofty Theme convey.   20
          VI [verse 8]
Thunder, and Lightning, Fire, and Hail
     Swift Heralds of the Lord,
In all your dreadful Forms appear,
     To speak his mighty Word.
          VII [verse 7]
Vast Monsters of the raging Deep
     Praise ye his awfull Name,
Let all the Brute Creation Praise
     The GOD from whom they came.
          VIII [verses 10–13]
Mortals assume a nobler strain,
     While meaner Creatures siing,   30
Chant thro' the wide-extended World;
     The Glories of your KING.

Here is Adams's "Hallelujah Attempted, In Imitation of the
148th Psalm," as published in original form in *The New-England
Weekly Journal* of 12 May 1735:

     LET all the Works of Heaven's Eternal KING,
Conspire his Praises in their spheres to sing.
Ye Heaven's, his Praises thro' your realms resound,
And let all nature catch the circling Sound.
The flaming Orb, which lights the Fields of Day,
The Moon, which marks in Heaven her silver Way,
And Stars, whose steady beams the shades display;
With Planets winding in elliptick Spheres,
And erring Comets red with sweeping Hairs;

With glowing Meteors shooting thro' the Skies,   10
In one united Voice and Chorus rise;
Your living Lamps with endless Oil he feeds,
Points all your Flames, and Revolutions leads.
He gilds the short liv'd Gellies[74] that ascend;
And Rockets in the Air, their sudden Glories spend.
Praise God, you smooth Serene,[75] and every Cloud
Which does the vivid Face of Phœbus shrowd.
He streaks the Light upon your fleecy Folds,
And black with Tempests in His Chambers holds;
Gives down the finer Drops of silver Dews,   20
Which o'er the glittering Lawns and Fields diffuse.
Drunk by the opening Mouths of spreading Flowers,
And fair Aurora paints the pearly Showers.
He frees the Sluices of suspended Rain,
And drives the rapid Torrents on the Plain:
He swells the ærial Vapours with a Storm,
Which shade the Scene of Heaven, and all the Sky deform;
The sweeping Winds drive furious o'er the Seas,
Or sport with scattering bows, & snap the bending Trees;
The roaring Forest bows before the sound,   30
And the high dashing Waves to Heaven resound.
Ye winding Rills in chrystal Mirrours rove,
Murmur his Praises, and reflect each Grove,
And you, ye artless Chorus of the Sky,
On painted wings, on wings of Musick fly.
He form'd the Nightingale's melodious Throat,
And on the vocal Forest pours each Note.
Ye Trees & Groves whose towring shades ascend
With humbler Greens which tremble to the Wind
Be deck'd with Leaves, with ripen'd Fruitage bend;   40
Let every Branch their verdant Honours bow,
To him who stain'd their Leaves, and made their Fruitage
    glow.
Flourish you Flowers, your painted Streaks unfold,
Ye Daffodills which drink the noon day Gold;
Or Violets, ting'd with a celestial blue,
Or, gaudy Tulips varied to the View.
Ye Lillies fairer than the new fall'n Snow.
Or Roses blushing with Aurora's Glow,
Let every Honour of the Garden own,
Who sunk their Dies, and put their Raiment on.   50
Praise God ye Tribes which in the Ocean teem,
Or gliding sparkle thro' the limpid Stream;

With liquid Silver bright or scaly Gold,
Or you whom oozy Beds inactive hold;
From him whose Shell contains the vivid Pearls,
To vast Leviathan who ponderous whirls
The foamy Waves, and sprinkles all the Skies
With the huge Streams that from his Nostrils rise;
Confess who sunk your Banks, or spread your Flood,
Who hung your Fins & who appoints your Food.   60
Ye Lions who thro' trembling Forests rove,
And all the Savage Horrors of the Grove,
In wilder Notes your Makers praise rehearse,
Who knit your Strength, & form'd you to be fierce;
And join in milder Sounds you tamer Tribe,
Who smooth the Lawn, or pierce the Sable Glebe.
And you with Garments Wove in speckled Dies
Before whose sting the frighted Traveller flies,
Drown every Hiss in Natures softer Lays,
Forget your Enmity, and learn to Praise.   70
Let Insects too, minute, which Glasses spy,
A new Creation crowding on the Eye;
Or green on Floods or labouring thro' the Leaf,
Be not exceeded in the vocal Strife;
Praise him ye countless Hosts who wondring flee,
A sand your Mountain, and a drop your sea.
But most in Man erect and form'd to Spy,
The pendent Scenes, & Blaze of all the Sky;
Let him, for he has skill to trace the Ways,
Of Nature, and unwind the lengthy Maze.   80
Let him to Natures Consort tune his Lyre,
And rank each Being in its proper Quire;
Then born from World to World the winding Strains,
Shall reach the Choir of Zion's warbling Plains.

These two eighteenth-century poems differ markedly from the King James Version and from each other. The word "part" in the title of the 1739 poem correctly indicates that the author did not attempt to translate all fourteen verses of Psalm 148. He ignores verses 5, 6, 9, and 14. This poem contains fewer words than the Authorized Version has for Psalm 148 (and has only slightly more words than the King James Version when verses 5, 6, 9, and 14 are removed from it). The author twice considers two or more verses in one stanza, twice addresses two stanzas in one verse, and twice uses one stanza to deal with one verse. He also inverts the order of verses 7 and 8 and takes a number of structural liberties with the text. Most of these stanzas rhyme *abcb* (ballad stanzas), but some rhyme *abab*. In content, the poem conveys straightforwardly the meaning of the verses in the Authorized Version. For our purposes, it is significant primarily to illustrate how a contemporary of Adams approached Psalm 148.

Whether Adams accounts for all the verses of this psalm is unclear. Often in this poem, determining the verse to which a line corresponds is difficult. Adams is less methodical than the author of the poem in *The New-York Weekly Journal*, but this does not mean that Adams composed this or other translations carelessly. He need not have treated the psalm verse by verse, or even made clear which verse he was translating in his lines. He is concerned with conveying the sense of the psalm, which he does effectively, though he violates its structure and possibly does not address verses 5, 6, and 14. In any event, Adams discusses the first two verses in his opening quatrain and begins addressing the third verse in line 5, concluding it probably at line 17. Lines 18–23 seem to treat verse 4. Adams apparently considers verse 7 in lines 51–60, verse 8 in lines 20–33, verse 9 in lines 38–50, verse 10 in lines 34–37 and 61–74, verse 11 in lines 75–78, and verses 12–13 in lines 79–84.

In translating the verses of this psalm, Adams includes important details (frequently quite visual) that do not appear in the King James Version, which is not the case with the other poet. For example, he augments verse 8 ("Fire, and hail; snow and vapours; stormy wind fulfilling his word") with, among other lines, the couplet

> He frees the Sluices of suspended Rain,
> And drives the rapid Torrents on the Plain.
>
> (ll. 24–25)

The two eighteenth-century texts also differ metrically. That in the *New-York Weekly Journal* has primarily ballad stanzas, while Adams's poem is in heroic couplets, with a few Alexandrines, which are lines of twelve syllables (lines 15, 27, 29, 42).

This psalm basically states that everyone and every thing should praise the Lord: angels, hosts, sun, moon, stars, heaven, waters, dragons, deeps, fire, hail, snow, vapors, wind, mountains, hills, fruit trees and cedars, beasts, cattle, creeping things, flying fowl, and all people, including kings, princes, judges, young men, maidens, old men, and children. It is concrete, not abstract. Four of the nine words in verse 9, for example, are nouns ("Mountains, and all hills; fruitful trees, and all cedars"), so it should be an easy verse to translate. The author of the translation in Zenger's newspaper avoids verse 9; Adams devotes thirteen lines to it. In fact, his treatment contains more than half as many words (101) as appear in the entire poem of 1739 (177).

Adams ignores mountains, hills, and cedars, focusing instead on what he calls "Trees & Groves." He handles trees generically before using the word "Fruitage" (l. 42) to connect his description with the Bible verse. He then shifts focus from trees to flowers. In eight lines unconnected in any obvious way to a word in verse 9 of the King James Version, he portrays the beauty of daffodils, violets, tulips, lilies, and roses, requesting that they acknowledge God as their creator. Adams adds numerous details to his treatment of this verse in order to amplify the point of the psalm. In being both selective (avoiding mountains, hills, and cedars) and inventive (introducing flora), he succeeds in making visual the main point of this verse.

Adams's most ambitious translations are of the entire books of Canticles and Revelation. Of the former, unfortunately, only a section of the fifth chapter is accessible because it is the sole part of Adams's version of Canticles to have been published. At one time, Matthew Adams possessed the complete manuscript of his nephew's poetic rendering of this book of the Bible. Although he discovered it missing as early as 1738, he apparently never retrieved it, despite offering a reward for its return, presumably so he could publish it.[76] But the translation of Revelation was published. In keeping with its position as the last book in the Bible, Matthew Adams made it the final poem in *Poems on Several Occasions*. At seventy-three pages, it is probably one of the longest of all poetic translations of a book of the Holy Writ. In this poem, Adams employs some of the same Blackmorean methods he uses in "On Society," most importantly antithetical rhymed couplets and many adjectives. Additionally, as David S. Shields observes, Adams enlivens this book through other techniques, such as creating analogies to augment metaphors and similes.[77] For example, he translates "His eyes were as a flame of fire" (19.12) as

> But the keen Glories of his flaming Eyes
> Not Light'nings rival, glancing thro' the Skies;
> Nor Stars which twinkle in the Saphire Plain,
> Nor Virgin-Light with all it's golden Train.
>
> (163.19–22)

He also makes events seem immediate by occasionally changing past-tense verbs to present, as in his treatment of the beginning of 6.12: "And I beheld when he had opened the sixth seal" in the King James Version becomes "A sixth, but dreadful, Vision now reveals" in Adams's poem (124.5).

Generally speaking, this translation of Revelation is more controlled than Adams's versions of other parts of the Bible, possibly because the poet did not want to make a long poem even longer. Yet he takes liberties with the text of this book as he does with the other Bible verses he translates. For example, the twenty-second (and last) chapter of Revelation contains twenty-one verses; Adams treats it in 118 lines. In the Authorized Version, the famous thirteenth verse of this chapter reads:

> I am Alpha and Omega, the beginning and the end, the first and the last.

Adams presents it in the following manner:

> Here Hell's tremendous Pit unwearied glows,
> There the bright Day of Heav'n, descending, flows:
> The *Alpha* and *Omega*, First and Last,
> Before My Word the springing Worlds were rais'd;
> And fading Nature withers at My Blast.
>
> (175.11–15)

Adams requires only one line (the third one quoted here) to convey the sense of verse 13. The other four lines go beyond the straightforward, brief, simple, and memorable statement of the King James Version of this verse; in so doing, they create a vivid image of hell and reveal the effect of Christ's word.

No matter how deftly Adams translated Revelation, his effort was not without risk, as is the case with anyone who translates the Bible. There is serious danger, which is extraliterary in nature. Two verses in this book presented Adams with a problem. According to Revelation 22.18–19, anyone tampering with the

Holy Writ risks incurring plagues and damnation. In the Authorized Version, the verses read as follows:

> 18   For I testify unto every man that heareth the words of the prophecy of this book, If any man shall add unto these things, God shall add unto him the plagues that are written in this book.
> 19   And if any man shall take away from the words of this prophecy, God shall take away his part out of the book of life, and out of the holy city, and from the things which are written in this book.

Adams modified slightly the meaning of these words that should have given him pause in his artistic and religious undertaking:

> YE, circling Tribes, My solemn Words attend,
> To whom the mystick Pages shall ascend.
> Who shall invent, and join ficticious Things
> To what from sacred Inspiration springs,
> The written Plagues, thro' all the Book display'd,
> Shall burst in Vengeance on his guilty Head.
> Or who shall blot, or alter what is writ,
> His Name, eras'd from Heav'n, shall perish quite:
> Nor flame the City's golden Streets for him,
> Nor the fair Visions of the Volume gleam.

(176.13–22)

The two verses in the Authorized Version characterize as damned anyone who will "add unto" the words of the Bible and who will "take away from the words of the book of this prophecy." Adams identifies such people as those "who shall invent, and join ficticious Things" to the Bible and who "blot, or alter what is writ." In translating these verses, he changes meaning, possibly in order to justify his own rendering of Revelation as being faithful to the words of St. John the Divine, the speaker of this book of the Bible. Adams easily could have rationalized the taking of poetic license with this book—or with any of the books of the Bible—by thinking that he had retained the main points and captured the spirit of the original while adding words to augment it, possibly making it more picturesque, musical, and understandable than it had been. From such a perspective, his version would be fundamentally faithful to the original and would not be fictitious, which is a key distinction, at least according to his treatment of verse 18. However, any translation necessarily alters the meaning of a text, the Bible included, at least to a degree. Even if a literal translation of the Hebrew and Greek original texts were possible, it would not be desirable because, as Eugene A. Nida states, the translator of the Bible "knows full well that reproducing the precise corresponding word may utterly distort the meaning. Accordingly, he has been obliged to adjust the verbal form of the translation to the requirements of the communicative process."[78] That is, translators strictly obeying the requirement of Revelation 22:18–19 not to add to or delete from the Bible would produce an unreadable text. In order to render God's word in a meaningful manner, translators—Adams included—must alter the words of the Bible, as he does. Adams, though, takes greater liberties with Revelation than necessary to convey John's words accurately, thus risking divine retribution.

In translating scripture into English verse, Adams is not an automaton. Instead of rendering the Holy Writ as literally as possible—word by word, phrase by phrase, or verse by verse—he is expansive, elaborating on words and adding details. While generally conveying the sense of selected Bible verses, he uses them as a springboard for his own end, poetic expression.

William Congreve, William Diaper, John Dryden, John Oldham, William Oldisworth, Alexander Pope, Matthew Prior, and Jonathan Swift are among the British writers who translated (imitated) Horace in the late seventeenth or early eighteenth century. Although John Adams also translated him, few eighteenth-century Americans did, possibly because they considered him "principally as a respository of numerous quotable commonplaces and practical maxims for living."[79] Within the context of transatlantic interest in Horace, though, Adams holds an important place because his version of book 2, ode 16, in *The New-England Courant* of 30 April 1726, is the first translation of Horace by an American to appear in a periodical, either in America or in England.[80]

Unlike many of the Hebrew and Greek texts of the Bible, odes are, by definition, verse. When translating Horace, then, John Adams had to address the issue of meter and rhyme. Some of the meters in the odes Adams translated are not easily reproduced in English, such as the Sapphic meter of book 1, ode 2, and book 2, ode 16; the Fourth Archilochean of book 1, ode 4; and the Al-

caic, Horace's favorite meter, of book 3, ode 1. The First Asclepiadean of book 1, ode 1, and the Third Asclepiadean of book 1, ode
24, can be handled more easily.[81] So how does Adams treat the
Latin meter? Perhaps because of its difficulty, he ignores it. With
the exception of the initial ode of the first book, which is in iambic
tetrameter, he translates Horace in heroic couplets, precisely as
he does most of his translations of the Bible, thereby solving the
problems of meter and rhyme. Horace's meter did not dictate
which of the odes he would translate. Adams might have decided
to render them into English verse because he had translated
them at Harvard, if not in grammar school. With the exception
of the sixteenth ode of book 2, they are among the most famous
Horatian odes.

Comparing Adams's treatment of the fourth ode of the first
book, which is addressed to Sestius, with two other eighteenth-
century translations of the same ode reveals Adams's method. In
five quatrains of Fourth Archilochean meter, the Latin text—the
source of all these versions—reads as follows:

> Solvitur acris hiems grata vice veris et Favoni
>   trahuntque siccas machinae carinas,
> ac neque iam stabulis gaudet pecus aut arator igni
>   nec prata canis albicant pruinis.
>
> iam Cytherea choros ducit Venus imminente luna,
>   iunctaeque Nymphis Gratiae decentes
> alterno terram quatiunt pede, dum gravis Cyclopum
>   Volcanus ardens visit officinas.
>
> nunc decet aut viridi nitidum caput impedire myrto
>   aut flore, terrae quem ferunt solutae.   10
> nunc et in umbrosis Fauno decet immolare lucis,
>   seu poscat agna sive malit haedo.
>
> pallida Mors aequo pulsat pede pauperum tabernas
>   regumque turris. o beate Sesti,
> vitae summa brevis spem nos vetat inchoare longam;
>   iam te premet nox fabulaeque Manes
>
> et domus exilis Plutonia; quo simul mearis,
>   nec regna vini sortiere talis
> nec tenerum Lycidan mirabere, quo calet iuventus
>   nunc omnis et mox virgines tepebunt.[82]   20

In 1850, William Sewell, inspired by the inability of his Oxford
students to render classical texts accurately, attempted to translate Horace literally, yet rhythmically. Here, I quote his version
of the fourth ode of book 1 in order to establish a basis for illustrating liberties Adams and other translators took with this
poem:

> MELTING is winter keen with grateful—change of spring, and
>   western wind,
>   And engines drag the dry keels from the shore;
> And Neither now doth flock in stalls—nor hind in hearth their
>   pleasure find;
>   Nor meads with hoary frosts stand silver'd o'er.
> Now Cythera's Venus leads her—choirs, with Luna o'er her head;
>   And hand in hand with Nymphs the Graces fair
> With foot alternate beat the ground, while—Vulcan, glowing hot, doth
>   bid
>   The Cyclops' pond'rous stithies blaze and glare.
> Now 'tis meet our glossy brow—either with green myrtle spray,
>   Or bloom to twine, which leas unfetter'd bear;   10
> Now, too, meet in groves embower'd—to Faun to offer, whether he
>   Ask with a lamb, or with a kid prefer.
> Ghastly Death, with foot impartial,—knocks at cabins of the poor,
>   And monarchs' towers. O Sextius, thou the blest,
> Life's brief span forbids our laying—plans for hopes of distant hour;
>   Thee soon shall Night and fabled shades arrest,
> And the phantom hall of Pluto;—whither, soon as thou hast gone,
>   Neither the wine-throne thou with dice wilt share;
> Nor young Lycides admire, with—whom at present all the town
>   Is charm'd, and soon will glow our maidens fair.[83]   20

Three eighteenth-century translations of this ode differ dramatically from Sewell's version and from one another. Here, the
first two are important for the light they shed on the last, the
translation by Adams.

Englishman Philip Francis presents the poem in the following
manner, modifying Horace most obviously by using iambic meter
and lengthening the poem by four lines:

> NOW Winter melts in vernal Gales,
> And grateful Zephyrs fill the spreading Sails;
> No more the Ploughman loves his Fire,
> No more the lowing Herds their Stalls require,

> While Earth her richest Verdure yields,
> Nor hoary Frosts now whiten o'er the Fields.
>   Now joyous through the verdant Meads,
> Beneath the rising Moon, fair Venus leads
>   Her various Dance, and with her Train
> Of Nymphs and Graces treads the flowery Plain,   10
>   While Vulcan's glowing Breath inspires
> The toilsome Forge, and blows up all its Fires.
>   Now crown'd with Myrtle, or the Flow'rs,
> Which the glad Earth from her free Bosom pours,
>   Whatever Victim Pan approves,
> Grateful shall bleed amid the sacred Groves.
>   With equal Pace, impartial Fate
> Knocks at the Palace, as the Cottage Gate,
>   Nor should our Sum of Life extend
> Our growing Hopes beyond their destin'd End.   20
>   When sunk to Pluto's shadowy Coasts,
> Oppress'd with Darkness, and the fabled Ghosts,
>   No more the Dice shall there assign
> To thee, the jovial Monarchy of Wine.[84]

Unlike Sewell, Francis is more concerned with creating a poem that stands on its own merit than with adhering as faithfully as possible to Horace's text. Although Francis translates this ode more poetically and readably than Sewell, he retains Horace's ideas while using only two verbs ("leads" and "knocks") and approximately half the nouns, or synonyms for them, of the Oxford tutor. Francis's 1742 translation is a paraphrase, according to Dryden's definition, because it takes some liberty with the original; it displays "a disciplined creativity."[85] This is not a literal translation—a metaphrase—as, basically, is Sewell's; nor is it a free translation—an imitation—as is at least the first of the two eighteenth-century versions that follow.

At mid century, Charles Woodmason, who had recently arrived in South Carolina from England, translated this ode in rhymed couplets and in an irregular meter that is primarily dactylic tetrameter.[86] "Hor. B. I. Ode iv. Imitated" was published in *The Gentleman's Magazine* (London) in May 1753:

> AT length our fine winter for spring has made way,
> And full loaded ships without fear put to sea:
> *Negroes* leave their smoak'd huts—cattle quit the rice field,
> Myrtles, lawrels, and bays, shady canopies yield

By moon-light, our ladies, bright, cheerful, and gay,
Walk the town round for air, and turn night into day.
Eastern gales cease to blight, or make our *bar* roar,
And *wild-ducks* retire to *Africa*'s shore.
   Now in groves and savanna's, 'midst beautiful flow'rs,
And blossoms expanding, enjoy the fleet hours: 10
Let's each hold a gen'rous *barbicu* feast,
And with toddy and punch drink rich wine of the best;
For death between mortals no diff'rence makes.
A king, or a beggar, he equally takes:
Hope of distant enjoyment, the present allays,
And sickness your vitals may suddenly seize;
Who can tell what delights will attend us below?
Or order'd how soon our last journey to go?
No *Chloe* or *Phillis*, who warm'd your fond breast,
Nor jovial companions whom once you carest,   20
Will heighten your laughter, distend your fat sides,
Or add to your pleasures where *Pluto* resides.
Then live while you may—make this minute your own,
For the flow'r of life will be quickly o'erblown.

                    (240–41)

Although Woodmason uses five of Sewell's nouns ("winter," "spring," "groves," "death," and "Pluto") while conveying the seasonal change and carpe diem theme of the ode, his is a creative endeavor. Woodmason takes great freedom with Horace's poem, primarily by making it topical. He mentions "Negroes," for example, thus implying the issue of slavery. He alludes to stylish women walking in Charleston and includes geographical features (savannas) of South Carolina that were presumably still new to him. He proposes enjoying life by having drinks and barbecued meat with friends. Such local color makes Woodmason's imitation appealing. How faithful it is to Horace is another question.

In heroic couplets, Adams's poem is metrically different from Francis's and Woodmason's treatments of Horace's ode. It is also the longest of these translations by far:

THE *Winter*, which bound up our frozen Plains,
Is disentangled from its melted Chains;
While in its Stead the graceful Spring returns,
And *Zephyrs* in enchanting Murmurs mourns.
No more our Ships, dry on the burden'd Land,

By Engines forc'd the Ocean to descend;
Nor now the solitary Cotts invite
The Cattle sighing for the cheerful Light:
Nor Peasants seek the feeble Force of Fire
Their Limbs to warm, but *Phœbus'* Aid require.
And now the Fields, in native Beauty drest,
Are by the Arms of Frost no more carest.
The Cytherian *Goddess* graceful moves,
Incircl'd with a Crowd of blooming Loves;
Whose nimble Steps fly o'er the verdant Meads,
While the gay Morn her Silver Lustre sheds.
The Graces, who with heavenly Features glow,
And comely Nymphs, whose Eyes Destruction throw
O'er the soft Grass lead up a bright and solemn Show.
Now, Vulcan with his brawny *Cyclops* sweats,
And on his Anvil glowing Irons beats;
While trembling *Etna* echo's with a Groan,
And *Jove*'s-Bolts Thunder, e'er from Heav'n they're thrown.
Let everlasting Laurels clasping spread,
And weave their verdant Honours round our Head;
Or blushing Flowers, with mingled Beauty shine,
And o'er our Front in amorous Kisses twine:
Protected by the Grove's delightful Shade;
To Pan the humble Sacrifice be made:
Whether a tender Lamb the *God* requires,
Or brouzing Goat shall smoak upon his Fires.
With equal Pace pale Death, in dreadful Steps,
Strikes at the Cott, or in the Palace leaps;
Our Lives, condemn'd in narrow Bounds to rove,
Forbid us long to hope for what we love:
Even now eternal Night projects its Gloom,
And fabled Ghosts haunt thy retiring Room.
Now in dire *Pluto*'s dusky Realms you stray,
And vainly wish the dawning Gleams of Day;
There, Friend, the circling Youth will never crown
Thy sumptuous Feast, and quaff the Nectar down:
Nor more shall beauteous Maids thy Love inspire,
And fill thy glowing Soul with am'rous Fire.

(62.1–64.6)

Like Francis, Adams uses only a modest number of Sewell's verbs ("lead" and "beat") and about half of Sewell's nouns, or synonyms for them, all of them faithful to Horace's Latin. For example, in his twelve-line treatment of the first stanza, Adams employs "winter," "spring," "zephyrs" (for "wind"), "ships" (for "keels"), "engines," "land" (for "shore"), "cotts" (for "stalls"), "cattle" (for "flock"), "fire" (for "blaze"), and "fields" (for "leas"). By translating many of Horace's words accurately, as does Sewell, Adams indicates that he is fundamentally faithful to the original, despite taking liberties with the Latin text.

Of these translations, Francis's is the most literal; Woodmason follows the example of seventeenth-century English poet John Oldham in making Horace "speak, as if he were living and writing now," as may be seen in such lines as

> Let's each hold a gen'rous *barbicu* feast,
> And with toddy and punch drink rich wine of the best.[87]
>
> (ll. 11–12)

Adams takes more liberties with the text than Francis, but fewer than Woodmason. Like a jazz musician improvising on a melody, Adams retains the basic features of the original and embellishes them, using two lines, on average, for every one of Horace's. He does not stray far from the Latin text; in fact, both he and Francis translate Horace's "aequo . . . pede" as "with equal pace."

The differences between Woodmason's and Adams's translations of this ode are obvious: Adams does not imbue his version with local color. Other than length, the dissimilarities between Francis's version and Adams's are less obvious. Their treatments of Horace's first line typify their approach to the text generally. The literal Sewell renders it "MELTING is winter keen with grateful—change of spring, and western wind" (l. 1); Francis,

> NOW Winter melts in vernal Gales,
> And grateful Zephyrs . . . ;
>
> (1–2)

Adams,

> THE *Winter*, which bound up our frozen Plains,
> Is disentangled from its melted Chains;
> While in its Stead the graceful Spring returns,
> And *Zephyrs* in enchanting Murmurs mourns.
>
> (62.1–4)

Although both Francis and Adams convey the sense of Sewell's (and Horace's) line, Francis introduces no new idea and uses fewer words than Sewell. Adams includes original material and employs more than twice as many words as Sewell. Adams presents winter as active by depicting it as having frozen the land, while at the same time characterizing it as passive, as something enchained. He also makes the line personal by using "our" for the first of several times in the translation. He characterizes spring as "graceful" and refers to the "enchanting Murmurs" of the winds. Because of these liberties—and similar ones throughout the poem—Adams's lines are more sensual and memorable than those of either Sewell or Francis. Although he captures the spirit of Horace's ode, Adams is less literal than either Sewell or Francis in rendering it into English verse. This treatment of the beginning of Horace's poem illustrates that Adams, a poet, was interested in expressing himself, as well as in presenting Horace's ideas in a readable, poetic manner. This was the goal in all his translations of the Latin poet.

Assessment

The poems of John Adams possess obvious strengths and weaknesses, although, as we have seen, determining how accurately the texts of the verses in *Poems on Several Occasions* reflect his wishes is impossible to determine. Some of the shortcomings stem from employing old modes of expression; several of the positive qualities derive from Adams's embracing of newer poetic values and techniques. This is not to say, though, that one cannot compose poems successfully in old modes or that writing in more current styles necessarily leads to effective expression.

The translations of Horace occasionally repeat key words when synonyms would enliven the texts, as in the fourth ode of the first book with "Cotts"/"Cott" (62.7; 63.23), "verdant" (63.5, 15), and "amorous"/"am'rous" (63.17; 64.6). These poems also contain old-fashioned, inflated diction. This same ode includes the even-then tired "poetic" word "Meads" (63.5) as a synonym for "meadows." For "sea," the first ode from the initial book uses "Deep" (60.24) and "Main" (61.2). It contains the word "coursers" (60.7), which also appears, as a singular, in the first ode of the third book (71.17). The translation of the sixteenth ode of the second book employs "Pinions" (68.19), "Steeds" (69.8), and "Glades" (69.15). "Purple" (for "blood") occurs in several odes, including the second ode of the first book (66.18). Furthermore, in the translations of Horace and elsewhere Adams employs periphrasis, a technique of using several words instead of a common word. In his translation of the second ode of Horace's first book, for example, he uses "scaly Brood" for "fish" (66.1). In the translation of Psalm 148 he uses "fleecy Folds" (4.3) for "clouds"; in "Dedicated to the Honour of Christ," "briny Torrents" (14.6) for "tears"; and in the elegy on Cotton Mather, "flaming Bolts" (84.15) for "lightning." These tendencies—and especially the inclination to use inflated diction and periphrasis—weaken the poems artistically. In the verse of poets like Milton, Dryden, or Pope, such techniques are generally effective. In Adams's poems, they appear as dated mannerisms.

We do not know if Adams was aware of the debate in British literary circles over the use of the Alexandrine in poems written in heroic couplets, often as the third line of a triplet. He uses the Alexandrine with some frequency, as in his rendition of the second chapter of Lamentations (54.16), in his version of the fourth ode of Horace's first book (63.9), and in "On the Death of . . . Cotton Mather" (85.10). He employs it most deftly in "David's Elegy Paraphras'd" (76.24). Here, the lengthened line reflects the stretched-out body of his dead friend Josiah Winslow: "He, falling on the Ground, projects his dreadful Length." Adams might have been inspired to use the Alexandrine by Dryden, who favored it. In "To the Memory of Mr. Oldham" (1684), for example, the English poet includes an Alexandrine as the last line in this triplet:

> Thy generous fruits, though gather'd ere their prime
> Still shew'd a quickness; and maturing time
> But mellows what we write to the dull sweets of Rime.[88]

The Alexandrine fell from favor after Swift burlesqued it at the conclusion of "A Description of a City Shower" (1710), where he uses one in the third line of the following triplet:

> Sweepings from Butchers Stalls, Dung, Guts, and Blood,
> Drown'd Puppies, stinking Sprats, all drench'd in Mud,
> Dead Cats and Turnip-Tops, come tumbling down the Flood.[89]

In *An Essay on Criticism*, published the next year, Pope derides it memorably in a couplet, where the second line is an Alexandrine:

> A *Needless Alexandrine* ends the Song
> That like a wounded Snake, drags its slow length along.[90]

Adams uses the Alexandrine in the straightforward manner of Dryden, not ironically, as do his contemporaries Swift and Pope. Adams honors the old way.

In the translation of Revelation and elsewhere, many of Adams's rhymes seem forced, as in the last three lines of his treatment of Revelation 22:13:

> The *Alpha* and Omega, First and Last,
> Before My Word the springing Worlds were rais'd;
> And fading Nature withers at My Blast.

The second of these lines presents a problem: the word "rais'd" does not seem naturally to rhyme with "Last" and "Blast." He could have replaced "rais'd" with a synonym, but which? Neither "Elevated" (which would make the line an Alexandrine), "levitated" (which would also create an Alexandrine), "heaved," "hoisted," nor "lifted" would solve the problem. He uses "rais'd" apparently because of these words it is the one closest in sound to "last" and "blast" and because it is a word of one syllable, which permits a line of iambic pentameter. Yet being the least objectionable of these words does not make it palatable. Unless people of Adams's time pronounced the vowel sound in "rais'd" as they did in "last" and "blast," Adams might better have rewritten the line so as to create a more effective rhyme than this triplet contains. This is not an isolated problem. A similar situation occurs with a triplet in Revelation 3, where the words that should rhyme do not obviously do so:

> *Laodicea*, hear the Great AMEN,
> For ever true His Witness will remain;
> And rising at His Word the World began. . . .

(114.5–7)

In mentioning Adams's idiosyncratic rhymes in his translation of Revelation, I intend primarily to call attention to possible difficulties, although I am not the first person to do so. In a book published in 1821, Samuel Knapp mentions Adams's inadequate rhymes in Revelation.[91] However, because we cannot know precisely the pronunciation of Adams and his contemporaries, he should not be held strictly accountable for what might strike us as ineffective rhymes.

Adams's verse also possesses strengths. Although he is no Pope, Adams composes serviceable heroic couplets in poems that helped introduce neoclassical verse to America. He creates antitheses in his couplets and knows how to emphasize a key word by setting it off with commas, with the caesuras accentuating its value. Adams renders ancient texts creatively in accessible English verse. In doing so, he elaborates upon the originals with some engaging lines of his own and indicates his awareness of Dryden's theory of translation. His greatest artistic strength is as a creator of images. Not every one is effective, as his likening of Katherine to ivy in "A Consolatory Letter to a Near Relative" illustrates. But many are. I have identified as felicitous images the lion in "David's Elegy Paraphras'd," the earthquake in "On the Sudden Death of Messieurs George and Nathan Howell," the light and dark in "On the Death of . . . Cotton Mather," and the stream in "To My Honoured Father on the Loss of His Sight," "On Society," the translation of Psalm 104, and the elegies on Mather and Katherine. Adams is important for his accomplishment in the Blackmorean mode, especially in "On Society" where he creates vivid descriptive passages while showing the connection between earthly order and God's power. His comments about theory in "An Address to the Supreme Being" are noteworthy. He is most approachable through his personal poems, where he attempts to console the survivors of recently departed friends and probable acquaintances by reflecting on their lives. These and other aspects of Adams's verse reflect the nature of the decade of the 1720s, which was one of cultural change. While honoring the old, he embraced the new. He was in the poetic vanguard of his time and place.

Because Adams lived when, in the context of English poetry to his time, there was no great American verse (however defined), possibly little good American verse, and arguably only barely adequate American verse, to say that he was among the foremost American poets of his day might mean little. But to dismiss him and others, such as Mather Byles, because their work is not readily available and is therefore generally unknown, because literary historians and critics ignore or in several instances disdain their productions, because they wrote according to the taste of their day, or because most of their work is often ordinary or flawed is to consign to oblivion usually modest yet historically significant and sometimes accomplished literary achievements.

3

Essays

THE PRESENCE OF NEWSPAPERS IN BOSTON ALLOWED FOR THE PUBLI-cation of a type of literature popular in England but not previously produced by Americans: the cultivated secular essay. Had writers wished to compose such an essay before the advent of newspapers, where would they have published it? Probably not in books; conceivably, but not likely, as broadsides. Newspapers were the perfect medium for such literature because they include numerous short selections. Beginning in 1704, the first Boston paper to have more than one number, *The Boston News-Letter*, published news from abroad (greatly delayed), from other American colonies, and from Boston. Shipping information was important, as was social news. This was a news paper, a publication informing readers about events of general interest. It did not publish what might be called literature, although in the 1720s it began including religious essays in its pages.[1] The next newspaper began publication in 1719. *The Boston Gazette* featured many of the same kinds of information as *The Boston News-Letter*, although it included a "Prices Current" section that proved valuable to merchants, farmers, and other people involved in trade.[2] The third paper, James Franklin's *The New-England Courant* (first published in 1721), was far livelier than the other two periodicals, but it made enemies by attacking religious and political figures. Its contributors, the Couranteers, occasionally reflected the influence of Addison, Steele, and the London urbane essay generally, with young Benjamin Franklin being the most adept of these writers. Not until the appearance of the next newspaper, *The New-England Weekly Journal*, did a Boston periodical feature literature prominently. Beginning in its inaugural year of 1727 and continuing for fifty-two weekly issues, on the first page it published Addisonian essays by American authors. Not until the decade of the 1720s, then, did some Americans fully assimilate the nature of such essays, write their own versions of them, and have them published on a regular basis. Essays published in *The New-England Courant* and especially *The New-England Weekly Journal* indicate, therefore, that a major shift occurred in American newspapers during this time: the publishers provided and readers welcomed literature, which was missing from *The Boston News-Letter* and *The Boston Gazette*. And this was not just any literature. It was the best that American writers could produce in the style mastered by Addison and other sophisticated English authors.

The age had become polite. In the context of Adams's era, Charles E. Clark defines "polite" as well as anyone. He explains that the term means less good manners than it does the polished arts, especially literature. He writes convincingly that politeness "was an ideal explicitly at odds with the 'plain style' of writing, preaching, and illustrating professed and practiced by several generations of New England Puritans."[3] Who better to illustrate the passing of the plain style than Cotton Mather, the arch-Puritan of the day. Much of his prose draws attention to itself. It is often ornate, some of it studded with Latin and Greek passages, as in *Magnalia Christi Americana* (1702). No one could mistake his style for that, say, of William Bradford, who wrote masterfully in the plain style in the seventeenth century. Yet "politeness" also includes the concept of gentlemanliness. *The Oxford English Dictionary* defines a gentleman as someone "in whom gentle birth is accompanied by appropriate qualities and behaviour; hence, in general, a man of chivalrous instincts and fine feelings." Cotton Mather's concluding comments about style in *Manuductio ad Ministerium* (1726) indicate how significant gentlemanliness had become in the 1720s. He writes, "Since every Man will have his own Style, I would pray, that we may learn to treat one another with mutual *Civilities*, and *Condescensions*, and handsomely *indulge* one another in this, as gentlemen do in other Matters."[4] The great cleric desires civility; he wants people to act as gentlemen, to demonstrate "chivalrous instincts and fine feelings." He does not ask them to demonstrate Christian love, as he possibly would have done a decade earlier. Here, he is concerned with easing social interaction, an interest that would have been alien to his grandfathers Richard Mather and John Cotton, if not to his father Increase Mather. Cotton Mather, though, was not the only American author of the time to write in a non-plain style and encourage gentlemanly social intercourse. So too did Mather Byles, Matthew Adams, and John Adams, though their prose is much less ornate than Mather's.

As John Adams helped introduce modern English poetic ideas to America in the 1720s, so did he assist in exposing his countrymen to the sophisticated Addisonian essay during the same decade. Four months before moving from Boston to Newport in August 1727, he began collaborating with Matthew Adams and Mather Byles on Proteus Echo. Following Benjamin Franklin's Dogood papers that appeared in *The New-England Courant* in 1722, Proteus Echo is the second essay series published in American periodicals. Belletristic in nature, these essays, which occasionally include poems, were published in fifty-two consecutive issues of *The New-England Weekly Journal*, from 10 April 1727 to 1 April 1728.

While Franklin's Dogood papers are well known, if only by reputation, to anyone familiar with the history of American literature, few readers, including scholars, are aware of Proteus Echo. It is not mentioned in the most comprehensive recent survey of Adams's life and career, that by John C. Shields. When Bruce Granger published an edition of Proteus Echo in 1986, it was greeted by silence. I have located no review of his book, not even in *Early American Literature*, the journal that would most obviously be interested in it. *American Literary Scholarship*, the annual that evaluates everything of even passing interest in the realm of American literary studies, ignores it. Joseph T. Buckingham analyzes the series in his discussion of *The New-England Weekly Journal* in *Specimens of Newspaper Literature* (1852), pointing out similarities between the American essays and those in *The Spectator* and *The Tatler*. Buckingham prints excerpts from several of the Proteus Echo essays. Before Granger's edition, the sole twentieth-century critics seriously to examine the series as literature are Elizabeth Christine Cook in 1912 and Granger himself in 1978. After the publication of Granger's *Proteus Echo*, one critic, Charles E. Clark, in 1994, investigates it. Cook and Clark consider the essays while examining *The New-England Weekly Journal* in studies of early American newspapers; Granger evaluates them in a discussion of early American essay serials.[5]

In 1727, the printer Samuel Kneeland established *The New-England Weekly Journal*, which Cook characterizes as the second

American newspaper to have "literary pretensions."[6] James Franklin's *The New-England Courant*, for which Kneeland worked and Matthew Adams and John Adams wrote, is the first. Although she identifies Byles, Judge Samuel Danforth, and Thomas Prince as the editors of Kneeland's publication (with the information gleaned from Isaiah Thomas's *The History of Printing in America* and affirmed by Charles E. Clark) and makes a number of observations about the series, her primary goal in analyzing Proteus Echo is to show its indebtedness to English periodicals, *The Spectator* and *The Tatler* in particular, as Buckingham did in the previous century.[7] She observes, for example, that both Proteus Echo and the Spectator have societies with comparable kinds of members and that the clubs are detailed in the second number of each series. She also identifies similar subject matter and language.

Charles E. Clark builds on the work of Cook. Like her, he places the series in the context of British periodicals, although he records more similarities and differences than she. He also compares Proteus Echo, generally unfavorably, with Franklin's Dogood papers. Most importantly, by focusing on John Adams's prose in the thirty-first contribution to the series (6 November 1727), Clark identifies the structure of some of the Proteus Echo "lucubrations" as that of the Puritan sermon. In this essay about fear resulting from an earthquake, Adams begins by introducing his topic in human terms before becoming general. He claims a universality of fear, states that one cannot escape its cause, and concludes by suggesting that people can overcome it through faith.[8] Given the theological training and interest of John Adams, his use of such a structure should not be surprising.

Although Granger offers only a brief introduction to his edition of Proteus Echo, in *American Essay Serials from Franklin to Irving* he examines more fully the contributions of Byles and the two Adamses to *The New-England Weekly Journal*. He makes various points by quoting, occasionally extensively, from individual essays. After identifying the members of the Proteus Echo club, he mentions the disappointments of Proteus Echo (the character), comments on the nature of some of the essays, deems them didactic rather than humorous, and focuses on ones dealing with writing. Granger values this series, but he concludes, reasonably, by finding it less vital and energetic than—

and lacking the American idiom and context of—the Silence Dogood papers of the young Benjamin Franklin.[9]

The first published allusion to Proteus Echo appears on page 1 of the initial number of *The New-England Weekly Journal* (20 March 1726/27). The last of four paragraphs introducing the newspaper to what Kneeland surely hoped would be a large audience reads as follows:

> This may serve as a Notification, that a Select number of Gentlemen, who have had the happiness of a liberal Education, and some of them considerably improv'd by their Travels into distant Countries; are now concerting some regular Schemes for the Entertainment of the ingenious Reader, and the Encouragement of Wit & Politeness; and may in a very short time, open upon the Publick in a variety of pleasing and profitable Speculations.

Who wrote this prose? The author implies that he is not one of the "Gentlemen" who will submit essays to the paper. If this is so, then he could be Judge Danforth or Thomas Prince—or conceivably Samuel Kneeland. Given the whimsical nature of some of the Proteus Echo essays, the author could actually be one of the "Gentlemen," writing ironically. Of them, Mather Byles— who would become celebrated as a wit—is the one most likely to have composed this paragraph that deceives by characterizing the contributors as being widely traveled. He was, as Charles E. Clark observes, "probably the prime instigator" of Kneeland's newspaper, although we cannot know this for certain.[10]

The question of authorship is not only of historical interest; it was also an issue in 1727. In the first Proteus Echo essay (10 April 1727), Byles, writing as E., notes that numerous people have attempted to identify the author of the advertisement for the series. While it might actually have generated curiosity among readers, saying that it did creates intrigue and constitutes good marketing. If some readers had not pondered the identity of its author, they might now wonder about him and therefore would read the "Speculations" with the hope of learning his name. In the opening essay, though, E. mentions "the Advertisement which I lately published" (1), thus implying Byles's possible authorship of the announcement.[11] "I" could refer, however, not to Byles but to Proteus Echo, the ostensible author of all the essays, and therefore to any one of the three contributors, or to a combination of them. Perhaps in an effort to conceal himself—while at the same time offering his qualifications for commenting on various issues—E. repeats a point in the advertisement by stating, preposterously, that as a young man he traveled to China, Japan, and Bantam (Java), thus qualifying him as someone "improv'd by . . . Travels into distant Countries" (1).

On 27 March 1727, one week after the advertisement, a statement of unknown authorship appeared in the same newspaper: *"By reason of the absence of one of the principal members of our Society, the Speculative entertainments which were propos'd the last week to the Publick, cannot conveniently be exhibited, 'till the second Monday in April"* (2). Although the announcement implies that the main members of the Proteus Echo society must be present before the series can begin and, once begun, progress, such was not the case. Because John Adams resided in Newport during most of the time the series was published, he, Byles, and Matthew Adams undoubtedly did not meet each week or even frequently to discuss Proteus Echo. The statement of 27 March might have been necessitated by the inability of Byles, the author of the first essay, to meet the deadline because of illness, absence from Boston, unpreparedness, or some other reason. In any event, delaying publication of a series already announced again constitutes good marketing. If prospective readers had begun discussing the series following publication of the advertisement, then further delaying the start of the series could possibly generate even more interest. Once the series began on 10 April, it continued for a year on a weekly basis without interruption.

Although John Adams contributed more essays to the series than Matthew Adams or Byles—eighteen complete ones plus parts of at least two others—Byles might have conceived of the project. Not only did he probably help establish *The New-England Weekly Journal*, but he composed the first and last numbers, thereby introducing the character Proteus Echo and providing the valediction. His words frame the whole.

In the first number, Byles's E. presents Proteus Echo to the public. Despite having been born in Salem in 1666 and therefore having been a young adult at the time of the witchcraft hysteria and trials in his hometown, Proteus Echo is not the conjurer that people have accused him of being. As a child he was effective at mimicry, a skill that will serve him well as he writes as an imitator (when criticizing bombastic prose, for example, he will convey his thoughts in a bombastic style). When traveling following his degree from Harvard, presumably in 1684, he made weekly journal entries about his experiences. This habit inspired him to name his newspaper the *Weekly Journal*.[12] Although he was once poor in arithmetic, he ultimately mastered it enough to become "a wealthy old Curmudgeon" (2), a fact he mentions hoping to attract readers who will pay him deference and will know that he is not writing for financial gain. Because he cannot now recall his real name, correspondents may address him as Proteus Echo in letters sent to Kneeland.

The next week, E. does not fulfill his promise of describing the members of his society. In the second number (17 April 1727), Matthew Adams, writing as M., introduces them. They are the merchant Charles Gravely, the intellectually impaired Timothy Blunt, the apparently sociable and somewhat penurious Christopher Careless, the cynical prognosticator Will. Bitterly, and the literary Mr. Honeysuckle, whose name derives from that of the fop Will Honeycomb of the Spectator Club.[13] Matthew Adams, through M., created these characters, or at least M. is the first of the contributors' narrators to mention them. In the last paragraph, which stands out because all lines after the first are doubly indented, M. concludes by mentioning two clergymen who complete the membership of the society:

> I might add the Character of Two Divines, who sometimes does us the Honour to set with us half an Hour, and improve us with their Excellent Conversation: But these Gentlemen are above the reach of my Pen to do them Justice. Their Lives are regular and Exemplary; their Learning Solid and Profound, and in the Pulpit, they Command the Attention of their Audience with the Gracefulness of their Air, the Musick of their Voice, and the noble Majesty of their Eloquence. These Gentlemen will have no inconsiderable Hand in these Weekly Entertainments.

By admitting an inability to describe the divines adequately, M. avoids having to identify, other than in general terms of adulation, the men who will assist his creator, Matthew Adams, in composing the Proteus Echo series. We can see clearly now that M. refers to two recent Harvard graduates, one who would soon become a minister in Newport and the other who would receive a master's degree from Harvard in 1728 and become a clergyman in Boston in 1733, remaining in this position until his Tory sympathies led to his dismissal in 1776. These men are, respectively, John Adams and Mather Byles. Whether the readers of the column in 1727 could have recognized them from M.'s description cannot be known.[14]

The Proteus Echo series does not sustain the humorous tone of the first two numbers, although some of the other essays are amusing. The anonymous twenty-eighth selection about a laughing club (16 October 1727) is the most obviously witty one. Occasionally the contributions merely elucidate such an unpromising subject as virtue, and to John Adams fell, by choice or assignment, the responsibility of writing more often than the others about these topics. In various essays, he discusses idleness, envy, politeness, avarice, taciturnity, jealousy and suspicion, vapors, the relative merits of solitude and society, God's power, and the appropriateness of being both religious and gentlemanly. (*The Spectator* addresses some of these subjects.) This is not to say that his essays on these topics are without merit or interest or even lightheartedness, as we shall see. The ability to deal with them engagingly is one measure of his success as a prose writer.

For Proteus Echo, John Adams wrote most frequently and importantly about literary theory. He discusses this subject in almost half of his pieces, but especially in his first three essays—numbers 5 (8 May 1727), 7 (22 May 1727), and 10 (12 June 1727). Here, at the beginning of his professional prose-writing career—these essays antedate the publication of his ordination sermon—Adams recognizes a problem neither new to his age nor alien to our own: to what degree, if any, should authors compromise their artistic integrity to gain general acceptance? (He does not identify writers who have lowered themselves for this reason.) There is a tendency among the literati to view a serious author's popular success as a sign of selling out, of pandering to common taste. The assumption behind such thinking is that most readers are unsophisticated, unintelligent, and unperceptive, unwilling to read meaningful literature either because they cannot understand it or because of the effort this type of reading occasionally entails. If this is the case, must not serious authors violate the supposed purity of their calling in order to gain acceptance and thereby ultimately earn a living?[15] John Adams considers aspects of these issues in some of his Proteus Echo essays.

Although John Adams is, in his initial contribution to the series, concerned with theory and is critical of other writers (such as Edward "Ned" Ward), R., his narrator, argues against criticism on religious grounds. Before addressing his major points, R.—writing as adviser to leading authors—posits that because we are all God's children, censuring a fellow mortal is tantamount to chiding the Supreme Being. R. acknowledges that while sin has made minds faulty, authors should dismiss hostile criticism of their work.[16] Although he invokes the brotherhood of man, R. assumes a critical stance, part of which concerns his attitude toward audience. Specifically, he values only learned readers; common ones he holds in contempt. As a result, he provides instruction to serious writers who have not earned the approval of the "vulgar." These authors should first remain serene in the face of popular criticism or indifference; second, be content with merit as its own reward; third, be confident that the best judges, including God, "the great Original of Truth" (1), will approve of all superior work, including theirs; and fourth, attempt to please everyone, at least initially. If people fail to respond positively to serious writing, authors should not cater to them. That is, they should not compromise.

R. avers further that because the unenlightened masses "are more eager after what glitters, and dazzles upon their Imaginations, than what instructs their Reason" (1) and because their taste is confined by their senses, they are incapable of understanding truth that, according to R. without illustration, is generally conveyed abstractly. While most readers of this essay, perhaps in 1727 but definitely now, would, in all likelihood, disavow the harshness of R.'s sentiments and some of his words, most would probably also agree that R. deals with a serious and continuing artistic issue.

Adams offers a variation on the theme of the fifth Proteus Echo essay in his next contribution, number 7, in which T. addresses the universal urge to learn—universal, that is, to everyone except the "Monsters" who "are not the Standards but the Excrescencies of the Species" (1). Yet even these unfortunates seem to possess a latent desire for knowledge that will become ignited if they receive the proper fuel. Although T. fails to identify the fuel, he probably means brains, or possibly good instruction. He also establishes what amounts to a hierarchy of people who seek various kinds of knowledge. They range from the most exalted to the lowly, from people with lofty minds wanting to know about everything to crass businessmen caring only about their concerns and the news of the day. In between, T. values, in descending order of importance, people who study divinity, metaphysics, mathematics and philosophy, medicine, geography, history, and grammar. After them but before businessmen he ranks witty and polite people, human beings who observe rather than participate in life, and lighthearted folk. Ranking businessmen last might indicate T.'s and Adams's disappointment with the increasing commercialism of the 1720s.

As does R. in the fifth essay, in the seventh one T. addresses the topic of a writer's sense of audience and how far authors should go to satisfy readers. He disagrees with R., who recommends that they not lower themselves to the level of their potential audience. In his assertion that "I have taken upon my self to please all or most of" the people "who thirst after Knowledge" (1), T. implies his fidelity more to others than to himself. But he goes on to discuss his writing briefly in terms of reception. People less well endowed intellectually than he will almost certainly disapprove of his sublime productions, while his light ones will disappoint his most perceptive readers. In other words, T. knows, and laments, that whatever he composes will irritate some group whose approbation he desires. Furthermore, he notes, in a voice doubtless ironic, that in order to keep numerous critics from attacking him because of his fame, he will intentionally make his creations imperfect so commentators will criticize these insignificant errors exclusively. For such infelicities he hopes "at least to be pardoned, if I am not so happy as to gain the Applause of my sober and ingenious Countreymen" (1), thus preserving his larger reputation. In this selection, then, T. indicates an awareness of his readers and wishes for their acceptance of his work.

Of the entire Proteus Echo series, the best known essay is the third (24 April 1727). Here, Mather Byles, writing as L., discusses bombastic (pompous, illustrated by the prose of George Brimstone) and grubstreet (mindless, akin to the free-writing theory of the late 1970s) prose while detailing how to write incorrectly. This essay is important, especially for its time and place; yet its celebrity far surpasses that of the other numbers—indeed, it is probably the only one known—primarily because of its inclusion in Perry Miller and Thomas H. Johnson's *The Puritans*, an anthology used by many students of early American literature, history, and culture from its publication in 1938 until 1994, when it went out of print.[17] This essay is not markedly superior to the tenth one in the series, John Adams's contribution that is narrated by R.

Although R. does not address bombastic style, he focuses on grubstreet writing in Adams's most masterful prose composition. For R., grubstreet style is bad writing generally, and is not limited to inane creations, as is the case in Byles's essay.[18] R. illustrates his point by creating the character Dick Grubstreet to personify embarrassing prose and to embody the writing admired by common people. After denigrating Dick's ancestors and proclaiming Grubstreet stupid, tasteless, and rude, R. notes that the vulgar admire Dick and explains why. The prolific Grubstreet is popular both in England and America. Abroad, he has supplied similes to Ned Ward, author of *The London Spy*, and has ingratiated himself with famous but unnamed English poets to the degree that he contributes to their creations.[19] He is responsible for the less exalted parts of the great poets' productions, as well as for much of the writing to appear under the names of more modest literary figures, such as Ward. To Grubstreet also belongs the credit—or blame—for the farcical parts of tragedies, for the abundance of dedicatory epistles, for flattering panegyrics, for ribaldry, for much of the periodical literature and juvenile poems that serve as soporifics, and, ultimately, for anything less than elegant in British literature. The weaknesses in contemporary letters may be traced to him.

In America, Dick Grubstreet functions less as author than as oratorical attorney, although the results of his endeavors are similar to those of his writing in England. Given to harangues, he attempts to sway juries with the volume of his presentations rather than by the reasonableness of his arguments. When called upon to address important issues, though, he is invariably silent. Yet even in America he remains a writer, in particular a composer of widely circulated poems and elegies. Despite initial popularity, Dick's productions have been used to light pipes in taverns and line the bottom of pie pans; some people have set his verses ablaze and sent them heavenward; many of his productions gather dust on booksellers' shelves. Dick's creations might serve utilitarian purposes, but the thoughts they contain are ignored. The problem, aside from Grubstreet's lack of ability, is that the age has become polite and therefore does not value Dick's compositions. Because of this reality, Grubstreet wishes to regain popularity as an author by assisting Proteus Echo in writing essays for the series. By believing that his infusions would permit the masses to appreciate Proteus Echo, he implies, possibly correctly, that the general readership ignores these essays that appear in *The New-England Weekly Journal.* Dick is apparently unaware of R.'s attitude toward readers who would likely appreciate Grubstreet's literary productions. Predictably and respectfully, R. declines Dick's offer. This is the end of Dick Grubstreet, except for his letter to Proteus Echo, which concludes this essay. Its last sentence characterizes the nature of Dick's prose style: "For my part, I'm as stout as you are proud, I scorn to ax any thing of you agin, I don't care a Fig for you, and you may go whisle for all me" (1). By printing this letter, R. lets Dick Grubstreet damn himself.

Such a piece as Benjamin Franklin's seventh Dogood paper on kitelic verse possibly laid the groundwork for Adams's witty yet serious literary criticism in the tenth number of Proteus Echo. The humor comes primarily from having Dick Grubstreet evidence numerous writing deficiencies and from having him confront Proteus Echo, through R., thus permitting the two attitudes toward writing to speak for themselves. Although Dick's letter constitutes an early example of the vernacular in American literature, it stands—especially in its diction—as R.'s indictment of the vulgar. R. claims that good writing matters, and that he himself writes well. For these and other reasons, Miller and Johnson might have as easily selected Adams's essay as Byles's for inclusion in their anthology.

In addition to rejecting common readers and poor writers, John Adams's narrators theorize about other aspects of literature, often in passing, but without employing humor, which Adams uses in the tenth essay, or displaying arrogance, as in the fifth. For example, X. devotes a substantial part of the twenty-ninth selection (23 October 1727) to the issue of style, specifically as it relates to politeness. After discussing the ancients and the moderns and lamenting that an adequate level of refinement will not be attained until the great classical authors are properly known (Harvard graduates in particular are unfamiliar with the proven masters of good writing, X. notes), he identifies the styles of writing he considers impolite. They are impolite because they fail "in the true Spirit of Composure" (1): luscious writing, which is too fanciful; blustering and bombastic, which aspires to the great rather than the natural; puerile, which is too witty; pedantic, which favors quotations rather than reasoning; stiff, which is too consciously learned; perplexed, which is too obscure; loose, which is redundant; and grubstreet.

X. does not stop with detailing impolite writing. He also explains what constitutes a polite author. Such a writer

> weighs his Subject wisely and exactly before he ventures to chuse or write upon it; then draws a clear and regular Scheme of it in his own Mind, which being the most natural is also the most easy: Endeavours to find out what Sentiments are the most proper for his Subject, and what Words will paint them in the most clear, strong and genuine Colours: Who uses a plain, sublime, nervous or soft Stile, according to the various Themes upon which he Treats, and so gracefully turns his Sentences, as to make them flow in the most musical Periods to the Ear; and understands when he has said enough. (1)

X. perceives polite writing as considered, natural, organic, and musical, qualities vague enough, as he describes them, to be embraced by authors of any time and place. In defining as well as Adams does such an elusive term as polite writing (he also addresses this same topic elsewhere, most fully in Proteus Echo number 21), he succeeds more than might reasonably be expected.

Also within the context of literary theory, in the seventh Proteus Echo essay Adams's narrator, T., praises poets. He believes that they are those imaginative authors

> whose Fancies teem with Images, into whose Breasts Nature has infused a Cælestial flush of Spirits, and who feel the inspiring Divinity inform their inmost Soul: They disdain to walk in the dull common pace of Prose; but bound and fly aloft upon the Pinions of Sublime Thoughts, and harmonious Numbers, till reaching their native Skies, they at the same time become the Admiration and Envy of all Mankind. (1)

T. values verse more than prose and views poets as potentially elevating forces for mankind generally. To his credit, Adams discusses these and other literary issues seriously. He also accepts his own counsel: in his poems he uses—or attempts to use—

devices that narrator T. values in theory. Aware of the importance of imagery, for example, Adams employs it effectively (a lion being killed by javelins in "David's Elegy Paraphras'd"), but not always (likening the loving Katherine to ivy and her husband to a tree in "A Consolatory Letter to a Near Relative").

These examples of literary theorizing in Proteus Echo indicate that Adams pondered issues relating to composition, both prose and poetry. His views compare favorably with Mather Byles's opinions on the same topic in the third essay. They also approximate the sophistication and importance of remarks about the theory of writing by Cotton Mather in *Manuductio ad Ministerium*, which was published the year before the Proteus Echo series began and which Perry Miller and Thomas H. Johnson call "undoubtedly the best essay 'of poetry and style' written in the American colonies."[20]

One need consider nothing more than some of John Adams's Proteus Echo essays to illustrate how dramatically, by the "polite" decade of the 1720s, the focus of New England culture had changed from the late seventeenth century. In encouraging people to be sociable, the narrators of Adams—a Congregational divine—are far removed from earlier Puritan ministers who directed parishioners and readers to consider their lives mainly in relation to Judgment Day. When criticizing "*Gynecandrical Dancing*, or that which is commonly called *Mixt* or *Promiscuous Dancing, viz.* of Men and Women . . . together," for example, Increase Mather, writing in 1684, has Christ address parents who expose their children to such an activity: "What will you say in the day of the Lords pleading with you?" (By Adams's time, there were dancing schools in Boston.)[21] Of course Adams was not the first Boston Congregationalist to emphasize the importance of sociability. In a diary that covers the years 1674 to 1729, Samuel Sewall—who was not a clergyman—presents himself as a man savoring society, most famously, perhaps, when detailing his unsuccessful courtship of Katherine Winthrop in 1720.[22]

Adams is concerned with sociability because he is interested in community, in people getting along with each other and enhancing the quality of their lives. In Proteus Echo number 43 (29 January 1727/28), X. argues for graceful social intercourse as he discusses the topic of conversation. Because he assumes a general agreement that loquaciousness is among the worst of traits, he focuses on taciturnity as practiced by Will. Formly and

Ruth le Grand. Formly says little because he wishes to offend no one, thus becoming "The Laughing-Stock of the Ladies [and] the Tool of the Men of Wit," while gaining "the Admiration of Ideots" (1). Le Grand's monosyllabic expressions become offensive when accompanied by her haughtiness. But these two characters are extreme cases. In general, X. prefers reservedness to verbosity because one learns more by listening than by talking. Wise people listen; fools talk. Ultimately, X. wants conversation to progress smoothly, with everyone participating in it.

As X. wishes for no one to dominate conversation or for anyone to withdraw or be excluded from it, so does X. elsewhere argue for inclusion. In Proteus Echo number 40 (8 January 1727/28), for example, the narrator addresses the issue of jealousy. This feeling should be avoided because a jealous or suspicious person prefers solitude to society and therefore becomes an observer of life rather than a participant in it. The best way to cure jealousy is through "Benevolence to Mankind" and "Beneficence to [one's] Fellow-Creatures," which lead one back into society and its greatest pleasure, "undissembled Freedom" (1). Yet X. warns that participating in society exposes people to the risk of placing confidence in every person they meet, which is as foolish as trusting no one. X. encourages people to be honorable and prudent.

While encouraging social interaction, X. acknowledges, in Proteus Echo number 35 (4 December 1727), that society is necessarily imperfect, that aspects of it—such as pointless conversation—occasionally grate. As a result, all people need the relaxation that solitude affords. When alone, they learn to know themselves and can contemplate God's creation, which leads to ultimate happiness. Reading permits them to improve their conversational skills. X. warns, however, that while "he who lives too much Retired very often catches the Spleen and Ill Manners, he that Converses too much, is too vain and Empty." Furthermore, "solitude is most Improving, and Conversation most Diverting: One is to be Preferred, the other not to be Neglected" (1). That is, X. suggests that a life lived exclusively in society or in solitude is a life misspent, that people must both interact with others and spend time by themselves. As elsewhere, here Adams, through X., favors the middle course between extreme positions.

X. makes a significant statement about society and religion in Proteus Echo number 21 (28 August 1727). He rejects the notion that people cannot be both religious and gentlemanly. To X., the politeness of his time is an improvement over the roughness of an earlier period, aspects of which continue in the present through boring religious individuals, by which he presumably means ministers. X. believes "that whereas these deceived good Men think to advance Religion by their Dulness and Unsociableness, there are no Men in the World who cast such a Gloom upon it, and bring it under such Disgrace" (1). (One would like to know which clergymen X. considers dull.) X. finds these people so tedious that if forced to choose between them and society, he would select the latter. He refuses to sacrifice things he values—he mentions reason, a pleasant nature, love of society, and good behavior—for the messages of pompous divines. In fact, he would rather "dye like a well-bred and reasonable Atheist" (1) than live in a manner suggested by dull Christians. He concludes his essay by recommending not the life of the bleak, even frightening cleric, but rather that of the man of refinement: "All the World is charmed with a Gentleman who at the same Time that he is religious, is also complaisant and obliging, who wears Chearfulness in his Aspect, and whose Years seem to slide away in a perpetual Content; till at last looking with Pleasure upon so beautiful an Example, they are irresistibly drawn to imitate what they admire" (1). I am aware of nothing in American literature of this period—and especially nothing by a Congregational clergyman— that so strikingly condemns the old-style religion then still being practiced and at the same time so unreservedly praises a religiously-informed sociability as this essay by Adams. To guarantee that no one would misunderstand him, he introduces this twenty-first Proteus Echo selection with an epigraph from Pope's *An Essay on Criticism: "And to be dull, was constru'd to be good"* (1), by which Pope and Adams mean that dullness is neither good nor desirable.[23]

I have examined the major themes in Adams's Proteus Echo essays: literary theory, society, and religion. They are also addressed in *The Spectator* and other influential English periodicals of the early eighteenth century. Many, if not most, of the additional, less promising topics on which Adams writes are also derived from essays in these publications; among the subjects are idleness, politeness, avarice, and jealousy. Adams's treatment of envy illustrates his indebtedness to such a writer as Joseph Addison and demonstrates that Adams could think seriously about moral issues in a manner both secular and religious.

Addison personifies envy in *The Tatler* number 81 (15 October 1709). In the eighty-third number of *The Spectator* (5 June 1711), he depicts envy as a painter; he devotes the entirety of number 253 (20 December 1711) to discussing the aversion of superior people to envy and detraction; he praises some results of people's envy in number 355 (17 April 1712); and he derides envious critics in number 592 (10 September 1714). As Addison addresses envy more than once, so does Adams, twice, in Proteus Echo essays numbers 18 (7 August 1727) and 23 (11 September 1727).

We cannot know why Adams decided to devote two complete essays to envy or the specific audience, if any, he envisioned. Were he envious of other people, he could have written these pieces primarily for himself. If he sensed that others envied him or his friends and collaborators Matthew Adams and Mather Byles, he might have hoped to convince them of the folly of admiring these writers. Adams arrived in Newport two days before the first of the essays on envy was published. Could he have anticipated that Nathaniel Clap, the father of Newport Congregationalism, would envy the newcomer, who would gain the backing of the church establishment in the dispute over the desire of Clap's parishioners to receive Holy Communion? Could young Adams have envied Clap or been intimidated by him, even before meeting him? We do not, and presumably cannot, know. Perhaps he wished merely to address an unattractive, even dangerous human trait, which he terms a "Disposition" (1). Whatever the reason, in this essay he offers moral instruction to his readership, precisely as he would immediately begin doing with his Newport congregation through sermons.

To make his position clear, narrator T. opens the first of the essays about envy with a thesis: "no Person envies another, unless it be upon the Account of some supposed or real Excellency or Advantage, he possesses or enjoys above him" (1). He proves this assertion by citing examples from ancient history to his own time. Greeks banished Aristides partly because his rectitude embarrassed them; they also exiled Themistocles, who had helped save them from Persian attack. As Zoilus criticized Homer for creating fables, so did Bavius and Mævius subject Virgil to "vile Obloquies" (1), Brutus and Cassius betray Caesar, and the British humiliate Sir Francis Bacon. T. also supports his argument by offering illustrations from the early eighteenth century. He cites *The Tatler* and *The Spectator* as examples of superior publications that small-minded people and *The Examiner*, a Tory periodical, cannot abide.[24] T. also mentions ministers (self-servingly for Adams?) and doctors as favorite targets of the envious vulgar and observes that "the groveling Populace hate a *Saul* who tow'rs Head and Shouldiers above them" (1).

At the conclusion of Proteus Echo number 18, T. promises to return to the topic of envy in a later essay. In the next of Adams's contributions (number 21), however, narrator X. discusses not envy but the appropriateness of being both religious and gentlemanly. Adams addresses envy in his next submission, essay number 23. Because it was published five weeks after the eighteenth number, readers could have been excused for forgetting that T. had promised a sequel of sorts to his initial musings on this topic. Narrator T. connects the second of these essays on envy to the initial piece: "I Have already considered Envy, as to the Universality of its Influence." He then states his main point: "In this Paper I shall endeavour to shew the Passion [of envy] it self, and by discovering the bad Consequences of it, discourage every one of my Readers from harbouring such a Fury in his Breast" (1). Giving examples of envy, as T. does in the earlier essay, is easy; describing the passion of this feeling would seem difficult.

After defining passion as "a Disposition of the Mind" (1), T. divides the topic into parts and discusses, in turn, the qualities that constitute an envious mind. They are pride ("the excess of Self-love"), desire ("a sort of coveting to be our selves the Persons we Envy"), and malice ("hatred") (1). Of them, pride is the most significant, both because of the disproportionate amount of space T. gives to it and because it seems to cause desire and malice. Although T.'s description of envy is unexceptional, his cure for this passion is not. T. argues that if people would understand that God has given certain skills and competencies to each person, they would accept their seeming superiors and would not envy them, wish to possess their abilities, or despise them. That is, because talented people are not responsible for being more gifted than others, less adept individuals should not feel hostility toward them.

This religious appeal resonates throughout much of the remainder of the essay, and T. augments it with fitting imagery.

For example, he likens an envious person to "a Serpent . . . who shoots out his venemous sting most of all at that Creature who is the confessed Lord of the Creation," characterizes the envious breast as "a perfect Hell," and, in the last paragraph, uses such language as "internal fiend" and "Devils" before concluding that "Envy is a Serpent whose stings will never be taken out, but rankle in our Breasts throughout the Eternity of our Existence" (1). In other words, in an essay that is mainly psychological in nature, T. supports his observations and recommendations with references and allusions to God and Satan, heaven and hell. Attempting to alter the feelings of his readers, T. states, threateningly, that envious people will reside eternally with the devil.

Adams, through T., discusses envy in detail in these two essays, and he proves his contentions in graceful prose. Logical and insightful, he urges readers not to envy other people, although one wonders if intellectual resolve can affect feelings. His accomplishment with this topic is similar to that in his creations on virtue, politeness, fear and terror, avarice, and like topics that might, in the abstract, seem unpromising. The second of the essays on envy possibly derives, in the importance it places on pride, from *The Spectator* numbers 33 (7 April 1711), composed by Richard Steele, and 621 (17 November 1714), by Addison. If these two Proteus Echo essays are less sophisticated than the English writers' creations, they nevertheless present Adams's reasonable views in the manner here described. Adams does not merely ape his transatlantic models.

The nature of the majority of his essays indicates that Adams preferred composing relatively sober (but not boring) ones to lighthearted pieces. T. expresses this attitude explicitly at the beginning of Adams's reflections on idleness in Proteus Echo number 12 (26 June 1727):

> But since Virtue is of all other things the most important to our present and future Felicity, and on the contrary Vice the most detrimental; I chuse rather to be thought dully Sober, than foolishly Merry; and shall make it my perpetual endeavour to strike at those Irregularities which deform humane Life, and place them in the most odious View. (1)

This is not an idle comment; Adams, through his narrators, treats serious issues, precisely as T. indicates will be the case.

The word "perpetual," though, misleads because it implies that Adams will write only reflective essays. He did not and would not. We have observed humorous elements in the tenth Proteus Echo, and his most whimsical creation is the fifteenth in the series (17 July 1727), his next contribution after essay number 12.

Selections by Mather Byles and Matthew Adams published before the fifteenth essay contain letters from supposed readers requesting that their poems appear in Proteus Echo. Indeed, these epistles introduce Byles's poems "Eternity" in submission number 6 (15 May 1727) and "To My Friend" in number 9 (5 June 1727), and Matthew Adams's "The Sequel of Commencement" in number 13 (3 July 1727). John Adams concludes Proteus Echo number 10, in which he discusses grubstreet writing, with a letter from Dick Grubstreet.[25] The fifteenth essay, though, deals with fictional readers' missives in a manner different from those in numbers 6, 9, 10, and 13. In it, Adams's narrator, X., presents letters from five writers: Simon Hearty, Sam. Wildfire, Clarissa, Will Pedant, and Dick Snarle. X. frames this number of Proteus Echo with a one-sentence introduction to the correspondence and a two-sentence conclusion in response to Snarle. The format is similar to that of several numbers of *The Spectator*, including numbers 8 (9 March 1710/11), 205 (25 October 1711), and 245 (11 December 1711). Through these letters to Proteus Echo—all written by John Adams—Adams demonstrates his humor and playfulness, thereby illustrating his ability to write effectively without making solemn moral pronouncements.

An epigraph, characters' names, and resonance with *The Spectator* (which Will Pedant mentions in his letter) and possibly *The Tatler* indicate the amusing nature of Proteus Echo number 15. Adams introduces this submission with a quotation from Virgil. "*Continuo audite voces vagitus et ingens*" [Low voices crying loud were heard at once] suggests, in light of what follows, that the author, John Adams, considers the correspondents' complaints not altogether seriously.[26] He reinforces this impression by giving amusing names to the writers. At least two of them, Will Pedant and Sam. Wildfire, possibly derive from essays in British periodicals. *The Tatler* discusses pedants and pedantry in numbers 158 (13 April 1710) and 165 (29 April 1710), while *The Spectator* addresses these topics in number 105 (30 June 1711). The second of these publications introduces the widow Wildfire (her husband was John, not Sam.) in number 561 (30

June 1714). In the letter from Simon Hearty to Proteus Echo, the appearance of characters named Jack Airy, Tim. Flash, and Jo. Dapperwitt indicates something of the tone of this correspondence. The last of these characters was inspired by Tom Dapperwit in *The Spectator* number 530 (7 November 1712), whom Will Honeycomb recommends to succeed him as a member of the Spectator Club.[27]

Simon Hearty is perplexed. A serious, honest man, he cannot understand why witty people less virtuous than he ridicule him. One person implies Hearty's priggishness by calling him "Mr. *Honesty*." Proud of his association with good authors and his ability to appreciate their work, Simon inspires a wag to say that he, Hearty, *"is an honest Fellow, but no Judge of good Writing."* Someone else comments that he has "no Soul"; another, that he is "too honest to be Rich"; another, that he is, because of his dullness, poor company; and yet another, that "any one might make a Fool of" him. "Young Revellers" complain that Simon is worthless because he cannot drink a "Bottle with them every Night, and give Nature an Escapade by being heartily fudled." Aware that he is the object of ridicule—"I have the unhappiness to be thought dull, because I will not be profane"—Simon hopes that the publication of his letter to Proteus Echo "will put a stop to the unjust Calumnies which are thrown upon me" (1). Despite—or because of—Hearty's plea for understanding, however, this missive of arrogant self-justification would probably be counterproductive. Human nature being what it is, certain people would delight in subjecting Simon to greater ridicule than previously because they can see that their criticisms have been effective: they have hit home; they have irritated him. In this letter, the narrator creates a man, Simon Hearty, so stuffy that he would benefit from the humanizing effect of mockery. X. succeeds in conveying sympathy not for Hearty but for his critics.

Simon's letter illustrates Adams's skill in composing a humorous sketch; it also reflects an aspect of the temper of the age. In expressing befuddlement at being criticized as an inadequate judge of good writing, Hearty cannot fathom why someone would think that his obvious and professed honesty would disqualify him from "relishing any thing polite" (1), thereby acknowledging that the best literature of the day is polite, a judgment that Adams, through his narrator, expresses elsewhere, as we have seen.

Simon Hearty is the first of five correspondents to Proteus Echo in the fifteenth contribution to the series. Adams, through X., juxtaposes Hearty's letter and the next one so as to contrast their supposed authors through the similarity of their requests.

Sam. Wildfire, the second writer, is troubled. As lighthearted and affable as Hearty is serious, he, unlike Simon, acknowledges a problem with his personality. At least the first correspondent is true to himself, unattractive though his reality might be. Wildfire presents a false face to the world. Hardly the gregarious person he appears in a social context, Sam., when alone, is frightened. A headache terrifies him, he hides from thunder, the pleasant sounds of nature upset him, and he runs from his shadow. Although Wildfire does not address directly the cause of this disjunction between appearance and reality, he hints at it: drink. Sam. concedes that "when the dull World is drowned in Sleep I am so in Drink; by which I have painted my Countenance with a fresh and lively Red, and desire the deepest Purple to vie with that in my Cheeks." To protect himself from a recent outbreak of illness, he drinks "two Bottles a Day." He has frightening thoughts after his "fancy is a little heated by a Debauch" (1). Bachelor Wildfire must bolster himself in order to become the genial person he appears to be with people, as with the ladies at their toilet. He gains confidence by imbibing alcohol immoderately. Although doing so might help sustain him in certain contexts, it affects him adversely in solitude, making his private moments terrifying.

After characterizing himself as "*Your melancholy humble Servant,*" Sam. concludes his letter with a postscript. Announcing that he and the members of his unnamed club are dull (Wildfire's public persona notwithstanding), he tells Proteus Echo that "your Men of Vertue are the most happy" (1) of mortals. Not only does he laud Proteus Echo for being virtuous and therefore content, he also implies admiration for people like Simon Hearty, whom he does not mention. Despite the characteristics that open Hearty to mockery, he is, according to Sam.'s reasoning, happy because he is honest. In public, the ostensibly affable Wildfire would probably join others in ridiculing Simon, doubtless in order to be one with the crowd and to conceal his own deficiencies. The hostility of Sam. and his friends ultimately makes him and them less appealing—and less content and less moral—than the laughable Hearty, a judgment with which Sam. himself, in his honest moments, would probably concur. And since he belongs to a club of people similar to himself, they too are inferior to Hearty. Simon's forthrightness and contentment trump Wildfire's falsity and anguish.

Despite the different concerns Hearty and Sam. express in their letters (the first worries about how he—his genuine self—is perceived, while the second wrestles with his true nature), they write to Proteus Echo for the same reason: they need advice. Hearty begins his letter with the sentence, "AS you profess to vindicate the abused, I know of none I may better apply to, under the Wrongs which are offered me, than your Self." He wants Proteus Echo to help rectify an unfortunate and painful situation. Wildfire, in his plea to Proteus Echo, is more direct than Simon. He states explicitly, "I desire your Advice upon my present Circumstances" (1). These two fictional epistles are among the first letters, if not the first ones, to an American newspaper requesting assistance in solving a problem. As such, they are progenitors of a genre of literature that mutated over time into the advice-to-the-lovelorn column that reached its greatest popularity, probably, in the columns of Abigail Van Buren (Dear Abby) and Ann Landers, beginning in the middle of the twentieth century, and that inspired Nathanael West's novel *Miss Lonelyhearts* (1933).

The other three letters in the fifteenth number of Proteus Echo are less significant than the initial two. The first of them, signed "Clarissa," complains about the depiction of women in an earlier submission to the series.[28] Here Adams writes as a woman, as Benjamin Franklin does in the Dogood papers. In the next letter, Will Pedant criticizes Proteus Echo for being less qualified than he "to write Speculations" (1), or essays, and declares himself the enemy of Proteus Echo. In a humorous postscript, though, Will promises friendship if Proteus Echo will publish one of Pedant's own essays in Latin or Greek on a monthly basis. In the last letter, Dick Snarle chides Proteus Echo for erring in stating his, Proteus Echo's, age. The addressee responds amusingly by saying that he can compute only figures having to do with money.

Proteus Echo number 15—John Adams's fifth contribution to the series—delights. It demonstrates that Adams—who generally wrote about serious topics—possessed a sense of humor that is not substantially different from that which Byles demonstrates in some of his Proteus Echo essays. Had Adams not demonstrated this trait, one might wonder about how "normal" a person he was. During the life of Proteus Echo, he was young, having had his twenty-second birthday in March 1727 (the series began on the first day of the next month). Even in the early eighteenth century people of such an age—including those schooled to become ministers—could have been expected to cut capers, crack a joke, have funny thoughts, or pull a prank. From Adams, therefore, unalleviated seriousness would have been unnatural and possibly even suspect. Proteus Echo number 15 humanizes him.

Authorship

The name of John Adams does not appear in the Proteus Echo series. He signs his pieces with initials, as do the other contributors. We can discuss his compositions, confident that he wrote them, because of the research of C. Lennart Carlson in 1940. Over two centuries after the series concluded in 1728, he provided the key for determining which of the men—Byles or one of the Adamses—composed a particular essay.

Carlson notes that forty-seven of the selections are signed with initials. In the last essay in the series, narrator Z. records that one author identified himself as C., E., L., O., I., Z., and A.; another, R., T., and X.; and a third, M., U., S., and Æ. Although Z. states the obvious in noting that the person writing as R. wrote the paraphrase of Psalm 104 in the thirty-third number of Proteus Echo (20 November 1727) and that this person therefore also wrote as T. and X., the presence of this poem in John Adams's *Poems on Several Occasions* means that this Adams wrote the selections narrated by R., T., and X. Poems appearing in both the Proteus Echo series and Byles's collection *Poems on Several Occasions*, such as "The God of Tempest" (the thirty-first Proteus Echo [6 November 1727], signed Z.), indicate that Byles used the first set of initials. In a copy of Byles's and other authors' *A Collection of Poems* (which Carlson calls *Poems by Several Hands*) in the Massachusetts Historical Society, Carlson discovered notations, probably by Byles, that identify Matthew Adams as the author of "A Poetical Lamentation"; the same poem appears in the forty-fifth number of Proteus Echo (12 February 1727/28) above the initial M. Matthew Adams therefore wrote as M., U., S., and Æ. On the basis of this evidence, Bruce Granger, in *Proteus Echo*, attributes twenty of the contributions to John Adams (numbers 5, 7, 10, 12, 15, 16, 18, 21, 23, 25, 27, 29, 31, 33, 35, 38, 40, 43, 46, 49), fourteen to Byles (numbers 1, 3, 6, 9, 11, 14, 17, 20, 22, 24, 30, 34, 37, 52), and thirteen to Matthew Adams (numbers 2, 4, 8, 13, 19, 26, 32, 36, 39, 42, 45, 50, 51). Granger does not identify the authors of five selections (numbers 28, 41, 44, 47, 48).[29]

Specifying the authorship of two of the selections is not as easy as Granger makes it seem. He attributes the unsigned sixth (15 May 1727) and twenty-second (4 September 1727) pieces to Byles. Indeed, because they both include poems that appear later in Byles's *Poems on Several Occasions* and because the second of them bears Byles's name—not just an initial—in *The New-England Weekly Journal*, Byles wrote these verses. In the newspaper, however, both poems are preceded by prose by an unidentified author. We cannot assume that Byles wrote this material. Not only is it unsigned, but the thirty-first and thirty-third selections, which Granger designates as John Adams's creations, contain prose by an author using one set of initials and poetry by a writer employing another. For the first of these two submissions, John Adams (as R.) composed the prose; Byles (Z.) wrote the poem. In the second, Byles (O.) was responsible for the prose; Adams (R.), the poem. Therefore, because two of the men collaborated, in a manner of speaking, on two of the numbers, one of the Adamses might have written the prose that accompanies Byles's poems in the sixth and twenty-second numbers of Proteus Echo.

Granger fails to attribute authorship to the prose of the forty-first contribution (15 January 1727/28) because he overlooks two initials in it.[30] Most importantly, the letter Z. concludes the essay, although Granger does not record this letter in *Proteus Echo*. Furthermore, correspondence to Proteus Echo (addressed as "*Sublimist Metropolitan*" [2]), signed E., precedes the paragraph signed Z. Because Z. and E. are letters Byles used with his lucubrations, he wrote the prose. This number of Proteus Echo concludes with an unsigned poem beginning "ROUZE up my Soul, awake thy active Pow'rs" (2), which was reprinted a week later in the *Boston Gazette*.[31] Its author is unknown. The two instances of one person writing the prose for a specific number of

Proteus Echo and someone else composing the accompanying poem (numbers 31 and 33) indicate that the author of the prose in the forty-first number, Byles, did not necessarily write the poem.

External evidence indicates that Byles wrote the essay in Proteus Echo number 41. Four contributions to the series (3, 11, 41, and 48) were published in *The Boston Magazine* in 1783–84.[32] In 1931 Lyon Richardson observed that James Freeman, a member of the editorial board of this publication, had annotated his copy of it. In so doing, Freeman identified the authors of several of the selections.[33] Indeed, Freeman records that Byles wrote three of the Proteus Echo essays appearing in the magazine, including what had originally been Proteus Echo numbers 3 and 11. The last of the three is the first eleven paragraphs of Proteus Echo number 41, now titled "An Essay on Flattery" and signed Honestus.

Freeman also observes that "Rev. S. Parker" wrote "Useful Inventions for Barren Writers," signed John Crotchet, which appears in *The Boston Magazine* of February 1784. Initially, this was the unsigned and therefore unattributed Proteus Echo number 48, which includes a letter to Proteus Echo from John Crotchet. (Crotchet is derived from Ralph Crotchet, who wrote to Mr. Spectator in *The Spectator* number 251, dated 18 December 1711.) S. Parker is Samuel Parker, Episcopal clergyman and member of the editorial board of *The Boston Magazine*. Brother-in-law of Mather Byles Jr., Parker was so intimate with the senior Byles that he sat at the bedside of his dying friend.[34] Because Parker was born in 1744, though, he could not have written any number of the Proteus Echo series. So why does Freeman attribute to Parker the essay that had been Proteus Echo number 48? He probably does so because "Useful Inventions for Barren Writers" contains material not in the text of 4 March 1727/28 and that was doubtless written for publication in *The Boston Magazine*. The later version deletes the first two paragraphs from the essay as originally published, replacing them with a new paragraph. It also substitutes a new sentence for the final two sentences and omits the concluding poem. If Freeman records correctly that Parker wrote this piece, he means that Parker composed its first paragraph and last sentence.

What, then, should one make of the appearance of these four numbers of Proteus Echo in *The Boston Magazine* over half a century after their initial publication? As Richardson observes,

John Norman and Joseph White, publishers of *The Boston Magazine*, were primarily printers who entrusted editorial policy and therefore responsibility for the contents to some eminent Bostonians. Among these men were James Freeman and Samuel Parker.[35] It seems unlikely that any of the editors could recall the Proteus Echo series in a newspaper from so long ago. If this is the case, then they must have learned of it from Samuel Parker, who probably knew of it from his friend Mather Byles, who might have supplied copies of Proteus Echo essays to Parker or directed him to them. If Byles was the source, which is a reasonable inference, then the understandable vanity of an old man might have caused him to give Parker only essays that he himself had written. We know that the essays originally numbered 3 and 11 are his; Freeman provides evidence for confirming that Byles also wrote number 41. And if Byles gave Parker exclusively his own compositions, then Byles also wrote Proteus Echo number 48, which Freeman attributes to Parker. Therefore, of the five previously unattributed essays, number 41 may be assigned to Byles with confidence, while at least the prose of number 48 is probably his.

In *Proteus Echo*, Granger identifies as Q. the author of the forty-fourth essay (5 February 1727/28). Because Carlson's findings indicate that none of the men used the letter Q. to sign compositions, Granger does not attribute authorship to this essay. In fact, the letter is O., not Q.[36] Therefore, Byles—who wrote as C., E., L., O., I., Z., and A.—composed Proteus Echo number 44.

My research leads to the following conclusions about the authorship of the Proteus Echo series. John Adams wrote the entirety of eighteen of the numbers: 5, 7, 10, 12, 15, 16, 18, 21, 23, 25, 27, 29, 35, 38, 40, 43, 46, 49; Matthew Adams, thirteen: 2, 4, 8, 13, 19, 26, 32, 36, 39, 42, 45, 50, 51; and Mather Byles, thirteen: 1, 3, 9, 11, 14, 17, 20, 24, 30, 34, 37, 44, 52. John Adams wrote the prose to Proteus Echo 31, which includes a poem by Byles; for number 33, Byles provided the prose that introduces a poem by John Adams. Byles contributed verse to the unsigned numbers 6 and 22, but the author of the accompanying prose cannot be determined. Although the author of the poems in numbers 41 and 48 is unknown, Byles wrote the prose in the first of these and more than likely composed the prose in the second. The authorship of any aspect of Proteus Echo numbers 28 and 47 is still a mystery.

REPUBLICATION

Despite the slight attention given to Proteus Echo in recent times, in the eight decades after the conclusion of the series two periodicals other than *The Boston Magazine* (1783–84) reprinted some of the individual essays. The third number of the original series, by Byles, serves as the preface to the second volume of *The American Magazine and Historical Chronicle* (1745). Then, in 1807, at a time when essay series were a popular feature in American periodicals, Oliver C. Greenleaf discovered Proteus Echo and began reprinting it in *The Emerald*, a Boston literary weekly he owned and edited. Ultimately, he published twenty-two of its numbers.[37]

Greenleaf obviously thought highly of the series. In a prospectus, he mentions the various types of literature that will appear in his publication. Part of his statement reads as follows:

> There are in the possession of some persons of curiosity and research, some valuable *Essays*, written in former times in this country; from which we propose to select the best, and publish them occasionally for the pleasure of our readers. They will evince the state of learning in America a century ago, and perhaps induce some gentleman of enterprise to trace our progress in literature from that period until now.[38] (3)

These essays that Greenleaf so praises are from the Proteus Echo series, and, since his statement, Joseph T. Buckingham, Elizabeth Christine Cook, Bruce Granger, and Charles E. Clark are the sole scholars to have regarded them as seriously as he thought they should be considered.

In *The Emerald* of 19 December 1807, Greenleaf announces that he has found Proteus Echo in newspapers "among the lumber of an antiquary's library" (97), although he neither identifies the antiquary nor states that the essays appeared originally in *The New-England Weekly Journal*. He compares his discoveries favorably with contemporary literature:

> we have met with a series of essays, some of which would not have discredited the pen of Addison. If the appetites of general readers be not entirely vitiated by the literary whip-syllabub, which is served up in the trash publications of the present time, they must relish the solid fare on which our ancestors regaled. (97)

That readers in 1727 and 1728 delighted in Proteus Echo can be assumed only by observing that the series lasted for a year. Greenleaf believed in its quality because the essays are substantial, but he probably valued them primarily because he was frustrated by what he perceived as the lack of significant literature during his own time, the early years of the nineteenth century. Furthermore, surely he was pleased as a businessman to find something that no other publisher knew about and that he could depend upon to fill the pages of *The Emerald*. In order to protect what might be seen as his investment, he places the series in historical perspective and praises it, as any good entrepreneur would.

Yet Greenleaf was not finished commenting on Proteus Echo. In *The Emerald* of 7 May 1808 he again addresses it. To raise the issue of authorship he quotes from the prospectus ("valuable essays, that would evince the state of learning in America a century ago"), repeats that the series had been celebrated ("extremely popular"), compares it favorably to *The Spectator*, and expresses pleasure at being able to arrest its *"flight to the gulph of oblivion"* (337). He assumes, mistakenly, that one person wrote all numbers of Proteus Echo and infers, reasonably but incorrectly, that, because of the author's familiarity with the classics, he was an Englishman living in America. John Adams would have approved of Greenleaf's logic because, as X. states in the twenty-ninth essay of Proteus Echo, Harvard students of his time were ill informed about the great classical writers. Ultimately, Greenleaf published seven productions by John Adams (numbers 12, 18, 21, 23, 25, 29, and 46) and six each by Matthew Adams (numbers 2, 4, 8, 26, 32, and 39) and Mather Byles (numbers 1, 11, 17, 30, 34, and 37). One, original number 31, contains John Adams's prose and Byles's poem; another, original number 41, includes prose by Byles and a poem whose author cannot be determined; and another, original number 47, cannot be attributed to any of the three writers.

At least some of the Proteus Echo selections were republished in the eighteenth (*The American Magazine and Historical Chronicle* and *The Boston Magazine*), nineteenth (Greenleaf's *The Emerald* and Buckingham's *Specimens of Newspaper Literature*), and twentieth (Miller and Johnson's *The Puritans* and

Granger's *Proteus Echo*) centuries, which suggests something about the enduring, if limited, appeal of these essays. As the second essay series in American newspapers, Proteus Echo is historically important. It demonstrates the influence of such British periodicals as *The Spectator* and *The Tatler*. The fact that *The New-England Weekly Journal* published it for a year indicates that it appealed to readers and probably reflected their interests; by emphasizing secular concerns (society, politeness) as well as moral issues—or what Joseph T. Buckingham characterizes as "most of the human passions, virtues and vices"[39]—it reveals the changing values of the time. In the manner of the day in England, John Adams, Matthew Adams, and Mather Byles write engagingly about subjects serious and lighthearted in a mode still new to their country.

Norman Grabo believes that the Proteus Echo essays "unfortunately have been overlooked by American literary historians and critics."[40] Indeed, the series deserves attention not only because of its inherent value but also because of questions it raises. It is fertile ground for the literary sleuth. The precise origin of the series remains obscure. To what degree did Byles, Judge Danforth, and Thomas Prince participate in the operation of *The New-England Weekly Journal*? What role, if any, did Samuel Kneeland play in Proteus Echo? Issues of authorship remain unresolved. Which of the contributors, for example, composed numbers 28 and 47, the only two selections to which even partial authorship cannot be attributed? Who wrote the unassigned parts of numbers 6, 22, 41, and 48? Someone needs to evaluate the contributions of Matthew Adams and Mather Byles. How did Oliver C. Greenleaf know of these essays? And what does his publishing of so many of them in *The Emerald* indicate about his view of readers' taste early in the nineteenth century? How appropriate are the epigraphs that introduce the essays? Do American advice-to-the-lovelorn newspaper columns date, ultimately, from the letters by Simon Hearty and Sam. Wildfire in Proteus Echo number 15, written by John Adams? A book about the entire series is needed. Such an undertaking might appeal to an enterprising scholar concerned with the history of American printing, publishing, newspapers, essays, poetry, or early American literature and culture generally, including transatlantic influences. Anyone undertaking such a project will find, though, that John Adams composed the greatest number of complete selections—eighteen, or approximately 40 percent of the essays to which a single author can be assigned—and that for this reason alone he assumes importance as an early eighteenth-century American prose writer.

Conclusion

Anyone wishing to understand American culture in the decade of the 1720s could do so through the works of Cotton Mather and Benjamin Franklin. By nearly any measure, they were the most significant men of the time, although Mather had been important for decades, and Franklin, who was only in his mid twenties by 1730, would make his greatest contributions to American life after this period. Religion and science were joined in Mather, a Congregational divine who supported the verdicts in the Salem witchcraft trials in the 1690s yet was elected to membership in the Royal Society twenty years later. The skeptic and autodidact Franklin did not share the older man's religious views but far surpassed Mather in scientific accomplishment. Mather was formed by seventeenth-century thought; Franklin, by that of the early eighteenth century. Mather died in the 1720s, and Franklin was then a young man, which suggests not only the changing nature of the decade, but also that change would continue, as it did, precisely as William Burgis implies in his artistic rendering of the Boston waterfront.

There was only one Cotton Mather; there was but one Franklin. But numerous other men provide insight into the transitional nature of the age, including John Adams, who was born the year before Franklin. By becoming involved in the controversy over which people qualify for receiving Holy Communion, Adams embraced, at least to a degree, the liberal Congregational view originally expressed by Solomon Stoddard, while Nathaniel Clap, Adams's adversary, hewed to the way of the early American Puritan fathers in his establishment of strict qualifications for receiving the Lord's Supper. With the assistance of Clap's frustrated parishioners and the councilors who adjudicated the dispute between the two men, Adams defeated Clap; the new vanquished the old.

In his writing, Adams also reflects the changing spirit of his day. Although he had one foot firmly planted in the past, another was solidly in the present. He was Janus-faced. Theologically trained, he wrote poems on religious topics and essays on quasi-moral issues in a manner that would have pleased Cotton Mather's father and grandfathers. Yet he was one of several authors who introduced American readers to contemporary English secular literary values, those espoused by Pope in poetry and Addison in prose, among others. Adams was neither a Pope nor an Addison, but in attempting to incorporate their style and substance into his own compositions, he was among the first Americans to acknowledge their significance and reflect their influence. Yes, he was imitative; yes, he was inferior to his models; yes, his accomplishments have gone largely unacknowledged—but he deserves credit for having attempted to succeed in the new styles of literary expression.

Unfortunately, Adams has had but two champions: his uncle Matthew Adams and, recently, David S. Shields. One can understand why no one has responded positively to Matthew Adams's praise of his nephew. It is too effusive, though understandably so. In fact, the only person to have reacted to it, Paul Dudley, takes Matthew Adams to task for commenting so unreservedly about John Adams, whom Dudley presumably knew. Shields, though, is restrained. Serious and analytical, he, alone among scholars, offers at least one good reason for considering John Adams seriously: his success in the Blackmorean mode.

Adams is significant for additional reasons. Although he failed in his ministry, he was the only divine between 1728 and 1740 to have delivered his own ordination sermon. *Jesus Christ an Example to His Ministers* was one of the first tracts published in Newport. His "To a Gentleman on the Sight of Some of His Poems" is the initial poem in *A Collection of Poems* (by Mather Byles and others), which is possibly the first anthology of American verse. Adams enhances some of his poems with compelling imagery, occasionally uses the caesura effectively, creates a memorable melancholiac in "Melancholly Discrib'd and Dispell'd," and, in "To a Gentleman on the Sight of Some of His Poems," raises the issue of an independent American literary tradition. Furthermore, he applied Dryden's theory of translation to renderings of Horace and the Bible; Adams was the first American to publish a translation of Horace and part of the Bible in an American or English periodical. His "A Consolatory Letter to a Near Relative" served as the basis for another poem. The republication in *Poems on Several Occasions* of Adams's five newspaper poems raises significant textual issues.

At a time when there were few American publications concerned with literary theory, Adams offered valuable comments on this topic in his poems and especially in his essays. In these writings, he is concerned primarily with how authors respond to readers. Should writers compromise their art in order to gain popular acceptance? In addressing literary style in Proteus Echo number 10, Adams creates his fictional masterpiece, Dick Grubstreet. In Proteus Echo number 15, Adams's Simon Hearty and Sam. Wildfire might well initiate the advice-to-the-lovelorn column that became and remains a staple in American newspapers. Adams reflects the spirit of his time by writing about and encouraging politeness and social intercourse, going so far, in the twenty-first Proteus Echo essay, as to have his narrator, X., prefer pleasant society to dull ministers. Few statements—especially by a Congregational divine—capture the transitional nature of the 1720s as accurately as this comment by John Adams.

Notes

INTRODUCTION

1. Harold Pinkham, "Massachusetts Engravers and Their Cities, 1722–1859," http://www.salem.mass.edu/sextant/v4n2/pinkham.html.

2. See I. N. Phelps Stokes and Daniel C. Haskell, *American Historical Prints: Early Views of American Cities, Etc., from the Phelps Stokes and Other Collections* (New York: New York Public Library, 1932), 21; and Richard B. Holman, "William Burgis," in *Boston Prints and Printmakers, 1670–1775*, Publications of the Colonial Society of Massachusetts, vol. 46 (Boston: Colonial Society of Massachusetts, 1973), 62–63, 78.

3. Edwin L. Bynner, "Topography and Landmarks of the Provincial Period," in *The Memorial History of Boston, Including Suffolk County, Massachusetts. 1630–1880*, ed. Justin Winsor (Boston: Osgood, 1881), 2:502.

4. Walter Muir Whitehill, *Boston: A Topographical History* (Cambridge: Belknap Press of Harvard University Press, 1959), 21.

5. Charles E. Clark, *The Public Prints: The Newspaper in Anglo-American Culture, 1665–1740* (New York: Oxford University Press, 1994), 124.

6. Marcus Rediker, *Between the Devil and the Deep Blue Sea: Merchant Seamen, Pirates, and the Anglo-American Maritime World, 1700–1750* (Cambridge: Cambridge University Press, 1987), 176.

7. Cotton Mather, *Useful Remarks. An Essay upon Remarkables in the Way of Wicked Men. A Sermon on the Tragical End, unto Which the Way of Twenty-Six Pirates Brought Them; at New Port on Rhode-Island, July 19, 1723* (New-London: T[imothy] Green, 1723), 15.

8. Ibid., 13.

9. Thomas Hutchinson, *The History of the Province of Massachusets-Bay, From the Charter of King William and Queen Mary, in 1691, Until the Year 1750* (Boston: Thomas and John Fleet, 1767), 231.

10. Herbert L. Osgood, *The American Colonies in the Eighteenth Century* (New York: Columbia University Press, 1924), 3:170.

11. John W. Raimo, *Biographical Directory of American Colonial and Revolutionary Governors, 1607–1789* (Westport, CT: Meckler Books, 1980), 139.

12. Ola Elizabeth Winslow, *A Destroying Angel: The Conquest of Smallpox in Colonial Boston* (Boston: Houghton Mifflin, 1974), 27, 45.

13. William Douglass, *A Summary, Historical and Political, of the First Planting, Progressive Improvements, and Present State of the British Settlements in North-America* (Boston: Daniel Fowle, 1751), 2:396; Winslow, *A Destroying Angel*, 89.

14. Winslow, *A Destroying Angel*, 38, 48.

15. Douglass, *A Summary*, 2:396.

16. Winslow, *A Destroying Angel*, 86.

17. "History of Church Music in America from the Colonial Period to the 21st Century," http://personal.lig.bellsouth.net/lig/m/u/musicedu/amhistry.htm#colonial.

18. See David W. Music, "Cotton Mather and Congregational Singing in Puritan New England," in *Studies in Puritan American Spirituality* 2 (1991): 1–30, and Karl Kroeger, "William Billings and the Puritan Musical Ideal," in *Studies in Puritan American Spirituality* 2 (1991): 31–50.

19. Linda R. Ruggles, "The Regular Singing Controversy: The Case against Lining-Out," *The Early American Review* (Fall 1997): http://www.animus.net/~earlya/review/fall97/sing.html.

20. See J. William T. Youngs Jr., *God's Messengers: Religious Leadership in Colonial New England, 1700–1750* (Baltimore: Johns Hopkins University Press, 1976), 98.

21. See Ruggles, "The Regular Singing Controversy."

22. Charles E. Clark, *The Public Prints*, 123.

23. Elizabeth Christine Cook, *Literary Influences in Colonial Newspapers, 1704–1750* (1912; reprint, Port Washington, NY: Kennikat Press, 1966), 9.

24. Charles E. Clark, *The Public Prints*, 123.

25. Ibid., 184.

26. See Samuel Eliot Morison, *Three Centuries of Harvard, 1636–1936* (Cambridge: Belknap Press of Harvard University Press, 1936), 58.

27. In a 1726 engraving titled *A Prospect of the Colledges in Cambridge in New England*, William Burgis offers his impression of the three Harvard colleges, Harvard, Stoughton, and Massachusetts Halls.

28. Morison, *Three Centuries*, 59–64.

29. David D. Hall, *The Faithful Shepherd: A History of the New England Ministry in the Seventeenth Century* (Williamsburg: Institute of Early American History and Culture; Chapel Hill: University of North Carolina Press, 1972), 274.

30. The first quotation is from Hall, *The Faithful Shepherd*, 276; the second is from Morison, *Three Centuries*, 63.

31. Benjamin Franklin, *Writings* (New York: Library of America, 1987), 1092–93.

CHAPTER 1

1. See Clifford K. Shipton, *Sibley's Harvard Graduates* (Boston: Massachusetts Historical Society, 1942), 6:423, 437–39, 439–67, 471–82, 488–89, 511–27, 527–28, 567–68, 574–82, 582–84. See Jane Colman Turell, *Memoirs of the Life and Death of the Pious and Ingenious Mrs. Jane Turell, Who Died at Medford, March 26th 1735 Ætat. 27*, collected by Ebenezer Turell (London: John Oswald, 1741); and Ebenezer Turell, *The Life and Character of the Reverend Benjamin Colman, D. D. Late Pastor of a Church in Boston New-England. Who Deceased August 29th 1747* (Boston: Rogers and Fowle for J[oseph] Edwards, 1749).

2. See Josiah Granville Leach, *Some Account of Capt. John Frazier and His Descendants, with Notes on the West and Checkley Families* (Philadelphia: Lippincott, 1910), 103–12; James Savage, *A Genealogical Dictionary of the First Settlers of New England, Showing Three Generations of Those Who Came before May, 1692, on the Basis of Farmer's Register* (Boston: Little Brown, 1860), 1:369; Barry M. Moody, "Adams, John," in *Dictionary of Canadian Biography*, ed. George W. Brown, et al. (Toronto: University of Toronto Press, 1974), 3:3–4; Shipton, *Sibley's Harvard Graduates*, 6:424–27; John Bartlet Brebner, *New England's Outpost: Acadia before the Conquest of Canada* (New York: Columbia University Press; London: King, 1927), 102–3. Also see "Descendants of Matthew Adams," *The New-England Historical and Genealogical Register* 10 (January 1856): 89–91, in which the anonymous author wishes that someone would provide "an account of Matthew Adams's ancestors," a need yet to be satisfied (90).

3. Benjamin Franklin, *The Autobiography of Benjamin Franklin*, ed. Leonard W. Labaree, et al. (New Haven: Yale University Press, 1964), 59.

4. C. B. E., "Notes on the Hon. John Adams of Nova Scotia and Boston," *New-England Historical and Genealogical Register* 32 (April 1878): 132–33; Everett S. Stackpole and Winthrop S. Meserve, *History of the Town of Durham New Hampshire (Oyster River Plantation)* (n.p.: Published by Vote of the Town [1913]), 2:1–5. E.'s findings are incomplete and inaccurate; Stackpole and Meserve's are probably comprehensive and authoritative. Two scholars claim that Adams was born in Boston on 26 March 1705, although I do not believe that such a statement can be substantiated. See Frederick Lewis Weis, *The Colonial Clergy and the Colonial Churches of New England* (1936; reprint, Baltimore: Clearfield, 1977), 17; and John C. Shields, "John Adams (1705–1740)," in *American Writers before 1800: A Biographical and Critical Dictionary*, ed. James A. Levernier and Douglas R. Wilmes (Westport, CT: Greenwood, 1983), 1:13.

5. Beamish Murdoch, *A History of Nova-Scotia, or Acadie* (Halifax: James Barnes, 1865), 398.

6. Shipton, *Sibley's Harvard Graduates*, 6:424.

7. Also note the title of A.'s "Remarks on the Poetical Character of the Rev. John Adams, A. M.," *The Massachusetts Magazine* 1 (April 1789): 232.

8. Youngs, *God's Messengers*, 11–12, 18.

9. I thank Harold F. Worthley of the Congregational Library in Boston for suggesting the possibility of Adams having received the degree *ad eundem gradum*.

10. For information about certain realities of travel between Boston and Newport shortly before Adams made his trip, see "Facilities for Traveling between Boston and Newport in 1720," *The Newport Historical Magazine* 4 (January 1884): 179.

11. Congregationalists of the time generally believed that a person should be ordained only after being called by a church. Ordination was not transferable from one church to another. See Williston Walker, *A History of the Congregational Churches in the United States* (New York: Scribner's, 1894), 224.

12. Clifford K. Shipton mentions Adams's involvement with the Society for Promoting Virtue and Knowledge (*Sibley's Harvard Graduates*, 6:425). For information about this society, see "Articles of the Society for Promoting Virtue

and Knowledge, by a Free Conversation," *The Newport Historical Magazine* 4 (October 1883): 67–71.

13. Paul Dudley, "Diary of Paul Dudley," *The New-England Historical and Genealogical Register* 35 (1881): 30. See "Articles of the Society," 67–71; Shipton, *Sibley's Harvard Graduates,* 6:425; Richard Webster, *A History of the Presbyterian Church in America, from Its Origin until the Year 1760* (Philadelphia: Joseph M. Wilson, 1856), 116; *A Report of the Record Commissioners of the City of Boston, Containing the Boston Records from 1729 to 1742* (Boston: Rockwell and Churchill, 1885), 114–15; *A Report of the Record Commissioners of the City of Boston, Containing the Records of Boston Selectmen, 1736 to 1742* (Boston: Rockwell and Churchill, 1886), 84; Thomas Prince, "Diary of the Rev. Thomas Prince, 1737," *Publications of the Colonial Society of Massachusetts: Transactions 1916–1917* (1918): 340; Stackpole and Meserve, *History of the Town of Durham,* 2:4; Ebenezer Parkman, "The Diary of Ebenezer Parkman, 1739–1744," ed. Francis G. Walett, *Proceedings of the American Antiquarian Society* 72, pt. 1 (1962): 110. Among the other subscribers to Prince's book were Matthew Adams, Mather Byles, and Nathaniel Clap, all significant men in John Adams's life. Clap, whose given name Prince spells Nathanael, ordered two copies. While there is confusion over the date and place of Adams's birth, at least one writer misstates the date of his death. George Champlin Mason incorrectly claims that Adams died on 6 January 1755 (Mason, *Annals of the Redwood Library and Athenæum, Newport, R. I.* [Newport: Redwood Library, 1891], 24 n. 19).

As early as 1829 someone lamented the lack of biographical information about Adams. Samuel Kettell writes: "The confident predictions of [Adams's] immortality, recorded in the preface to a little collection of his poems published after Mr Adams's death, serve only to excite a desire of knowing something of a character so lauded as his, but we are furnished with nothing that can gratify our curiosity" (Kettell, *Specimens of American Poetry, with Critical and Biographical Notices* [Boston: Goodrich, 1829], 1:67).

14. The obituary was republished, slightly revised, in "The Publisher to the Reader" in John Adams, *Poems on Several Occasions, Original and Translated* (Boston: D[aniel] Gookin, 1745), iv–v. A notation in Mather Byles's copy of this volume in the Widener Library, Harvard University, identifies Matthew Adams as the author of the preface. Matthew Adams claims authorship of the John Adams obituary in a letter to Josiah Cotton dated 31 January 1739/40 (Curwen Family Papers, box 3, folder 1, American Antiquarian Society).

15. Dudley, "Diary," 30.

16. In the revised obituary, "immortal Labours" becomes "immortal Writings" (John Adams, *Poems,* v).

In a letter to Josiah Cotton dated 31 January 1739/40, Matthew Adams offers additional impressions of his nephew:

> It is a melancholy Time with me, having lately lost my dear Friend & Nephew, the Rev Mr. *John Adams,* a short account of whose Death and burial, with a Hint at his Character, I have this Day given in the *Boston-Weekly News-Letter,* but is vastly Short of what I conceive is the just Desert of that truly great and vertuous Man—. He was Master of Nine Languages, and had read all the most famous Greek, Latin, Italian[,] French[,] and Spanish Authors, and has translated some fine pieces from several of

'em. The noblest Writers in our own Language, in Prose and Verse, he was so perfectly acquainted with, that he cou'd turn at once, upon Occasion, to any remarkable Passage, whether History, Philosophy, Poetry, Morality, or Divinity. Nor was his Genius inferior to his Learning. He had a bright and vigorous Fancy, and a fine taste for Polite Litterature, accompany'd with a solid Judgment, and a Capacity for reasoning with the greatest Strength and Perspicuity. And as to his Invention, I don't know Whether it was not without a Paralel. Some of the finest Sermons that he (or any Body else in these Parts, & of his Age) ever made—, I have known him compose, from the Beginning, to the End, in ye Space of about Seven or Eight Hours Time. And once I remember him to have walk'd about my room, dictating to Three Nimble Writers, alone and the same Time, upon Three different subjects, as well as in Three different sorts of Composition, for a whole Hour together, not suffering one of the Scribes to waite for Matter, but kept them constantly supplyd, attending at the same tyme to the Subject, the Stile, and Coherence of each Piece till the Three were completed: And they are all now in my Hands, and worthy of the Press, as well as that fine Volume of Divine Poems, & Sermons, he has left, which may shortly be printed, and which I wish you might think it worth your while to Subscribe for.

But that which was the Crown of all, in this fine Genius, was his great and undissembled Piety, which ran like a Vein of Gold thro' all his Life and Performances. And tho towards his Conclusion, he was something in a Cloud, for want of the free Use of his Reason, yet I trust he is risen bright in the Horizon of Glory.

The letter is in the Curwen Family Papers, box 3, folder 1, American Antiquarian Society.

17. For a comment on Clap's early years in Newport, see Sydney V. James, *Colonial Rhode Island: A History* (New York: Scribner's, 1975), 198–99. Councilors adjudicating the conflict between Clap and his parishioners address the charge against him in a document dated 3 April 1728, as transcribed by Ezra Stiles. About the issue of baptism they write as follows: "we find several things exceptional and very irregular objected against him, Particularly in the case of Mr. Randall Nicholls' child, and adult persons not being seasonably propounded" (John Comer, "The Diary of John Comer," ed. C. Edwin Barrows and James W. Willmarth, vol. 8 of *Collections of the Rhode Island Historical Society* [n.p.: Published for the Society, 1893], 52 n. 81). There are three copies of this document, one in the Massachusetts Historical Society, and two in the Historical Society of Pennsylvania. They render Nicholls's surname variously. Not one of the documents includes Nicholls's given name. C. Edwin Barrows apparently borrowed Nicholls's given name from a letter of 11 October 1727 in which nine men call for a council to hear their complaint against Clap. I read his name as "Kendall," not "Randall."

18. For a discussion of Clap as being principled, see Kreg H. Bryan, "Nathaniel Clap: Rhode Island's Last Puritan," *New England Reformed Journal* 6 (Winter 1998): 13–36. See William B. Sprague, *Annals of the American Pulpit* (New York: Robert Carter, 1859), 1:349; Norman S. Grabo, *Edward Taylor* (1961; revised, Boston: Twayne, 1988), 19; Gerald R. McDermott, *One Holy and Happy Society: The Public Theology of Jonathan Edwards* (University Park: Pennsylvania State University Press, 1992), 166.

19. All references to the Bible are to the Authorized King James Version. John Calvin, *Institutes of the Christian Religion*, ed. John T. McNeill, trans. Ford Lewis Battles (Philadelphia: Westminster Press, 1960), 2:1418–19.

20. *A Platform of Church Discipline Gathered out of the Word of God: and Agreed upon by the Elders: and Messengers of the Churches Assembled in the Synod at Cambridge in New England* (Cambridge: S[amuel] G[reen], 1649), 22.

21. *Propositions Concerning the Subject of Baptism and Consociation of Churches, Collected and Confirmed out of the Word of God, by a Synod of Elders and Messengers of the Churches in Massachusets-Colony in New-England* (Cambridge: S[amuel] G[reen] for Hezekiah Usher, 1662), 17–18. 1 Corinthians 10:16 reads as follows: "The cup of blessing which we bless, is it not the communion of the blood of Christ? The bread which we break, is it not the communion of the body of Christ?"

22. Increase Mather, *The Necessity of Reformation with the Expedients Subservient Thereunto, Asserted* (Boston: John Foster, 1679), 10.

23. Thomas M. Davis and Virginia L. Davis, eds., *Edward Taylor vs. Solomon Stoddard: The Nature of the Lord's Supper*, vol. 2 of the Unpublished Writings of Edward Taylor (Boston: Twayne, 1981), 27–28.

24. Ibid., 6.

25. See *Edward Taylor vs. Solomon Stoddard*, vol. 2 of the Unpublished Writings of Edward Taylor, ed. Thomas M. Davis and Virginia L. Davis (Boston: Twayne, 1981).

26. The writers of the preface to the Cambridge Platform address the issue that would confront Clap's frustrated parishioners:

> If the Ministers do dislike the way of those, whom they otherwise count their best members, & so refuse to joyn with them therin; yet if those members can procure some other Ministers to joyn with them in their own way, & still continue their dwelling together in the same town, they may easily order the times of the publick assembly, as to attend constantly upon the ministery of their former Church: & either after or before the publick assembly of the parish take an opportunity to gather together for the administratiō of Sacramēts, & Censures, & other church ordinances amongst themselves. (*A Platform of Church Discipline*, 6)

In 1728, Benjamin Bass became the initial minister of the First Congregational Church in Hanover, Massachusetts, which he served until his death in 1756. In surveying Bass's career, Frederick Lewis Weis does not mention Bass's time in Newport (Weis, *The Colonial Clergy*, 29). For information about Bass, see Shipton, *Sibley's Harvard Graduates*, 6:72–74. In November 1729, two months before Adams was dismissed from his ministerial position in Newport, Clap wrote a preface to one of Bass's sermons, thus indicating that he harbored no ill will toward the first minister his congregation called to assist him. (See Nathaniel Clap, preface to *Parents and Children Advised and Exhorted to Their Duty. Part of a Sermon, Preached at Newport on Rhode-Island, September 28. 1729*, by Benjamin Bass [Newport: n.p., 1730].) Clap would never be so charitable toward Adams, although he got along well with James Searing, Adams's successor. Clap officiated at Searing's wedding (James, *Colonial Rhode Island*, 199).

J. William T. Youngs Jr. notes that "the actual choice of a pastor remained under popular control throughout the eighteenth century" (Youngs, *God's Messengers*, 24). John Comer records the date on which Adams arrived in Newport

(Comer, "Diary," 101). See also Sprague, *Annals of the American Pulpit*, 1:349–50.

27. John Comer notes that "Adams was ordained over half Mr. Clap's church, *i. e.*, ye Brethren, viz., Richard Clark, John Reynolds, Nathan Townsend, Randall Nichols, James Carey, Job Bissel, Ebenezer Davenport" (Comer, "Diary," 51). See also Comer, 49, 101; Youngs, *God's Messengers*, 24–25; and *A Platform of Church Discipline*, 4, 11–12.

28. Rev. Nathaniel Clap, Request by council for his dismissal (11 October 1727), Simon Gratz Collection, courtesy of The Historical Society of Pennsylvania. An unknown person wrote on this document that "at this Time there were thirteen males in the Chh."

29. Samuel Sewall, *The Diary of Samuel Sewall, 1674–1729*, ed. M. Halsey Thomas (New York: Farrar, Straus and Giroux, 1973), 2:1058.

30. Comer, "Diary," 49.

31. Ibid., 52 n. 81.

32. Ibid., 52–53 n. 81.

33. J. William T. Youngs Jr. avers that eighteenth-century candidates for the Congregational ministry often had to honor the principles of the 1649 Cambridge Platform (Youngs, *God's Messengers*, 28), which probably governed actions relating to the Clap-Adams issue. This document permits withdrawing from a church, for example, only because of personal or general persecution, or for "*want* of competent subsistence" (*A Platform of Church Discipline*, 20). Thus, because Clap denied them the Lord's Supper, his disaffected worshipers were justified in separating from his church. In noting that one church may censure another, the Cambridge Platform also provides a basis for Clap's criticizing of the members of the Second Congregational Church and its minister, Adams (*A Platform of Church Discipline*, 24).

34. Comer, "Diary," 50–51.

35. Ibid., 51 n. 81.

36. Ibid., 50.

37. *The Interpreter's Bible*, ed. George A. Buttrick, et al. (New York: Abingdon Press, 1956), 5:943–44.

38. *The Interpreter's Bible*, 5:266.

39. See Comer, "Diary," 50.

40. Ibid., 51 n. 81.

41. John Adams, *Jesus Christ an Example to His Ministers. A Sermon Preach'd on the Day of His Ordination* (Newport: J[ames] Franklin; Boston: T[homas] Fleet, 1728). Also in 1728, James Franklin published John Webb's *The Believer's Redemption by the Precious Blood of Christ: A Sermon Preach'd at Newport, on Rhode-Island: On Lord's Day, December 31. 1727*. Webb was a member of the council that heard the Clap-Adams case. See *Rhode Island Imprints, 1727–1800*, ed. John Eliot Alden (New York: Bibliographical Society of American/R. R. Bowker, 1949), 1–4.

42. An advertisement in Adams's *Poems on Several Occasions* announces the pending publication by D[aniel] Gookin of a volume of Adams's sermons, "upon suitable Encouragement" (John Adams, *Poems*, vi). Such encouragement (subscriptions) was not forthcoming; the collection was not published. The manuscript sermons have apparently not survived. The titles of the ser-

mons that were to have been published, according to the advertisement, are these: "The Unknown God," "The Prince of Life Exalted," "The Christian Fighting for the Robes of Victory," "Poverty of Spirit, the Way to a Kingdom," "The Bounds of Christian Prudence, Stated and Adjusted," "The Nature, Causes, and Effects of Insincerity," "The Condescention of God in Accepting Our Charities," "How to Make Friends of the Mammon of Unrighteousness," "The Blind Restor'd, and the Miserable Reliev'd," and "Preparation for Death, the Best Remedy against the Suddenness of It."

43. Joseph Baxter, et al., preface to *Jesus Christ an Example to His Ministers, A Sermon Preach'd on the Day of His Ordination*, by John Adams (Newport: J[ames] Franklin; Boston: T[homas] Fleet, 1728), vi.

44. George Selement, "Publication and the Puritan Minister," *William and Mary Quarterly* 37 (1980): 237.

45. Ibid., 222–23.

46. Youngs, *God's Messengers*, 35.

47. Ibid.

48. In his sermon at the ordination of John Lowell, Foxcroft writes, "Truly glad shou'd I have been, if (pursuant to the Custom, which hath so long obtain'd among us) he cou'd have been prevail'd on to take up the Book at this time, & preach to us his own devout Thoughts & Purposes" (Thomas Foxcroft, *Ministers, Spiritual Parents, or Fathers in the Church of God. A Sermon Preach'd at the Ordination of the Rev. Mr. John Lowell, at Newbury, Jan. 19. 1725, 6* [Boston: B(artholomew) Green for Samuel Gerrish, 1726], 2).

49. John Adams, *Jesus Christ an Example*, 52–53.

50. Youngs, *God's Messengers*, 1.

51. Baxter, et al., iv.

52. Ibid., viii.

53. Youngs, *God's Messengers*, 35–36.

54. John Adams, *Jesus Christ an Example*, 34.

55. Ibid., 45–46.

56. Ibid., 46–47.

57. Ibid., 48.

58. Ibid., 58.

59. Ibid., 59.

60. For a discussion of the behavior people needed to exhibit before being permitted to join Congregational churches—and the controversy surrounding this issue—see Youngs, *God's Messengers*, 82–84. Also see the twelfth chapter of *A Platform of Church Discipline*, 16–18.

61. John Adams, *Jesus Christ an Example*, 71. For a discussion of the Congregational ordination procedure, including the charge and the right hand of fellowship, see Walker, *A History of the Congregational Churches*, 225–26.

62. See *Edward Taylor vs. Solomon Stoddard*, 63–66.

63. Clap's letter was transcribed by Ezra Stiles on 10 February 1767. Rev. Nathaniel Clap, To— (6 May 1728), Simon Gratz Collection, courtesy of The Historical Society of Pennsylvania.

64. *The Interpreter's Bible*, 1:983.

65. Ibid., 1:1070–71.

66. Rev. John Adams, To Mr. Clap (11 May 1728), Simon Gratz Collection,

American Colonial Clergy, case 8, box 21, courtesy of The Historical Society of Pennsylvania.

67. *The Interpreter's Bible*, 1:718–22.

68. Richard M. Bayles, ed., *History of Newport County, Rhode Island. From the Year 1638 to the Year 1887, Including the Settlement of Its Towns and Their Subsequent Progress* (New York: Preston, 1888), 445, 446. For a more generous assessment of Clap, see Bryan, "Nathaniel Clap."

69. Ezra Stiles records this information in his introductory note to Clap's letter to Adams dated 6 May 1728.

70. Comer, "Diary," 54.

71. Rev. John Adams, Request for his own dismissal (25 February 1729/30), Simon Gratz Collection, courtesy of The Historical Society of Pennsylvania.

72. Youngs, *God's Messengers*, 103–4.

73. Timothy Alden, *A Collection of Epitaphs and Inscriptions with Occasional Notes* (New York: n.p., 1814), 4:45.

74. David S. Shields, *Civil Tongues & Polite Letters in British America* (Williamsburg: Institute of Early American History and Culture; Chapel Hill: University of North Carolina Press, 1997), 244.

75. Rev. John Adams, Approval for his dismissal (25 February 1729/30), Simon Gratz Collection, courtesy of The Historical Society of Pennsylvania. "Nemine Contradicente" means "no one contradicting"; the vote was unanimous.

76. Comer, "Diary," 101.

77. See Youngs, *God's Messengers*, 104.

78. C. Edwin Barrows reproduces Stiles's transcript in John Comer, "Diary," 51–53 n. 81. Stiles's original is in the Second Congregational Church Records, Book #828 B, pp. 1–4, Vault A, Newport Historical Society.

79. Ezra Stiles, note dated 10 February 1767 appended to Clap's letter to Adams dated 6 May 1728, housed in The Historical Society of Pennsylvania.

80. Alden, *A Collection of Epitaphs*, 47.

81. For information about ministers' length of service, see Youngs, *God's Messengers*, 29, 143.

In eulogizing Clap, John Callender possibly refers to the controversy with Adams in the following:

> He [Clap] was zealously attached to what he tho't to be the true Doctrines of Grace, and the Forms of Worship. . . . You will remember the little Value he had for a meer Speculative, Local, Nominal Christianity, and a Form of Godliness without the Power. He insisted most on those Things, on which our Interest in Jesus Christ, and our Title to Eternal Life must depend; that *Faith* by which we are Justified and have peace with God thro' our Lord Jesus, and that *Repentance* toward God and new Obedience, which is the necessary Effect and Evidence of our Regeneration, and the proper Exercise of Christianity.

See John Callender, *A Discourse Occasioned by the Death of the Reverend Mr. Nathaniel Clap, Pastor of a Church at Newport on Rhode-Island, on October 30 1745. in the 78th Year of His Age* (Newport: Widow Franklin, 1746), 27.

CHAPTER 2

1. Taylor's "Extract of a Letter" appears in Cotton Mather, *Right Thoughts in Sad Hours, Representing the Comforts and the Duties of Good Men under All Their Afflictions; and Particularly, That One, the Untimely Death of Children* (London: James Astwood, 1689).

2. The standard anthology of early American poetry includes only Bradstreet, Wigglesworth, and Taylor as major writers. See Harrison T. Meserole, ed., *American Poetry of the Seventeenth Century* (1968; reprint [as *Seventeenth-Century American Poetry*], University Park: Pennsylvania State University Press, 1985).

3. Ibid., 37.

4. Roy Harvey Pearce, *The Continuity of American Poetry* (Princeton: Princeton University Press, 1961), 56.

5. Hyatt H. Waggoner, *American Poets, from the Puritans to the Present* (Boston: Houghton Mifflin, 1968).

6. Pearce, *The Continuity of American Poetry*, 56.

7. Sixteen-year-old Benjamin Franklin, writing as Silence Dogood a year after Adams's graduation from Harvard (Franklin was less than ten months Adams's junior), notes that American verse of that time—primarily elegies—is "wretchedly Dull and Ridiculous." Yet in recommending "An Elegy upon the Much Lamented Death of Mrs. Mehitebell Kitel," Franklin identifies one of the major problems with contemporary American verse and anticipates, by more than a century, Emerson's "Merlin" in noting that the great poet's "Muse scorns to be confin'd to the old Measures and Limits, or to observe the dull Rules of Criticks." See "To the Editor of the *New-England Courant*, No. VII," *The New-England Courant* 18–25 June 1722, 1–2. For a succinct discussion of the poetic theories of the time, see the entry on neoclassical poetics in *The New Princeton Encyclopedia of Poetry and Poetics*, ed. Alex Preminger and T. V. F. Brogan (Princeton: Princeton University Press, 1993), 825–31.

8. Alexander Pope, *An Essay on Criticism*, in *Pastoral Poetry and An Essay on Criticism*, ed. E[mile] Audra and Aubrey Williams, The Twickenham Edition of the Poems of Alexander Pope (London: Methuen; New Haven: Yale University Press, 1961), 273, l. 298.

9. John Adams, *Poems*, ii.

10. A., "Remarks," 232.

11. John Eliot, *A Biographical Dictionary, Containing a Brief Account of the First Settlers, and Other Eminent Characters among the Magistrates, Ministers, Literary and Worthy Men, in New-England* (Salem: Cushing and Appleton; Boston: Oliver, 1809), 3–4; Samuel L. Knapp, *Biographical Sketches of Eminent Lawyers, Statesmen, and Men of Letters* (Boston: Richardson and Lord, 1821), 145; Kettell, *Specimens of American Poetry*, 1:68; Evert A. Duyckinck and George L. Duyckinck, *Cyclopædia of American Literature* (New York: Scribner, 1855), 1:133; Francis S. Drake, *Dictionary of American Biography, Including Men of the Time* (1872; reprint, Detroit: Gale Research, 1974), 6; Moses Coit Tyler, *A History of American Literature, 1676–1765* (1878; reprint, Williamstown, MA: Corner House, 1973), 2:55.

12. Oscar Fay Adams, *A Dictionary of American Authors* (1904; reprint, De-

troit: Gale Research, 1969), 4; Samuel Marion Tucker, "The Beginnings of Verse, 1610–1808," in *The Cambridge History of American Literature*, ed. William Peterfield Trent, et al. (New York: Putnam's; Cambridge: University Press, 1917), 1:161; Stanley J. Kunitz and Howard Haycraft, eds., *American Authors, 1600–1900: A Biographical Dictionary of American Literature* (New York: H. W. Wilson, 1938), 11; C. Lennart Carlson, "John Adams, Matthew Adams, Mather Byles, and the *New England Weekly Journal*," *American Literature* 12 (1940): 347; Shipton, *Sibley's Harvard Graduates*, 6:424; Theodore Hornberger, "The English Colonies, 1588–1765," in *The Literature of the United States: An Anthology and a History*, ed. Walter Blair, et al. (Chicago: Scott Foresman, 1946), 1:43; John C. Shields, "John Adams (1705–1740)," 1:15; David S. Shields, "The Religious Sublime and New England Poets of the 1720s," *Early American Literature* 19 (Winter 1984/85): 231–48; *American Colonial Writers, 1606–1734*, ed. Emory Elliott, vol. 24 of Dictionary of Literary Biography (Detroit: Bruccoli Clark/Gale Research, 1984); *Columbia Literary History of the United States*, ed. Emory Elliott (New York: Columbia University Press, 1988); *The Cambridge History of American Literature*, ed. Sacvan Bercovitch (Cambridge: Cambridge University Press, 1994), 1:311, 326, 339; David S. Shields, "Eighteenth-Century Literary Culture," in *The History of the Book in America: The Colonial Book in the Atlantic World*, ed. Hugh Amory and David D. Hall (Cambridge: American Antiquarian Society/Cambridge University Press, 2000), 1:450, 469, 471.

13. See J. A. Leo Lemay, *A Calendar of American Poetry in the Colonial Newspapers and Magazines and in the Major English Magazines through 1765* (Worcester: American Antiquarian Society, 1972), 14, item 74.

14. The introductory prose reads as follows:

—Imprimis Venerare Deum. Virg.
ALMOST every Author of Note, has a way of Writing peculiar to himself, which distinguishes him from all other Writers whatsoever. It is the Happiness of a fine Genius, that he is able to taste the several various Excellencies, which Compose the differing Characters of each Author about which he is conversant. If a Capacity to relish the various Qualities of Authors be such an admirable Talent, the Art to imitate them in their several ways must be much greater. This Observation will reflect a just Honour and Penegyrick upon the Author of the following Lines. The Polite Reader will take notice, that besides his natural manner of Writing (of which there have been applauded Specimens in some of my former Papers) he is able to vary his manner as he pleases & appear beautiful in the Garb of another. I need not observe to the Gentlemen who are acquainted with *Sir RICHARD BLACKMORE's* noble Poem on the *Creation*, that the following Translation is written for Style, Diction, and Sentiment, in imitation of that admiral Piece; of which they will perceive it bears a very nice Similitude & Resemblance.

O.

Evidence for concluding that Byles is O. may be found in Carlson, "John Adams," 347–48.

15. While there are few alterations to this poem, such changes should be noted, both here and in Adams's other poems where two texts exist. David S. Shields, Adams's best critic, mistakenly assumes that the two texts of Psalm 104 are identical. He quotes the first ten lines from it, dating them 1727; they

are from the final version of 1745. Revised, these lines omit one word and change two words from the newspaper text. See David S. Shields, "The Religious Sublime," 238.

16. In quoting from John Adams's *Poems on Several Occasions*, I cite page number(s) followed by line number(s).

17. Having God bless mankind is Adams's invention. In this couplet, the poet interprets verse 23, but does so in the second of these lines, not the first. Verse 23 reads: "Man goeth forth unto his work and to his labour until the evening."

18. For a statement about the differences between the words "charity" and "love" in 1 Corinthians, see *The Interpreter's Bible*, 10:166–67.

19. For the evolution of "love" and "charity" as synonyms, see "charity" in *The Oxford English Dictionary*.

20. For a discussion of why both "charity" and "love" are appropriate, see "charity" in *The Oxford English Dictionary*.

21. An unsigned letter to *"the Worshipful Master* JANUS*"* introduces Adams's poem in *The New-England Courant*. (Janus was James Franklin, printer and publisher of this newspaper.) The author of the letter states, "with some Assurance, that if the Reception is but correspondent to the Merit of the Performance, it will obtain a considerable Applause; at least with those who have an Acquaintance with the Charms of the Original" (1). If, as implied, the letter writer was not John Adams, then he was possibly Matthew Adams. According to Benjamin Franklin's handwritten comments in the first forty-three numbers of *The New-England Courant* (less numbers 7, 9, 12, 13, and 19) housed in the British Library, Matthew Adams's four contributions to these numbers make him, with John Eyre, the sixth most prolific contributor to them. The men appearing more frequently than Matthew Adams in the newspaper are Mr. Gardner, James Franklin, Dr. Douglass, Captain Taylor, and Benjamin Franklin. Matthew Adams contributed to numbers 17 (27 November 1721), 22 (1 January 1722), 30 (26 February 1722), and 39 (30 April 1722). See Worthington Chauncey Ford, "Franklin's New England Courant," in *Proceedings of the Massachusetts Historical Society* 57 (February–April 1924): 336–53.

Joseph T. Buckingham identifies this submission—the letter to Janus and the translation of Horace—as "the last original article" to be published in Franklin's newspaper (Joseph T. Buckingham, *Specimens of Newspaper Literature: With Personal Memoirs, Anecdotes, and Reminiscences* [Boston: Charles C. Little and James Brown, 1850],1:82). He reproduces the entire submission on 82–84 but does not address the issue of authorship or mention the names of John Adams or Matthew Adams.

22. In *The New-England Weekly Journal*, Adams's poem is preceded by an anonymous prose paragraph about the psalm. It is not included in *Poems on Several Occasions*.

23. In *The New-England Weekly Journal*, the poem, which is signed T., is preceded by two prose paragraphs that do not appear in Byles's book. For evidence that John Adams wrote this poem, see Carlson, "John Adams," 347–48.

24. I here list the substantive textual changes to Adams's original text. Following the line number appears the word or words from *The New-England Weekly Journal* (1727); after the close bracket is the word or words used in Byles's (and other poets') *A Collection of Poems* (Boston: B[artholomew] Green [Jr.] for D[aniel] Gookin, 1744):

13 your] *his*
77 While we] We too
96 strains,] scenes,
103 a] the

There are several changes in accidentals between the two texts.

25. Cotton Mather, *Manuductio ad Ministerium. Directions for a Candidate of the Ministry* (Boston: Thomas Hancock, 1726), 42, 45.

26. In seeking inspiration from God and disavowing the muse, Adams reflects an attitude expressed most memorably in seventeenth-century American verse by Michael Wigglesworth. In "A Prayer unto Christ the Judge of the World," a proem to *The Day of Doom*, Wigglesworth addresses God (*"Dearest Dread"*): "Thee, thee *alone I'le invocate, / For I do much abominate / To call the* Muses *to mine aid*." (See Michael Wigglesworth, "A Prayer unto Christ the Judge of the World," in *The Poems of Michael Wigglesworth*, ed. Ronald A. Bosco [Lanham, MD: University Press of America, 1989], 9, ll. 5–7.) The date of Adams's "An Address to the Supreme Being" cannot be determined because it appears, undated, only in the posthumous *Poems on Several Occasions*.

27. Pope emphasizes individual expression in *An Essay on Criticism*, 255–59, ll. 141–68. He comments on the vulgar on 288, l. 424.

28. For examples of new contexts in which to view eighteenth-century American culture, including poetry, see David S. Shields, *Civil Tongues*. Also see his "Eighteenth-Century Literary Culture." Philip F. Gura summarizes scholarship in this area in "Early American Literature at the New Century," *William and Mary Quarterly*, 3d series, 57 (2000): 599–620. Among the scholars suggesting fertile areas of inquiry are Michael P. Clark, "The Persistence of Literature in Early American Studies," *William and Mary Quarterly*, 3d series, 57 (2000): 641–46; Gura, "Early American Literature"; Carla Mulford, "The Ineluctability of the Peoples' Stories," *William and Mary Quarterly*, 3d series, 57 (2000): 621–34; and David S. Shields, "Joy and Dread among the Early Americanists," *William and Mary Quarterly*, 3d series, 57 (2000): 635–40.

29. Adams addresses this same issue from another perspective in the fifteenth number of the Proteus Echo essays (*The New-England Weekly Journal*, 17 July 1727, 1–2). Here Adams, writing as X., berates Will Pedant by having Pedant criticize Proteus Echo's writing and so describe his own: "I would never write in your dull correct Manner, but give the Publick my first hasty Thoughts, which have always the most Fire." Adams criticizes Pedant for refusing to control his emotions, as Adams controls his.

30. John Adams, *Poems*, iii.

31. For a different interpretation of these lines, see David S. Shields, "The Religious Sublime," 246.

32. Samuel Johnson, *Lives of the English Poets*, (1779–81) (1905; reprint, New York: Octagon, 1967), 2:35–52; John Locke, *The Correspondence of John Locke* (Oxford: Clarendon Press, 1981), 142–45; Cotton Mather, *The Diary of Cotton Mather, 1709–1724* (New York: Frederick Ungar, [1957]), 105, 141; Cotton Mather, *The Christian Philosopher*, ed. Winton U. Solberg (1721; Urbana: University of Illinois Press, 1994), 44, 226; John Dryden, *Fables Ancient and Modern* (London: Jacob Tonson, 1700), preface (where Blackmore is "the City Bard,

or Knight Physician"); Jonathan Swift, *The Prose Works of Jonathan Swift, D.D.*, ed. Temple Scott (London: George Bell, 1902), 10:376 (where Blackmore is an "insipid . . . scoundrel"); Alexander Pope, *Peri Bathous*, in *Alexander Pope*, ed. Pat Rogers (Oxford: Oxford University Press, 1993), 205; Alexander Pope, *The Dunciad*, in *Alexander Pope*, ed. Pat Rogers (Oxford: Oxford University Press, 1993), 477–78, ll. 259–60.

33. David S. Shields, "The Religious Sublime."

34. Harry M. Solomon, *Sir Richard Blackmore* (Boston: Twayne, 1980), 122,

35. Ibid., 129.

36. David S. Shields, "The Religious Sublime," 236.

37. Ibid., 241.

38. Although I am aware of the danger of identifying a poetic voice as the author, I refer to it as Adams throughout this study because the speaker of the poems seems so obviously the poet himself.

39. Lines 55–86 from the second canto of "On Society" appear in *A Library of American Literature: From the Earliest Settlement to the Present Time*, ed. Edmund C. Stedman and Ellen M. Hutchinson (New York: Charles L. Webster, 1890), 2:366–67.

40. David S. Shields, "The Religious Sublime," 241.

41. Ibid.

42. For details of Winslow's life, including his brief military career, see Shipton, *Sibley's Harvard Graduates*, 6:587–89. Adams, apparently writing soon after Winslow's death, possibly did not know of two other Winslow elegies that might have been written before his own tribute. See Cotton Mather, "The Tragedy of Green-Island, and the Memorable End of Captain Josiah Winslow," in *Edulcorator. A Brief Essay on the Waters of Marah Sweetened. With a Remarkable Relation of the Deporable [sic] Occasion Afforded for It, in the Præmature Death of Captain Josiah Winslow, Who [with Several of His Company] Sacrificed His Life, in the Service of His Country; Engaging an Army of Indians, May 1. 1724* by Cotton Mather (Boston: B[artholomew] Green, 1725), 27–34; Mather Byles, "To the Memory of a Young Commander Slain in Battle with the Indians, 1724," in *Poems on Several Occasions*, by Mather Byles (Boston: S[amuel] Kneeland & T[imothy] Green, 1744), 34–38, in which Winslow is unnamed.

43. See Jeffrey A. Hammond, "The Puritan Elegaic Ritual: From Sinful Silence to Apostolic Voice," in *Studies in Puritan American Spirituality* 2 (1991): 77–98.

44. Texts of classical Greek authors were available in the Harvard library before 1682; Sophocles's plays are mentioned in the 1723 library catalogue. See *Catalogus Librorum Bibliothecæ Collegij Harvardini Quod Est Cantabrigiæ in Nova Anglia* (Boston: B[artholomew] Green, 1723), 61; and Samuel Eliot Morison, *Harvard College in the Seventeenth Century* (Cambridge: Harvard University Press, 1936), 199.

45. For genealogical information and for an account of Cotton Mather's amazing attitude toward and actions against Nathan and George Howell's father, see M. Halsey Thomas, ed., *The Diary of Samuel Sewall, 1674–1729* (New York: Farrar, Straus and Giroux, 1973), 2:817–18 n. 20. One Boston newspaper notes the drownings: "On Monday last Two Young Persons who were

Brothers and only Children, viz. Mr. *George & Nathan Howell*, diverting themselves by Skating at the Bottom of the Common, the Ice braking under them, they were both Drowned; their Dead Bodies were taken up a few Hours after; and were very decently buried on Thursday last" (*The New-England Weekly Journal*, 15 January 1728, 2). Neither the obituary nor Adams's poem mentions the children's father.

46. Writing as R. in Proteus Echo number 31 (*The New-England Weekly Journal*, 6 November 1727, 1), Adams uses the recent earthquake as the basis for his essay on fear. For an account of the earthquake, see Cotton Mather, *Selected Letters of Cotton Mather*, ed. Kenneth Silverman (Baton Rouge: Louisiana State University Press, 1971), 417–19. Among the clergymen delivering sermons on this event were James Allen, John Barnard, Benjamin Colman, William Cooper, Cotton Mather, Thomas Prince, and Joseph Sewall.

47. Cotton Mather, *Selected Letters*, 404. See Cotton Mather, *The Temple Opening. A Particular Church Considered as a Temple of the Lord. In a Sermon Preached on a a* [sic] *Day, When Such a Church Was Gathered, and a Pastor to It Ordained* (Boston: B[artholomew] Green for S[amuel] Phillips, 1709).

48. James, *Colonial Rhode Island*, 199.

49. Knapp, *Biographical Sketches*, 145.

50. Adams writes:

> THE slow, the cruel Power of a Disease,
> Has given the kindest Charmer a Release:
> Rude was the Wound, too piercing to the Sight,
> When with her every Pleasure took its Flight.

> (89.23–26)

51. Near the beginning of the poem, Adams implies his closeness to the couple. He writes:

> She, who could raise our Joys, or charm our Ears,
> Receives the gliding Current of our Tears;
> Which, to her ever-pleasing Mem'ry just,
> Fall from our Eyes, and mingle with her Dust.

> (89.19–22)

52. See "Descendants of Matthew Adams," 89; and Stackpole and Meserve, *History of the Town of Durham*, 2:5.

53. "A Consolatory Letter to a Near Relative, on the Death of His Agreable Consort, July 22. 1751" reads as follows:

> FOR you, *dear Sir*, the Muse unus'd to sing,
> With artless Fingers bends the solemn String:
> Pardon if much, yet less concern'd I tell,
> A Loss whose Fulness only you can feel.
> Perhaps the Measure of my friendly Muse,
> May thro' your pensive Mind some Joy diffuse;
> And make those Sorrows, which no Words can paint,
> Retire before the Glories of the Saint.

> The tender Partner, from your Bosom torn,
> Is to sequester'd Vales, and lonely Silence Borne:
> Her closed Lids exclude the graceful Day,
> Nor more her Cheeks the Crimson Stain display.
> Pale are her Lips, not now the Purple Flood
> Distends her Veins, nor winds the mazy Road.
> Still are her Limbs, her beating Heart no more
> Receives, or gives the ever-circling Store.
> She, who could raise our Joys, or charm our Ears,
> Receives the gliding Current of our Tears;
> Which, to her ever-pleasing Mem'ry just,
> Fall from our Eyes, and mingle with her Dust.
> The slow, the cruel Power of a Disease,
> Has given the kindest Charmer a Release:
> Rude was the Wound, too piercing to the Sight!

> Ah! fade ye Greens, and weep ye gliding Rills,
> Drop all ye Flowers, in Vapours rise ye Hills:
> Ye Zephyrs into mourning Murmurs turn,
> And gather Clouds of Tears for MARTHA'S Urn.
> The tender Tyes of nuptial Life she grac'd,
> And all the Mother to the Child express'd:
> The best of Daughters in her Carriage shone,
> She felt the Friend, and charm'd the weeping Town.
> Few were her Words, but chose and weighty too,
> We could not blame, but griev'd they were so few.
> Consider then, with various Passions tost,
> The Saint possesses what the Husband lost.
> Remov'd from desart Plains, and gloomy Groves,
> In fairer Fields of boundless Bliss she roves.

54. Letter to author from Brenda Dunn, project historian for Parks Canada in Halifax, Nova Scotia, 17 December 1993.

55. Letter to author from Clarice Muntz of the Annapolis Valley Regional Library, Nova Scotia, 23 January 1990; letter to author from Brenda Dunn, 28 January 1990.

56. In all probability, John Adams—and not Matthew Adams—linked the two parts of this poem. This may be inferred from the presence of the complete poem (as "An Epistle to the Reverend Mr. Ebenezer Turell, Occasioned by the Death of His Late Virtuous Consort") in Benjamin Colman, *Reliquiæ Turellæ, et Lachrymæ Paternæ. The Father's Tears over His Daughter's Remains. Two Sermons Preach'd at Medford, April 6. 1735* (Boston: S[amuel] Kneeland and T[imothy] Green for J[oseph] Edwards and H[opestill] Foster, 1735). In 1735—the year Jane Turell and Elizabeth Taylor died, Adams wrote the poem, and *Reliquiæ Turellæ* was published—Adams had not yet begun suffering from delirium. If he cared enough to lament these women in verse and had the skill to do so, he was doubtless responsible for the final form of this poem. This elegy was also published, the year following Adams's death, in Jane Colman Turell, *Memoirs*. The poem includes the lines about Elizabeth Taylor.

57. Jeffrey A. Hammond, "The Puritan Elegaic Ritual," 81.

58. For Jane Colman Turell's verse, see Jane Turell and Martha Brewster,

Poems of Jane Turell and Martha Brewster, ed. Kenneth A. Requa (Delmar, NY: Scholars' Facsimiles & Reprints, 1979). Here, once again Turell shares posthumous publication with another woman.

59. Anne Bradstreet, "The Prologue," in *The Complete Works of Anne Bradstreet*, ed. Joseph R. McElrath Jr. and Allan P. Robb (Boston: Twayne, 1981), 7, ll. 25–26.

60. John Winthrop, *The Journal of John Winthrop, 1630–1649*, ed. Richard S. Dunn, et al. (Cambridge: Belknap Press of Harvard University Press, 1996), 570.

61. Moody, "Adams, John," 3–4.

62. Adams's poem appears, in a text improved (by Mather Byles?) from its newspaper appearance, in Byles's compilation, *Collection of Poems*, 3–8. It is therefore the initial poem in what is arguably the first anthology of American verse.

63. The pertinent lines are

> And now, my Muse, attempt one labour more,
> Let *Milton's* fame resound from shore to shore:
> *Milton* who in his works immortal lives,
> And in the deathless praise your Poem gives.
> You imitate his airy rapid flights,
> And mount with ardour to his godlike heights.
> How swift the vigour of your numbers fly,
> When the dread chariot bounds along the sky;
> While o'er the azure plains *Messiah's* driven,
> And hurls his foes precipitant from heaven!
> His eyes majestick flash with flames of fire,
> And kindle hell in those who dare his ire.
> You lead me through the gay delightful strains,
> Where paradise adorns the happy plains.
> Here nature's wing'd inhabitants repair,
> And chant their musick thro' the ravish'd air.
> Here rilling streams in winding mazes move,
> There towre the shady honours of the grove.
> There opening flowers breathe their refreshing sweets,
> And here a ripening fruit the singer greets:
> While courtly Zephyres wave the trembling trees,
> And fan their faces with a gentle breeze.
> Blest garden of primæval innocence!
> (But now surrounded with a flaming fence.)
> How longs my panting Soul to stretch my limbs,
> Near the soft running of thy cooling streams,
> Upon the verdure of a grassy mead,
> And rising turf a pillow for my head,
> Easy my thought, my prostrate length to lay,
> And waste in chearful joys the smiling day?
> Here dwelt the happy Pair dissolv'd in bliss,
> And heard unmov'd the Serpent's harmless hiss,
> While subject nature bow'd its humble neck,
> And every charm conspir'd the place to deck.

(ll. 84–117)

See Mather Byles, *Poems on Several Occasions* (Boston: S[amuel] Kneeland & T[imothy] Green, 1744), 25–34.

64. In a letter prefatory to the poem, N. S., the announced author of Adams's poem, states that he is submitting his poem because Adams and others have tried "to protect and cultivate the *New England* Muses." Adams wrote the letter; he possibly uses N. S. as a clue to his identity. He once lived in Nova-Scotia, where his family continued to reside in 1727. In writing "May *Milton's* force and *Dryden's* smoothness join," Adams probably alludes to "Where *Denham's* Strength, and *Waller's* Sweetness join," in Pope's *An Essay on Criticism*, l. 361.

65. See Noah Webster, *A Grammatical Institute, of the English Language, Comprising, an Easy, Concise, and Systematic Method of Education, Designed for the Use of English Schools in America*, part 1 (Hartford: Hudson and Goodwin, 1783). This book is generally known as the "Blue-Back Speller."

66. Sydney Smith, Review of Adam Seybert's *Statistical Annals of the United States of America, Edinburgh Review* (January 1820): 79.

67. Morison, *Three Centuries*, 26, 57, 103; Robert Francis Seybolt, *The Private Schools of Colonial Boston* (1935; reprint, Westport: Greenwood, 1970), 10.

68. Letter from Matthew Adams in Boston to Josiah Cotton, 31 January 1739/40. The letter is in the Curwen Family Papers, box 3, folder 1, American Antiquarian Society.

69. For a structuralist approach to translating Old Testament Hebrew, see Ruth apRoberts, "Old Testament Poetry: The Translatable Structure," *PMLA* 92 (October 1977): 987–1004. apRoberts uses as her major example Psalm 24, which Adams translated (*Poems*, 45–47), although she does not acknowledge his effort.

70. See Lemay, *A Calendar*.

71. John Dryden, "Preface to the Translation of Ovid's Epistles," in *Essays of John Dryden*, ed. W. P. Ker (1900; reprint, New York: Russell & Russell, 1926), 1:237–42.

72. Ibid., 1:239.

73. The translators explain their approach to the Holy Writ in the dedication of the Authorized Version to King James:

> For when Your Highness had once out of deep judgment apprehended how convenient it was, that out of the Original Sacred Tongues, together with comparing of the labours, both in our own, and other foreign Languages, of many worthy men who went before us, there should be one more exact Translation of the holy Scriptures into the *English Tongue*; Your Majesty did never desist to urge and to excite those to whom it was commended, that the work might be hastened, and that the business might be expedited in so decent a manner, as a matter of such importance might justly require. (par. 4)

74. *The Oxford English Dictionary* records "gelle" and "gellie" as obsolete forms of "jelly." Adams uses "gellies" in the sense of definition 2b of "jelly": "Applied to the alga *Nostoc*, which appears as a jelly-like mass on dry soil after rain, and was popularly supposed to be the remains of a fallen 'star' or meteor." The dictionary gives several examples of the word used in this sense, including one from around the time Adams published his translation of Psalm 148. It quotes William Somerville (1740), "Like that falling Meteor, there she lies, A jelly cold on Earth."

75. Adams uses "serene" in the sense of "a light fall of moisture or fine rain after sunset in hot countries" (*The Oxford English Dictionary*).

76. A poet other than Matthew Adams knew about John Adams's translation of Canticles. In a 1745 newspaper advertisement, Matthew Adams notes that his nephew's translation of Canticles is missing, a fact Nathaniel Gardner Jr., writing as Philo-Muses, laments a few months later when introducing his own translation of part of Canticles in another newspaper.

John Adams's fragment is published as "The Perfection of Beauty. From Cant. 5. 9,—ult.," in Adams's *Poems*, 6–9. Matthew Adams's advertisement, which appears in *The Boston News-Letter* (12 December 1745), reads as follows:

> LOST out of the House of Mr. *Matthew Adams* at the Town Dock, about seven Years ago, a Manuscript, written by the late Rev. *John Adams*: being a Translation of the whole *Book of Canticles*, which he wrote to rescue that Author of the *Fair Circasion* [Samuel Croxall]. It is in heroick Verse; and thought to be one of the best Translations of that Song of Songs that's in the English Language, and is a great Loss to the Public. Whosoever therefore will bring the said Manuscript, or a true Copy thereof, to the Printer [John Draper], shall have *Ten Pounds* Reward, and no Questions ask'd. (2)

Ironically, on the same page as Matthew Adams's advertisement appears a call for settling the accounts of the late Rev. Mr. Nathaniel Clap of Newport. Philo-Muses's statement is in *The Boston Gazette*, 11 March 1746, 1. David S. Shields identifies Nathaniel Gardner Jr. as Philo-Muses in "Nathaniel Gardner, Jr., and the Literary Culture of Boston in the 1750s," *Early American Literature* 24 (1989): 196–216.

77. David S. Shields, "The Religious Sublime," 240.

78. Eugene A. Nida, "Principles of Translation as Exemplified by Bible Translating," in *On Translation*, ed. Reuben A. Brower, Vol. 23 of Harvard Studies in Comparative Literature (Cambridge: Harvard University Press, 1959), 12.

79. Meyer Reinhold, *The Classick Pages: Classical Reading of Eighteenth-Century Americans* (University Park, PA: American Philological Association, 1975), 70.

80. See Lemay, *A Calendar*, 12, item 61.

81. I am indebted to Ward W. Briggs Jr. for information about Latin meter and Horace. For English translations of the odes in Horatian meters, see Horace, *The Odes of Quintus Horatius Flaccus*, trans. Justin Loomis Van Gundy (Monmouth, IL: Monmouth College, 1936); and *Translating Horace: Thirty Odes Translated into the Original Metres*, trans. J. B. Leishman (Oxford: Bruno Cassirer, 1956).

82. Horace, *Q. Horati Flacci Opera*, ed. Fridericvs Klingner (Leipzig: Teubner, 1970), 6–7.

83. Horace, *The Odes and Epodes of Horace, Translated Literally and Rhythmically*, trans. W[illiam] Sewell (London: Bohn, 1850), 6–7.

84. Horace, *The Odes, Epodes, and Carmen Seculare of Horace, In Latin and English*, trans. Philip Francis (Dublin: S[tephen] Powell for T[homas] Moore, 1742), 1:6–7.

85. Paul Hammond, "Figures of Horace in Dryden's Literary Criticism," in

Horace Made New: Horatian Influences on British Writing from the Renaissance to the Twentieth Century, ed. Charles Martindale and David Hopkins (Cambridge: Cambridge University Press, 1993), 147.

86. For a discussion of Woodmason, see Claude E. Jones, "Charles Woodmason as a Poet," *South Carolina Historical Magazine* 59 (October 1958): 189–94. Jones reproduces Woodmason's imitation of the fourth ode of Horace's first book (191).

87. In the advertisement to his own imitation of *Ars Poetica*, Oldham explains his approach to translating Horace:

> *Wherefore, being prevail'd upon to make an Essay, I fell to thinking of some course, whereby I might serve my self of the Advantages, which those, that went before me, have either not minded, or scrupulously abridg'd themselves of. This I soon imagin'd was to be effected by putting* Horace *into a more modern dress, than hitherto he has appear'd in, that is, by making him speak, as if he were living, and writing now. I therefore resolv'd to alter the Scene from* Rome *to* London, *and to make use of* English *names of Men, Places, and Customs, where the Parallel would decently permit, which I conceiv'd would give a kind of new Air to the Poem, and render it more agreeable to the relish of the present Age. . . . I have not, I acknowledg, been over-nice in keeping to the words of the Original, for that were to transgress a Rule therein contained. Nevertheless I have been religiously strict to its sence, and exprest it in as plain, and intelligible a manner, as the Subject would bear. Where I may be thought to have varied from it (which is not above once or twice, and in Passages not much material) the skilful Reader will perceive 'twas necessary for carrying on my propos'd design, and the Author himself, were he again alive, would (I believe) forgive me.*

See John Oldham, Advertisement to *Some New Pieces Never before Publisht* (London: M[ary] C[lark] for Jo[seph] Hindmarsh, 1681), i–ii. Poet C. H. Sisson reflects one of Oldham's opinions: "But the temptation is always there, for the poet who is as deeply concerned with his own art as with Horace's, to substitute local or contemporary references for those of the Latin" (C. H. Sisson, "Deniable Evidence: Translating Horace," in *Horace Made New: Horatian Influences on British Writing from the Renaissance to the Twentieth Century*, ed. Charles Martindale and David Hopkins [Cambridge: Cambridge University Press, 1993], 260).

88. John Dryden, "To the Memory of Mr. Oldham," in *Remains of Mr. John Oldham in Verse and Prose* (London: Jo[seph] Hindmarsh, 1684), v.

89. Harold Williams, the editor of Swift's poems, presents Swift's 1735 comments on these lines (lines 61–63):

> These three last lines were intended against that licentious Manner of modern Poets, in making three Rhimes together, which they call *Triplets*; and the last of the three, was two or sometimes more Syllables longer, called an *Alexandrian*. These *Triplets* and *Alexandrians* were brought in by DRYDEN, and other Poets in the Reign of CHARLES II. They were the mere Effect of Haste, Idleness, and want of Money; and have been wholly avoided by the best Poets, since these Verses were written.

(Swift, "A Description of a City Shower," in *The Poems of Jonathan Swift*, ed. Harold Williams [Oxford: Clarendon Press, 1937], 1:139–40.)

90. Pope, *An Essay on Criticism*, 280, ll. 356–57.

91. Knapp, *Biographical Sketches*, 145.

CHAPTER 3

1. Before the 1720s, *The Boston News-Letter* published one poem, four lines in Latin about the burning of the seminary at Quebeck (24 December 1705, 2). Samuel Sewall composed these lines, which constitute the first poem to have been published in an American newspaper.

2. See Sidney Kobre, *The Development of the Colonial Newspaper* (Pittsburgh: Colonial Press, 1944), 18–29; and David A. Copeland, *Colonial American Newspapers: Character and Content* (Newark: University of Delaware Press; London: Associated University Presses, 1997), 288–89.

3. Charles E. Clark, *The Public Prints*, 142.

4. Cotton Mather, *Manuductio ad Ministerium*, 46.

5. In *Specimens of Newspaper Literature*, Buckingham prints all but the last sentence of Proteus Echo number 1 (1:91–95); all except the first paragraph of number 2 (1:95–98); the seventh (less the first sentence), eighth, and ninth paragraphs of number 3 (1:98–99); the fifth and sixth paragraphs and the poem from number 31 (1:101–4); and snippets from a few other selections.

6. Cook, *Literary Influences*, 32.

7. See Charles E. Clark, *The Public Prints*, 144–46. Several Proteus Echo essays mention *The Spectator*. See, for example, the second sentence of number 25 (25 September 1727), written by John Adams.

8. Charles E. Clark, *The Public Prints*, 151–52.

9. See *Proteus Echo (1727–28)*, ed. Bruce Granger (Delmar, NY: Scholars' Facsimiles & Reprints, 1986); and Bruce Granger, *American Essay Serials from Franklin to Irving* (Knoxville: University of Tennessee Press, 1978), 25–40.

10. Charles E. Clark, *The Public Prints*, 145.

11. All quotations from Proteus Echo are from *The New-England Weekly Journal.* I cite dates and page numbers in my text.

12. Despite Byles's involvement with *The New-England Weekly Journal*, it was initially Kneeland's enterprise. Upon taking Timothy Green II as partner in 1726, Kneeland became less involved in its printing and publishing (Charles E. Clark, *The Public Prints*, 144). Kneeland and Green published Byles's *Poems on Several Occasions* in 1744.

13. Will Honeycomb is introduced in the second number of *The Spectator* (2 March 1710/11).

14. Writing in 1912, long before C. Lennart Carlson provided the key for identifying the authors of Proteus Echo, Elizabeth Christine Cook, following the logic of another scholar, Delano Goddard, argues that the two divines were Mather Byles and Thomas Prince (Cook, *Literary Influences*, 44–45).

15. I am aware that American authors of the early eighteenth century did not rely on writing for their livelihood.

16. No evidence suggests that Adams's sole publication to this time, his

translation of an Horatian ode in *The New-England Courant* (23–30 April 1726), had been received unfavorably, or received at all.

17. The essay appears in Perry Miller and Thomas H. Johnson, eds., *The Puritans* (1938; revised, New York: Harper, 1963), 2:689–94. The editors imply, incorrectly, that Byles's essay originally appeared in *The American Magazine* (1745): 1–4. It was published first in *The New-England Weekly Journal* (24 April 1727): 1–2. Paul Giles accepts their dating. See Paul Giles, *Transatlantic Insurrections: British Culture and the Formation of American Literature, 1730–1860* (Philadelphia: University of Pennsylvania Press, 2001), 36–37.

18. In the twenty-ninth Proteus Echo (23 October 1727), Adams, writing as X., describes grubstreet style as "slovenly, dull, and grovelling" (1).

19. Edward "Ned" Ward, noted for his grubstreet style, wrote *The London Spy* (1698–1700) in eighteen monthly numbers published in folio pamphlets. For information about Ward, see Howard W. Troyer, *Ned Ward of Grubstreet: A Study of Sub-Literary London in the Eighteenth Century* (Cambridge: Harvard University Press, 1946), 29–60, 247–52.

20. Miller and Johnson, *The Puritans*, 2:684.

21. Increase Mather, *An Arrow against Dancing. Drawn out of the Quiver of the Scriptures* (Boston: Samuel Green, 1684), 1–2, 30. See Carl Bridenbaugh, *Cities in the Wilderness: The First Century of Urban Life in America, 1625–1742* (London: Oxford University Press, 1938), 277.

22. Sewall, *Diary*, 2:956–68.

23. This twenty-first Proteus Echo essay was published twenty-three days after Adams arrived in Newport from Boston. Although the date he wrote it cannot be determined, in focusing on priggish clergy he could refer obliquely to Nathaniel Clap, whose theological stubbornness alienated his Newport congregation. Had Clap been more sociable (concerned with the temporal well-being of his flock) and less doctrinaire, his people might have remained content with him, thus avoiding the schism that led to Adams's presence in the city. See Pope, *An Essay on Criticism*, 317, l. 690.

24. Adams might recently have read *The Spectator* number 253, in which Addison uses Bavius's and Mævius's treatment of Virgil to illustrate the negative effects of envy. Jonathan Swift, who wrote for *The Tatler*, was involved with *The Examiner*.

25. The technique of using fictional missives in periodical essays did not originate with the contributors to Proteus Echo. It was by 1727 a staple in British literary periodicals, as may be seen in many issues of *The Spectator* such as number 53 (1 May 1711). Benjamin Franklin uses this technique in the Dogood essays.

26. Virgil, *The Aeneid*, trans. Robert Fitzgerald (New York: Random House, 1983), 174.

27. Adams's indebtedness to British periodicals may also be gleaned from his use of epigrams at the beginning of his essays. Some of them duplicate epigrams used in *The Spectator*, for example. Among them:

> *"Spectatum admissi risum teneatis?"* Horace
> [Admitted to the sight, would you not laugh?]
>
> Proteus Echo   *The Spectator*
> Number 10 (12 June 1727)   Number 5 (6 March 1711)

"*Jovis omnia plena.*"   Virgil
[All things are full of Jove]
    Proteus Echo   *The Spectator*
    Number 16 (24 July 1727)   Number 121 (17 July 1711)

"*Di bene facerunt, inopis me quodque pusilli*
Finærunt animi, raro et perpauca loquentis."   Horace
[Thank heaven, that made me of an humble mind;
To action little, less to words inclined!]
    Proteus Echo   *The Spectator*
    Number 23 (11 September   Number 19 (22 March 1711)
    1727)

English translations are from *The Spectator*, ed. George A. Aitken (London: Routledge; New York: Dutton, n.d.), 6:404, 415, 405.

28. Clarissa objects to the inelegant language narrator A. uses about a woman in Proteus Echo number 11 (19 June 1727), which was written by Mather Byles. A. states that the woman, pursued by a submissive man, "*beat him out of Doors with a Broomstick.*" Clarissa would have preferred a more delicate rendering of this scene, such as, she "*Patted him from her Presence with her Fan*" (1). The four male writers represented in Proteus Echo number 15 have first and last names; the sole woman writer, Clarissa, has but one. This might suggest the relative status of and respect for women during Adams's time.

29. *Proteus Echo*, 5 n. 1.

30. Granger also fails to record the letters T., at the conclusion of Proteus Echo numbers 12 (26 June 1727) and 27 (9 October 1727); C., at the end of number 24 (18 September 1727); and M., at the conclusion of number 45 (12 February 1727/28).

31. The poem eulogizes Elizabeth Perry Mascarene, who died on 2 January 1727/28. As a member of the English army, her husband, the French-born Paul Mascarene, was important in Annapolis Royal, Nova Scotia, for defending, before the composition of the poem, the fort against attacks by the French and Indians. Because the family of John Adams lived in Annapolis Royal, he and Matthew Adams could have known the Mascarenes. The Mascarenes also maintained a residence in Boston, Elizabeth's home, where they could have been friendly with any or all of the three contributors to Proteus Echo. See Peter Landry, "Early Acadians & Nova Scotians: 1700–1763," http://www.blupete.com/Hist/BiosNS/1700–63/Mascarene.htm; and Lemay, *A Calendar*, 15–16, items 81–82, 85.

32. Proteus Echo essays appear in the following numbers of *The Boston Magazine*: November 1783, 8 (part of Proteus Echo 3); December 1783, 49–51 (another part of Proteus Echo 3); February 1784, 140–43 (Proteus Echo 11 and 48); and March 1784, 183–85 (Proteus Echo 41).

33. Lyon N. Richardson, *A History of Early American Magazines, 1741–1789* (1931; reprint, New York: Octagon, 1966), 217. I am grateful to Jennifer Tolpa of the Massachusetts Historical Society for verifying Freeman's notations in *The Boston Magazine*.

34. See Richardson, 212; Shipton, *Sibley's Harvard Graduates* 16:81, where

Shipton attributes "Useful Inventions for Barren Writers" to Parker; and Arthur W. H. Eaton, *The Famous Mather Byles, the Noted Boston Tory, Preacher, Poet, and Wit, 1707–1788* (Boston: Butterfield, 1914), 202.

35. Richardson, *History of Early American Magazines*, 212–13. Norman and White appointed the editorial board following the publication of the first number of *The Boston Magazine* in October 1783. Members of the board first met on 25 November and therefore needed to act quickly to find contents for the second issue. Disregarding the number of October 1783, Norman and White began numbering the magazine with the issue of November.

36. I am grateful to Russell L. Martin III for confirming the letter O. in a copy of *The New-England Weekly Journal* at the American Antiquarian Society.

37. *The Emerald, (New Establishment) or Miscellany of Literature; Containing Sketches of the Manners, Morals, and Amusements of the Age.* In 1806 *The Emerald* succeeded *The Boston Magazine*, which in 1805 succeeded *The Boston Weekly Magazine*, which had begun publication in 1802. (This *Boston Magazine* is different from the periodical of the same title that published numbers of Proteus Echo in 1783 and 1784.) Greenleaf always ran Proteus Echo on the first page under the heading "Essays of the Last Century, by Proteus Echo," except for the first number, which appears under "Essays, by Proteus Echo." He numbered his Proteus Echo essays consecutively, without concern for the original numbering. They appear in the following issues of the third volume of *The Emerald* (Greenleaf styles it the first volume, as if the magazine began with his ownership):

Proteus Echo 1807–08	1727–28	"Emerald" Issue	Date	Pages
1	1	9	19 Dec. 1807	97–99
2	2	11	2 Jan. 1808	121–24
3	34	16	6 Feb. 1808	181–84
4	4	17	13 Feb. 1808	193–95
5	8	21	12 Mar. 1808	241–43
6	18	23	26 Mar. 1808	265–68
7	23	24	2 Apr. 1808	277–79
8	39	25	9 Apr. 1808	289–92
9	11	28	30 Apr. 1808	325–27
10	29	29	7 May 1808	337–40
11	26	32	28 May 1808	373–75
12	12	33	4 June 1808	385–87
13	21	36	25 June 1808	421–23
14	46	38	9 July 1808	445–47
15	41	40	23 July 1808	469–72
16	31	43	13 Aug. 1808	505–8
17	47	45	27 Aug. 1808	529–32
18	17	46	3 Sep. 1808	541–45
19	30	47	10 Sep. 1808	553–56
20	25	49	24 Sep. 1808	577–79
21	32	51	8 Oct. 1808	601–4
22	37	52	15 Oct. 1808	613–16

38. Greenleaf's undated "Prospectus of the Emerald" appears in four unnumbered pages prefatory to the third volume of *The Emerald* (1808).

39. Buckingham, *Specimens of Newspaper Literature*, 1:100.

40. Norman S. Grabo, "The Journalist as Man of Letters," in *Reappraising Benjamin Franklin: A Bicentennial Perspective*, ed. J. A. Leo Lemay (Newark: University of Delaware Press; London: Associated University Presses, 1992), 33.

Bibliography

A. "Remarks on the Poetical Character of the Rev. John Adams, A.M." *The Massachusetts Magazine* 1 (April 1789): 232–35.

Adams, John. *Jesus Christ an Example to His Ministers. A Sermon Preach'd on the Day of His Ordination.* Newport: J[ames] Franklin; Boston: T[homas] Fleet, 1728. Evans 2982.

———. *Poems on Several Occasions, Original and Translated.* Boston: D[aniel] Gookin, 1745. Evans 5527.

Adams, Oscar Fay. *A Dictionary of American Authors.* 1904. Reprint, Detroit: Gale Research, 1969.

Alden, Timothy. *A Collection of Epitaphs and Inscriptions with Occasional Notes.* Vol. 4. New York: n.p., 1814.

American Colonial Writers, 1606–1734. Edited by Emory Elliott. Vol. 24 of Dictionary of Literary Biography. Detroit: Bruccoli Clark/Gale Research, 1984.

apRoberts, Ruth. "Old Testament Poetry: The Translatable Structure." *PMLA* 92 (October 1977): 987–1004.

"Articles of the Society for Promoting Virtue and Knowledge, by a Free Conversation." *Newport Historical Magazine* 4 (October 1883): 67–71.

Baxter, Joseph, et al. Preface to *Jesus Christ an Example to His Ministers. A Sermon Preach'd on the Day of His Ordination,* by John Adams. Newport: J[ames] Franklin; Boston: T[homas] Fleet, 1728. Evans 2982.

Bayles, Richard M., ed. *History of Newport County, Rhode Island. From the Year 1638 to the Year 1887, Including the Settlement of Its Towns and Their Subsequent Progress.* New York: Preston, 1888.

Bradstreet, Anne. "The Prologue." In *The Complete Works of Anne Bradstreet.* Edited by Joseph R. McElrath Jr. and Allan P. Robb. Boston: Twayne, 1981.

Brebner, John Bartlet. *New England's Outpost: Acadia before the Conquest of Canada.* New York: Columbia University Press; London: King, 1927.

Bridenbaugh, Carl. *Cities in the Wilderness: The First Century of Urban Life in America, 1625–1742.* London: Oxford University Press, 1938.

Bryan, Kreg H. "Nathaniel Clap: Rhode Island's Last Puritan." *New England Reformed Journal* 6 (Winter 1998): 13–36.

Buckingham, Joseph T. *Specimens of Newspaper Literature: With Personal Memoirs, Anecdotes, and Reminiscences.* Vol. 1. Boston: Charles C. Little and James Brown, 1850.

Byles, Mather. *Poems on Several Occasions.* Boston: S[amuel] Kneeland and T[imothy] Green, 1744. Evans 5355.

————. "To the Memory of a Young Commander Slain in a Battle with the Indians, 1724." In *Poems on Several Occasions*, by Mather Byles. Boston: S[amuel] Kneeland and T[imothy] Green, 1744. Evans 5355.

[Byles, Mather, et al.] *A Collection of Poems*, by Several Hands. Boston: B[artholomew] Green[, Jr.] for D[aniel] Gookin, 1744. Evans 5365.

Bynner, Edwin L. "Topography and Landmarks of the Provincial Period." In *The Memorial History of Boston, Including Suffolk County, Massachusetts. 1630–1880*. Edited by Justin Winsor. Vol. 2. Boston: Osgood, 1881.

Callender, John. *A Discourse Occasioned by the Death of the Reverend Mr. Nathaniel Clap, Pastor of a Church at Newport on Rhode-Island, on October 30 1745. in the 78th Year of His Age*. Newport: Widow Franklin, 1746. Evans 5751.

Calvin, John. *Institutes of the Christian Religion*. Edited by John T. McNeill. Translated by Ford Lewis Battles. Vol. 2. Philadelphia: Westminster Press, 1960.

The Cambridge History of American Literature (1590–1820). Edited by Sacvan Bercovitch. Vol. 1. Cambridge: Cambridge University Press, 1994.

Carlson, C. Lennart. "John Adams, Matthew Adams, Mather Byles, and the *New England Weekly Journal*." *American Literature* 12 (1940): 347–48.

Catalogus Librorum Bibliothecæ Collegij Harvardini Quod Est Cantabrigiæ in Nova Anglia. Boston: B[artholomew] Green, 1723. Evans 2432.

Clap, Nathaniel. Preface to *Parents and Children Advised and Exhorted to Their Duty. Part of a Sermon, Preached at Newport on Rhode-Island, September 28. 1729*, by Benjamin Bass. Newport: n.p., 1730. Evans 3250.

Clark, Charles E. *The Public Prints: The Newspaper in Anglo-American Culture, 1665–1740*. New York: Oxford University Press, 1994.

Clark, Michael P. "The Persistence of Literature in Early American Studies." *William and Mary Quarterly*. 3d series. 57 (2000): 641–46.

Colman, Benjamin. *Reliquiæ Turellæ, et Lachrymæ Paternæ. The Father's Tears over His Daughter's Remains. Two Sermons Preach'd at Medford, April 6. 1735*. Boston: S[amuel] Kneeland and T[imothy] Green for J[oseph] Edwards and H[opestill] Foster, 1735. Evans 3888.

Columbia Literary History of the United States. Edited by Emory Elliott. New York: Columbia University Press, 1988.

Comer, John. "The Diary of John Comer." Edited by C. Edwin Barrows and James W. Willmarth. Vol. 8 of *Collections of the Rhode Island Historical Society*. N.p.: Published for the Society, 1893.

Cook, Elizabeth Christine. *Literary Influences in Colonial Newspapers, 1704–1750*. 1912. Reprint, Port Washington, NY: Kennikat Press, 1966.

Copeland, David A. *Colonial American Newspapers: Character and Content*. Newark: University of Delaware Press; London: Associated University Presses, 1997.

Davis, Thomas M., and Virginia L. Davis, eds. *Edward Taylor vs. Solomon Stoddard: The Nature of the Lord's Supper*. Vol. 2 of the Unpublished Writings of Edward Taylor. Boston: Twayne, 1981.

"Descendants of Matthew Adams." *The New-England Historical and Genealogical Register* 10 (January 1856): 89–91.

Douglass, William. *A Summary, Historical and Political, of the First Planting, Progressive Improvements, and Present State of the British Settlements in North-America.* Vol. 2. Boston: Daniel Fowle, 1751. Evans 6663.

Drake, Francis S. *Dictionary of American Biography, Including Men of the Time.* 1872. Reprint, Detroit: Gale Research, 1974.

Dryden, John. *Fables Ancient and Modern.* London: Jacob Tonson, 1700. Wing D2278.

———. "Preface to the Translation of Ovid's Epistles." In *Essays of John Dryden.* Edited by W. P. Ker. Vol. 1. 1900. Reprint, New York: Russell & Russell, 1926.

———. "To the Memory of Mr. Oldham." In *Remains of Mr. John Oldham in Verse and Prose.* London: Jo[seph] Hindmarsh, 1684. Wing O240.

Dudley, Paul. "Diary of Paul Dudley, 1740." *The New-England Historical and Genealogical Register* 35 (1881): 28–31.

Duyckinck, Evert A., and George L. Duyckinck. *Cyclopædia of American Literature.* Vol. 1. New York: Scribner, 1855.

E., C. B. "Notes on the Hon. John Adams of Nova Scotia and Boston." *New-England Historical and Genealogical Register* 32 (April 1878): 132–33.

Eaton, Arthur W. H. *The Famous Mather Byles, the Noted Boston Tory, Preacher, Poet, and Wit, 1707–1788.* Boston: Butterfield, 1914.

Edward Taylor vs. Solomon Stoddard: The Nature of the Lord's Supper. Vol. 2 of the Unpublished Writings of Edward Taylor. Edited by Thomas M. Davis and Virginia L. Davis. Boston: Twayne, 1981.

Eliot, John. *A Biographical Dictionary, Containing a Brief Account of the First Settlers, and Other Eminent Characters among the Magistrates, Ministers, Literary and Worthy Men, in New-England.* Salem: Cushing and Appleton; Boston: Oliver, 1809.

"Facilities for Traveling between Boston and Newport in 1720." In *The Newport Historical Magazine* 4 (January 1884): 179.

Ford, Worthington Chauncey. "Franklin's New England Courant." *Proceedings of the Massachusetts Historical Society* 57 (February–April 1924): 336–53.

Foxcroft, Thomas. *Ministers, Spiritual Parents, or Fathers in the Church of God. A Sermon Preach'd at the Ordination of the Rev. Mr. John Lowell, at Newbury, Jan. 19. 1725, 6.* Boston: B[artholmew] Green for Samuel Gerrish, 1726. Evans 2744.

Franklin, Benjamin. *The Autobiography of Benjamin Franklin.* Edited by Leonard W. Labaree, et al. New Haven: Yale University Press, 1964.

———. *Writings.* New York: Library of America, 1987.

Giles, Paul. *Transatlantic Insurrections: British Culture and the Formation of American Literature, 1730–1860.* Philadelphia: University of Pennsylvania Press, 2001.

Grabo, Norman S. *Edward Taylor.* 1961. Rev. ed. Boston: Twayne, 1988.

———. "The Journalist as Man of Letters." In *Reappraising Benjamin Frank-*

lin: A Bicentennial Perspective. Edited by J. A. Leo Lemay. Newark: University of Delaware Press; London: Associated University Presses, 1992.

Granger, Bruce. *American Essay Serials from Franklin to Irving.* Knoxville: University of Tennessee Press, 1978.

Gura, Philip F. "Early American Literature at the New Century." *William and Mary Quarterly.* 3d series. 57 (2000): 599–620.

Hall, David D. *The Faithful Shepherd: A History of the New England Ministry in the Seventeenth Century.* Williamsburg: Institute of Early American History and Culture; Chapel Hill: University of North Carolina Press, 1972.

Hammond, Jeffrey A. "The Puritan Elegaic Ritual: From Sinful Silence to Apostolic Voice." *Studies in Puritan American Spirituality* 2 (1991): 77–98.

Hammond, Paul. "Figures of Horace in Dryden's Literary Criticism." In *Horace Made New: Horatian Influences on British Writing from the Renaissance to the Twentieth Century.* Edited by Charles Martindale and David Hopkins. Cambridge: Cambridge University Press, 1993.

"History of Church Music in America from the Colonial Period to the 21st Century." http://personal.lig.bellsouth.net/lig/m/u/musicedu/amhistry.htm#colonial.

Holman, Richard B. "William Burgis." In *Boston Prints and Printmakers, 1670–1775.* Vol. 46 of Publications of the Colonial Society of Massachusetts. Boston: Colonial Society of Massachusetts, 1973.

Horace. *The Odes, Epodes, and Carmen Seculare of Horace, In Latin and English.* Translated by Philip Francis. Vol. 1. Dublin: S[tephen] Powell for T[homas] Moore, 1742.

———. *The Odes and Epodes of Horace, Translated Literally and Rhythmically.* Translated by W[illiam] Sewell. London: Bohn, 1850.

———. *The Odes of Quintus Horatius Flaccus.* Translated by Justin Loomis Van Gundy. Monmouth, IL: Monmouth College, 1936.

———. *Q. Horati Flacci Opera.* Edited by Fridericvs Klingner. Leipzig: Teubner, 1970.

———. *Translating Horace: Thirty Odes Translated into the Original Metres.* Translated by J. B. Leishman. Oxford: Bruno Cassirer, 1956.

Hornberger, Theodore. "The English Colonies, 1588–1765." In *The Literature of the United States: An Anthology and a History.* Edited by Walter Blair, et al. Vol. 1. Chicago: Scott Foresman, 1946.

Hutchinson, Thomas. *The History of the Province of Massachusets-Bay, From the Charter of King William and Queen Mary, in 1691, Until the Year 1750.* Boston: Thomas and John Fleet, 1767. Evans 10658.

The Interpreter's Bible. Edited by George A. Buttrick, et al. 12 vols. New York: Abingdon Press, 1952–57.

James, Sydney V. *Colonial Rhode Island: A History.* New York: Scribner's, 1975.

Johnson, Samuel. *Lives of the English Poets* (1779–81). Vol. 2. 1905. Reprint, New York: Octagon, 1967.

Jones, Claude E. "Charles Woodmason as a Poet." *South Carolina Historical Magazine* 59 (October 1958): 189–94.

Kettell, Samuel. *Specimens of American Poetry, with Critical and Biographical Notices.* Vol. 1. Boston: Goodrich, 1829.

Knapp, Samuel L. *Biographical Sketches of Eminent Lawyers, Statesmen, and Men of Letters.* Boston: Richardson and Lord, 1821.

Kobre, Sidney. *The Development of the Colonial Newspaper.* Pittsburgh: Colonial Press, 1944.

Kroeger, Karl. "William Billings and the Puritan Musical Ideal." *Studies in Puritan American Spirituality* 2 (1991): 31–50.

Kunitz, Stanley J., and Howard Haycraft, eds. *American Authors, 1600–1900: A Biographical Dictionary of American Literature.* New York: H. W. Wilson, 1938.

Landry, Peter. "Early Acadians & Nova Scotians: 1700–1763." http://www.blupete.com/Hist/BiosNS/1700-63/Mascarene.htm.

Leach, Josiah Granville. *Some Account of Capt. John Frazier and His Descendants, with Notes on the West and Checkley Families.* Philadelphia: Lippincott, 1910.

Lemay, J. A. Leo. *A Calendar of American Poetry in the Colonial Newspapers and Magazines and in the Major English Magazines through 1765.* Worcester: American Antiquarian Society, 1972.

A Library of American Literature: From the Earliest Settlement to the Present Time. Edited by Edmund C. Stedman and Ellen M. Hutchinson. Vol. 2. New York: Charles L. Webster, 1890.

Locke, John. *The Correspondence of John Locke.* Oxford: Clarendon Press, 1981.

Mason, George Champlin. *Annals of the Redwood Library and Athenæum, Newport, R. I.* Newport: Redwood Library, 1891.

Mather, Cotton. *The Christian Philosopher.* Edited by Winton U. Solberg. 1721. Urbana: University of Illinois Press, 1994.

———. *The Diary of Cotton Mather, 1709–1724.* New York: Frederick Ungar, [1957].

———. *Manuductio ad Ministerium. Directions for a Candidate of the Ministry.* Boston: Thomas Hancock, 1726. Evans 2772.

———. *Selected Letters of Cotton Mather.* Edited by Kenneth Silverman. Baton Rouge: Louisiana State University Press, 1971.

[———]. *The Temple Opening. A Particular Church Considered as a Temple of the Lord. In a Sermon Preached on a a [sic] Day, When Such a Church Was Gathered, and a Pastor to It Ordained.* Boston: B[artholomew] Green for S[amuel] Phillips, 1709. Evans 1408.

———. "The Tragedy of Green-Island, and the Memorable End of Captain Josiah Winslow." In *Edulcorator. A Brief Essay on the Waters of Marah Sweetened. With a Remarkable Relation of the Deporable [sic] Occasion Afforded for It, in the Præmature Death of Captain Josiah Winslow, Who [with Several of His Company] Sacrificed His Life, in the Service of His Country;*

Engaging an Army of Indians, May 1. 1724, by Cotton Mather. Boston: B[artholomew] Green, 1725. Evans 2668.

[————]. *Useful Remarks. An Essay upon Remarkables in the Way of Wicked Men. A Sermon on the Tragical End, unto Which the Way of Twenty-Six Pirates Brought Them; at New Port on Rhode-Island, July 19, 1723.* New-London: T[imothy] Green, 1723. Evans 2451.

[Mather, Increase.] *An Arrow against Dancing. Drawn out of the Quiver of the Scriptures.* Boston: Samuel Green, 1684. Evans 370.

————. *The Necessity of Reformation with the Expedients Subservient Thereunto, Asserted.* Boston: John Foster, 1679. Evans 263.

McDermott, Gerald R. *One Holy and Happy Society: The Public Theology of Jonathan Edwards.* University Park: Pennsylvania State University Press, 1992.

Meserole, Harrison T., ed. *American Poetry of the Seventeenth Century.* 1968 (as *Seventeenth-Century American Poetry*). Reprint, University Park: Pennsylvania State University Press, 1985.

Miller, Perry, and Thomas H. Johnson, eds. *The Puritans.* Vol. 2. 1938. Rev. ed. New York: Harper, 1963.

Moody, Barry M. "Adams, John." In *Dictionary of Canadian Biography.* Edited by George W. Brown, et al. Vol. 3. Toronto: University of Toronto Press, 1974.

Morison, Samuel Eliot. *Harvard College in the Seventeenth Century.* Cambridge: Harvard University Press, 1936.

————. *Three Centuries of Harvard, 1636–1936.* Cambridge: Belknap Press of Harvard University Press, 1936.

Mulford, Carla. "The Ineluctability of the Peoples' Stories." *William and Mary Quarterly.* 3d series. 57 (2000): 621–34.

Murdoch, Beamish. *A History of Nova-Scotia, or Acadie.* Halifax: James Barnes, 1865.

Music, David W. "Cotton Mather and Congregational Singing in Puritan New England." *Studies in Puritan American Spirituality* 2 (1991): 1–30.

The New Princeton Encyclopedia of Poetry and Poetics. Edited by Alex Preminger and T. V. F. Brogan. Princeton: Princeton University Press, 1993.

Nida, Eugene A. "Principles of Translation as Exemplified by Bible Translating." In *On Translation.* Edited by Reuben A. Brower. Harvard Studies in Comparative Literature 23. Cambridge: Harvard University Press, 1959.

[Oldham, John.] Advertisement. *Some New Pieces Never before Publisht.* London: M[ary] C[lark] for Jo[seph] Hindmarsh, 1681. Wing O248.

Osgood, Herbert L. *The American Colonies in the Eighteenth Century.* Vol. 3. New York: Columbia University Press, 1924.

Parkman, Ebenezer. "The Diary of Ebenezer Parkman, 1739–1744." Edited by Francis G. Walett. *Proceedings of the American Antiquarian Society* 72, pt. 1 (1962).

Pearce, Roy Harvey. *The Continuity of American Poetry.* Princeton: Princeton University Press, 1961.

Pinkham, Harold. "Massachusetts Engravers and Their Cities, 1722–1859." http://www.salem.mass.edu/sextant/v4n2/pinkham.html.

A Platform of Church Discipline Gathered out of the Word of God: and Agreed upon by the Elders: and Messengers of the Churches Assembled in the Synod at Cambridge in New England. Cambridge: S[amuel] G[reen], 1649. Evans 25.

Pope, Alexander. *The Dunciad.* In *Alexander Pope.* Edited by Pat Rogers. Oxford: Oxford University Press, 1993.

———. *An Essay on Criticism.* In *Pastoral Poetry and An Essay on Criticism.* Edited by E[mile] Audra and Aubrey Williams. Vol. 1 of The Twickenham Edition of the Poems of Alexander Pope. London: Methuen; New Haven: Yale University Press, 1961.

———. *Peri Bathous.* In *Alexander Pope.* Edited by Pat Rogers. Oxford: Oxford University Press, 1993.

Prince, Thomas. "Diary of the Rev. Thomas Prince, 1737." *Publications of the Colonial Society of Massachusetts: Transactions 1916–1917* (1918).

Propositions Concerning the Subject of Baptism and Consociation of Churches, Collected and Confirmed out of the Word of God, by a Synod of Elders and Messengers of the Churches in Massachusets-Colony in New-England. Cambridge: S[amuel] G[reen] for Hezekiah Usher, 1662. Evans 68.

Proteus Echo (1727–28). Edited by Bruce Granger. Delmar, NY: Scholars' Facsimiles & Reprints, 1986.

Raimo, John W. *Biographical Directory of American Colonial and Revolutionary Governors, 1607–1789.* Westport, CT: Meckler Books, 1980.

Rediker, Marcus. *Between the Devil and the Deep Blue Sea: Merchant Seamen, Pirates, and the Anglo-American Maritime World, 1700–1750.* Cambridge: Cambridge University Press, 1987.

Reinhold, Meyer. *The Classick Pages: Classical Reading of Eighteenth-Century Americans.* University Park, PA: American Philological Association, 1975.

A Report of the Record Commissioners of the City of Boston, Containing the Boston Records from 1729 to 1742. Boston: Rockwell and Churchill, 1885.

A Report of the Record Commissioners of the City of Boston, Containing the Records of Boston Selectmen, 1736 to 1742. Boston: Rockwell and Churchill, 1886.

Rhode Island Imprints, 1727–1800. Edited by John Eliot Alden. New York: Bibliographical Society of America/R. R. Bowker, 1949.

Richardson, Lyon N. *A History of Early American Magazines, 1741–1789.* 1931. Reprint, New York: Octagon, 1966.

Ruggles, Linda R. "The Regular Singing Controversy: The Case against Lining-Out." *The Early America Review* (Fall 1997). http://www.animus.net/~earlya/review/fall97/sing.html.

Savage, James. *A Genealogical Dictionary of the First Settlers of New England, Showing Three Generations of Those Who Came before May, 1692, on the Basis of Farmer's Register.* Vol. 1. Boston: Little Brown, 1860.

Selement, George. "Publication and the Puritan Minister." *William and Mary Quarterly* 37 (1980): 219–41.

Sewall, Samuel. *The Diary of Samuel Sewall, 1674–1729.* Edited by M. Halsey Thomas. Vol. 2. New York: Farrar, Straus and Giroux, 1973.

Seybolt, Robert Francis. *The Private Schools of Colonial Boston.* 1935. Reprint, Westport: Greenwood, 1970.

Shields, David S. *Civil Tongues & Polite Letters in British America.* Williamsburg: Institute of Early American History and Culture; Chapel Hill: University of North Carolina Press, 1997.

———. "Eighteenth-Century Literary Culture." In *The History of the Book in America: The Colonial Book in the Atlantic World.* Edited by Hugh Amory and David D. Hall. Vol. 1. Cambridge: American Antiquarian Society/Cambridge University Press, 2000.

———. "Joy and Dread among the Early Americanists." *William and Mary Quarterly.* 3d series. Vol. 57 (2000): 635–40.

———. "Nathaniel Gardner, Jr., and the Literary Culture of Boston in the 1750s." *Early American Literature* 24 (1989): 196–216.

———. "The Religious Sublime and New England Poets of the 1720s." *Early American Literature* 19 (Winter 1984/85): 231–48.

Shields, John C. "John Adams (1705–1740)." In *American Writers before 1800: A Biographical and Critical Dictionary.* Edited by James A. Levernier and Douglas R. Wilmes. Vol. 1. Westport, CT: Greenwood, 1983.

Shipton, Clifford K. *Sibley's Harvard Graduates.* Vols. 6 and 16. Boston: Massachusetts Historical Society, 1942, 1972.

Sisson, C. H. "Deniable Evidence: Translating Horace." In *Horace Made New: Horatian Influences on British Writing from the Renaissance to the Twentieth Century.* Edited by Charles Martindale and David Hopkins. Cambridge: Cambridge University Press, 1993.

Smith, Sydney. Review of Adam Seybert's *Statistical Annals of the United States of America. Edinburgh Review* (January 1820): 79.

Solomon, Harry M. *Sir Richard Blackmore.* Boston: Twayne, 1980.

The Spectator. Edited by George A. Aitken. Vol. 6. London: Routledge; New York: Dutton, n.d.

Sprague, William B. *Annals of the American Pulpit.* Vol. 1. New York: Robert Carter, 1859.

Stackpole, Everett S., and Winthrop S. Meserve. *History of the Town of Durham New Hampshire (Oyster River Plantation).* Vol. 2. N.p.: Published by Vote of the Town, [1913].

Stokes, I. N. Phelps, and Daniel C. Haskell. *American Historical Prints: Early Views of American Cities, Etc., from the Phelps Stokes and Other Collections.* New York: New York Public Library, 1932.

Swift, Jonathan. "A Description of a City Shower." In *The Poems of Jonathan Swift.* Edited by Harold Williams. Vol. 1. Oxford: Clarendon Press, 1937.

———. *The Prose Works of Jonathan Swift, D.D.* Edited by Temple Scott. Vol. 10. London: George Bell, 1902.

Taylor, Edward. "Extract of a Letter." In *Right Thoughts in Sad Hours, Representing the Comforts and the Duties of Good Men under All Their Afflictions; and Particularly, That One, the Untimely Death of Children*, by Cotton Mather. London: James Astwood, 1689. Wing M1147.

Thomas, M. Halsey, ed. *The Diary of Samuel Sewall, 1674–1729*. Vol. 2. New York: Farrar, Straus and Giroux, 1973.

Troyer, Howard W. *Ned Ward of Grubstreet: A Study of Sub-Literary London in the Eighteenth Century*. Cambridge: Harvard University Press, 1946.

Tucker, Samuel Marion. "The Beginnings of Verse, 1610–1808." In vol. 1 of *The Cambridge History of American Literature*. Edited by William Peterfield Trent, et al. New York: Putnam's; Cambridge: University Press, 1917.

Turell, Ebenezer. *The Life and Character of the Reverend Benjamin Colman, D. D. Late Pastor of a Church in Boston New-England. Who Deceased August 29th 1747*. Boston: Rogers and Fowle for J[oseph] Edwards, 1749. Evans 6434.

Turell, Jane Colman. *Memoirs of the Life and Death of the Pious and Ingenious Mrs. Jane Turell, Who Died at Medford, March 26th 1735. Ætat. 27*. Collected by Ebenezer Turell. London: John Oswald, 1741.

Turell, Jane Colman, and Martha Brewster. *Poems of Jane Turell and Martha Brewster*. Edited by Kenneth A. Requa. Delmar, NY: Scholars' Facsimiles & Reprints, 1979.

Tyler, Moses Coit. *A History of American Literature, 1676–1765*. Vol. 2. 1878. Reprint, Williamstown, MA: Corner House, 1973.

Virgil. *The Aeneid*. Translated by Robert Fitzgerald. New York: Random House, 1983.

Waggoner, Hyatt H. *American Poets, from the Puritans to the Present*. Boston: Houghton Mifflin, 1968.

Walker, Williston. *A History of the Congregational Churches in the United States*. New York: Scribner's, 1894.

Webb, John. *The Believer's Redemption by the Precious Blood of Christ: A Sermon Preach'd at Newport, on Rhode-Island: On Lord's Day, December 31. 1727*. Newport: J[ames] Franklin; Boston: T[homas] Fleet, 1728. Evans 3115.

Webster, Noah. Part 1 of *A Grammatical Institute, of the English Language, Comprising, an Easy, Concise, and Systematic Method of Education, Designed for the Use of English Schools in America*. Hartford: Hudson and Goodwin, 1783. Evans 18297.

Webster, Richard. *A History of the Presbyterian Church in America, from Its Origin until the Year 1760*. Philadelphia: Joseph M. Wilson, 1856.

Weis, Frederick Lewis. *The Colonial Clergy and the Colonial Churches of New England*. 1936. Reprint, Baltimore: Clearfield, 1977.

Whitehill, Walter Muir. *Boston: A Topographical History*. Cambridge: Belknap Press of Harvard University Press, 1959.

Wigglesworth, Michael. "A Prayer unto Christ the Judge of the World." In *The Poems of Michael Wigglesworth*. Edited by Ronald A. Bosco. Lanham, MD: University Press of America, 1989.

Winslow, Ola Elizabeth. *A Destroying Angel: The Conquest of Smallpox in Colonial Boston*. Boston: Houghton Mifflin, 1974.

Winthrop, John. *The Journal of John Winthrop, 1630–1649*. Edited by Richard S. Dunn, et al. Cambridge: Belknap Press of Harvard University Press, 1996.

Youngs, J. William T., Jr. *God's Messengers: Religious Leadership in Colonial New England, 1700–1750*. Baltimore: Johns Hopkins University Press, 1976.

Index

References to material in endnotes include page number, note number, and, in parentheses, the page in the text to which the note refers.

70, 94–95, 153; poetic influences on, 53, 57, 75; religious verse of, 54; as wit, 59. Works: *Collection of Poems*, 60–61, 68–69, 70, 144, 153; "An Essay on Flattery," 146; "Eternity," 140; "The God of Tempest," 144; *Poems on Several Occasions*, 94, 144, 145; Proteus Echo, #1: 125–27, 145, 147, 149; —, #3: 130–31, 134, 145–47, 148; —, #6: 140, 145, 147, 150; —, #9: 140, 145, 147; —, #11: 145–47, 149; —, #14: 145, 147; —, #17: 145, 147, 149; —, #20: 145, 147; —, #22: 145, 147, 150; —, #24: 145, 147; —, #30: 145, 147, 149; —, #31: 124, 144, 145–46, 147, 149; —, #33: 144, 145–46, 147; —, #34: 145, 147, 149; —, #37: 145, 147, 149; —, #41: 145–47, 149, 150; —, #44: 145, 147; —, #48: 145–47, 150; —, #52: 126, 145, 147; "To My Friend," 140; "Useful Inventions for Barren Writers," 146; "Verses Written in Milton's *Paradise Lost*," 94
Byles, Mather, Jr., 146

Caesar, 137
Callender, John: *A Discourse Occasioned by the Death of the Reverend Mr. Nathaniel Clap, Pastor of a Church at Newport on Rhode-Island, on October 30 1745. in the 78th Year of His Age*, 163 n. 81
Calvin, John, 27, 53
Cambridge, Massachusetts, 19, 21, 22, 25, 26
Cambridge History of American Literature, The (Bercovitch), 60
Cambridge Platform. See *A Platform of Church Discipline*
Campbell, John, 20
Canada, 24
Carlson, C. Lennart, 59, 144, 147
Cary, James, 30
Cassius, 137
Champney, Joseph, 23
"Charge" (Baxter), 40–41
charity (love), 37, 44, 63–64
"Charity. Being a Paraphrase on the

13th Chapter of the 1st of Corinthians," 62–64
Charleston, South Carolina, 113
Chaucer, Geoffrey, 54
Chauncy, Charles, 23, 31
Checkley, Anthony, 23
China, 126
Chronological History of New England in the Form of Annals (Thomas Prince), 25
Church, Benjamin, 56
Church, Thomas, 31
Church of England (Anglicans), 22, 23
Clap, Nathaniel: agrees with Mathers and Edward Taylor about Holy Communion, 52; arrives in Newport, 27; assisted by Bass, 29; assisted by John Adams, 25, 29; birth of, 27; and church councilors, 30–37, 43, 47, 159 n. 17 (27); correspondence with John Adams, 32, 41–48; and Cotton Mather, 52, 83; disserves Christ, 38; dispute with John Adams, 13, 27–52, 83, 152; Eells preaches from the pulpit of, 32; envy of John Adams, possible, 137; envied by John Adams, possibly, 137; establishes First Congregational Church, 27, 51; eulogy of, by Callender, 163 n. 81 (51); fails to bring people to Jesus Christ, 37; graduate of Harvard, 27; invokes Jesus Christ, 41–42; likened to Jacob, 33; likened to John Adams, 36; ministerial qualities of, 39; minister of the First Congregational Church, 13, 25, 27; as most significant Newport Congregational minister, 43, 137; obstinacy of, 38; ordination of, 27; parishioners of, 27–32, 36–39, 42, 48, 51, 52, 83, 137, 152; power of, 30; receives Holy Communion in Second Congregational Church, 51; reception of, 27; refuses to baptize, 27; rejects John Adams as colleague, 30–31; requirements of, for receiving Holy Communion, 40; sermons by, 32–34, 41, 48; sides with opponents of Stod-